PARTY OVER SECTION

American Presidential Elections

MICHAEL NELSON

JOHN M. MCCARDELL, JR.

PARTY OVER SECTION

THE ROUGH AND READY
PRESIDENTIAL ELECTION
OF 1848
JOEL H. SILBEY

UNIVERSITY PRESS OF KANSAS

Published
by the
University
Press of Kansas
(Lawrence,
Kansas 66045),
which was
organized by the
Kansas Board of
Regents and is
operated and
funded by
Emporia State
University,
Fort Hays State
University,
Kansas State
University,
Pittsburg State
University,
the University
of Kansas, and
Wichita State
University

Library of Congress Cataloging-in-Publication Data

Silbey, Joel H.
    Party over section : the rough and ready presidential
election of 1848 / Joel H. Silbey.
        p.   cm. — (American presidential elections)
    Includes bibliographical references and index.
    ISBN 978-0-7006-1640-4 (cloth : alk. paper)
        1. Presidents—United States—Election—1848.
2. Taylor, Zachary, 1784–1850. 3. Van Buren, Martin, 1782–1862.
4. Cass, Lewis, 1782–1866. 5. United States—Politics and
government—1845–1849. I. Title.
    E420.S55 2009
    324.973—dc22   2008044078

British Library Cataloguing-in-Publication Data is available.

Printed in the United States of America

10 9 8 7 6 5 4 3 2 1

The paper used in this publication is recycled and contains
30 percent postconsumer waste. It is acid free and meets the
minimum requirements of the American National Standard for
Permanence of Paper for Printed Library Materials z39.48-1992.

To Madeline S. R. Silbey and Her Fellow
Conspirators on the Main Line

CONTENTS

Editors' Foreword ix

Author's Preface xi

1 Troubled Political Times 1

2 "A Northern No!" 30

3 "The Sore-Headed Leaders in the State of New York"—
and Some Others—Nominate a President 45

4 "The Work to Be Done": The Parties Organize 86

5 "There Never Was an Election . . . of Greater Importance":
The Parties Define What Is at Stake 103

6 "The Presence of Every Man Is Necessary":
Zachary Taylor Is Elected 129

7 "A Conspicuous Milestone in the Antislavery
Journey"—or Not 147

Appendix A: Democratic National Platform, 1848 157

Appendix B: Whig Party Statement of Principles Passed
at a Mass Meeting after the National Convention 162

Appendix C: Free Soil National Platform, 1848 164

Appendix D: Zachary Taylor's Inaugural Address,
March 5, 1849 167

Notes 171

Bibliographic Essay 193

Index 199

The law of unintended consequences is nowhere more evident than in the political history of the United States in the years after 1845. "Manifest Destiny," as the historian Allan Nevins once noted, yielded bitter fruit. Yet few Americans in the middle 1840s anticipated such a harvest. Elected on a platform calling for the "reannexation of Texas and the reoccupation of Oregon," James K. Polk of Tennessee, the Democratic "dark horse," assumed office in 1845 with a clear agenda. During his single term, he proved remarkably effective in carrying that agenda out. Indeed, by the middle of Polk's term, the United States had extended its territorial domain to the Pacific.

Issues hitherto suppressed now demanded attention and resolution. How were the new territories to be organized and governed? By what process ought they to qualify for admission to the Union? Most important, should these territories be open to settlement by all Americans, and, if so, could those Americans take their property, which included their slaves, with them?

The matter of slavery's boundaries had been laid to rest in 1820. The Missouri Compromise had fixed the territorial limits of slavery within the area of the Louisiana Purchase. Though that act appeared successfully to remove slavery from the political arena, in fact, a small but vocal antislavery movement continued to agitate for the radical step of abolition. Abolitionists were few in number, however, and effectively isolated on the periphery of national politics by the so-called Gag Rule, a congressional decision automatically to table their petitions.

The acquisition of new territory changed all that. For the first time, Americans who harbored genuine reservations about the "peculiar institution" but were unwilling to interfere with slavery where it existed discovered a new and compelling intermediate position. Congressman David Wilmot, a Democrat from Pennsylvania, introduced a proviso to that effect in 1846. It passed the House, where nonslaveholding states were in the majority, but failed in the Senate, where North and South were evenly balanced. Almost immediately, all the other issues that seemed so pressing—banks, tariffs, internal improvements—and that had been the basis for the political party system pitting Democrats against Whigs seemed to recede into the background. "Free Soil," the belief that slavery should not be permitted to expand beyond its 1820 boundaries, quickly became part of the political vocabulary.

These momentous events set the stage for the tumultuous election of 1848, a story well told by a master historian. Joel Silbey notes the stresses placed upon the party system by the emerging issue of slavery but argues that party loyalty prevailed over sectional allegiance. We follow a three-way contest for the presidency that pits a slaveholding military hero against a Michigan senator and a former president from New York. Zachary Taylor prevails over both Lewis Cass and Martin Van Buren. Though unsuccessful, and perhaps a sacrifice on the altar of party, it is Van Buren's candidacy on the ticket of a new "Free Soil" movement that portends what will ultimately put the future of the Union at stake.

Meantime, Whigs and Democrats both are attracted by the Free Soil appeal even as party loyalists try, for the most part successfully, to hold their members in line. A new cast of characters, many of whom will assume major roles on the political stage in years to come, populates the narrative: Abraham Lincoln and Stephen A. Douglas, William Seward and Salmon P. Chase, Charles Francis Adams and William Lowndes Yancey, all have parts during this contest.

Slavery's defenders, fearing the tyranny of a sectional majority, take comfort in Taylor's victory. Slavery's opponents, augmented in numbers and more diverse in position, fear the consequences of defeat. Yet the issue remains unsettled, and the territorial question will continue to vex the country until, finally, separation comes in 1861.

Such omniscience, of course, was not present in 1848, which imparts to the narrative an element of genuine tragedy even as, from the perspective of the participants, party still seemed an effective antidote to the centrifugal force of the slavery issue. The route to civil war, as Professor Silbey reminds us, was neither direct nor necessarily inevitable. There can be no doubt, however, that it reached a significant crossroads, and was at least temporarily arrested, in a critical election in that momentous year.

For much of the western world, 1848 was a year of severe political challenge, popular unrest, violent uprisings against the status quo, and a
number of successful revolutions. From London to Paris to Vienna
empires shook, several monarchies collapsed under the assault against
them, and all over Europe, liberal reform ideas and democratic governments replaced what previously had been the dominant reactionary
political ethos of the continent. Across the Atlantic, the United States escaped the violence and the overthrow of conservative governing institutions and elites that occurred elsewhere that year. But it, too, experienced
an attack on the usual understandings and practices of its political world.
Specifically, although no one took to the streets (except in campaign rallies and parades), 1848 was a year of political challenge that vigorously
sought to limit the reach of what many considered to be a decadent social and economic system in the nation's southern states based on human slavery. For the first time, an organized political program calling
for the containment of slavery within then-established boundaries took
a primarily electoral focus in the platform of the Free Soil Party in an
attempt to win the presidency and other offices that year. More focused
and coherent than earlier advocates of limiting the institution had been,
the Free Soilers verbally assaulted the region that practiced slavery along
with a national political system in which most of the participants were
indifferent or hostile to their concerns and preferred to concentrate their
attention on other matters.

Although a pale echo of events in Europe, the battle between Zachary
Taylor, Lewis Cass, and Martin Van Buren to capture the presidency of
the United States was a rousing, hard-fought, and often bitter affair—"a
fierce political storm," as one contemporary characterized it.[1] It aroused
a great deal of sectional tension, energized hopeful reformers seeking to
improve their society through the electoral process, created much threatening drama, and seemed, for a time, to augur a new day on the national
landscape. "The crisis has come," the author of a Democratic Party address to the voters solemnly intoned as the contest got under way, and
proceeded to spell out what it was and why it had arrived.[2]

To be sure, beginning with the hotly contested election of 1800, and reinforced by the resurgence of partisan conflict in the 1820s, Americans were used to having their battles for office articulated in apocalyptic language; political leaders often told the people that they were confronted by the most dangerous situations the nation had ever faced—as well as a critical, last gasp opportunity to make things right if they voted correctly on election day. But, as the author of the quoted pamphlet explained, the last presidential election of the 1840s caught the eye of many contemporaries as being a turning point—a particularly critical moment in the nation's development that entailed its possible maturing into the society promised generations before in the Declaration of Independence in which all men were created equal.

Even as sectionally charged attitudes and appeals helped define the election of 1848 and played a significant role in what occurred then, they were not alone in shaping the battle for the presidency. The Free Soil Party appeared during an intensely partisan era in which sectional appeals were resisted and thwarted by a partisan force that was the primary influence on the nation's politics. Different conceptions of "the great political question of the country" therefore framed the presidential battle and its outcome.[3] Whatever the intensity of sectional anger in 1848, the intersectional national parties, the Whigs and Democrats, responded quickly to the challenge by seeking to persuade the electorate to stay with them. They brought forward other issues rooted in economic, cultural, and ideological differences that had divided the country for twenty years. The result was an election that turned on several fronts as the parties and candidates sought to win out over the rhetorical appeals of their rivals. It became a confrontation between the force of tradition and the powerful rise of a different way of thinking about the political world they all inhabited.

Historians have displayed a great deal of interest in the Free Soil election. Because of their many books and articles, we do not lack for information or perspectives on what occurred then. Still, I suggest that there is always more to consider as new research emerges concerning the events of that year. A fresh look at 1848 is useful in order to clarify, develop, and perhaps shift some of our current understanding about this apparent turning point in U.S. history. This book focuses on the interaction of the different forces in play then and their roles in shaping the direction of politics in the United States of the mid-nineteenth century.

A long time ago, a fine teacher and historian, Arthur C. Cole, directed my undergraduate honors thesis on the Barnburner Democrats in the election of 1848. It was an exceptional experience much appreciated, then and now, as it set me on a career-long path. As a result of Professor Cole's stimulation I have been engaged in research on the politics of the 1840s for many years. I have spent a great deal of time working in the collections of many libraries, including state historical societies and major university and public collections, most importantly, the Library of Congress, the New York Public Library, and, of course, the Cornell University Library. I have, in other work, thanked the staffs of each of these remarkable institutions and of the others I have visited, and repeat my gratitude here.

Much of the final research for this volume, and my first efforts at putting together what I wanted to say, occurred while I was the Harmsworth Professor of American History at the University of Oxford. I am in debt to my faculty colleagues in American History there, Richard Carwardine, Donald Ratcliffe, Jay Sexton, and Stephen Tuck, as well as Michael Heale, who was a visiting scholar at the time of my residence, for their conversations, suggestions, and hospitality. John Pinfold, then head of the Vere Harmsworth Library, was most helpful to a visitor. I am also grateful to Provost Alan Budd and the fellows of Queens College, home of the Harmsworth professorship, for much support. The current members of the Harmsworth family, led by Major Vyvyan Harmsworth, were most kind to the current chair.

The many historians who have written previously about U.S. politics in this era and the Free Soil moment have provided the foundation on which I have explored the election and built my own view. To Joseph Rayback, Frederick Blue, Richard Sewell, Holman Hamilton, William Shade, Ronald Formisano, Richard P. McCormick, Donald Cole, John Niven, K. Jack Bauer, Stephen Maizlish, and, most of all, Michael Holt, I owe a great deal for all they have contributed through their writings and personal exchanges to guide my understanding of these events even when I did not always agree with them. They are exemplary professionals. My U.S. history colleagues at Cornell University, equally exemplary, contributed in many ways as they always have to my efforts, and I thank them for being the kind of associates they are.

Allan G. Bogue, from when I first met him until now, remains in a class by himself as a teacher, stimulant, critic, and enabler even at a long distance. I can never thank him enough for all he has done for me.

Fred Woodward and his staff at the University Press of Kansas have been patient, gracious, and most attentive in supporting my efforts and bringing this work to publication. They, too, have earned my deep gratitude as have the coeditors of the American Presidential Elections series, Michael Nelson and John M. McCardell, Jr., for their helpful advice.

Finally, once more my family, Rosemary, Victoria, David, Tom, Mari, Abigail, Thomas, and Madeline have provided joy, comfort, support, and satisfaction while I have been engaged in this book as they always have. They know what they mean to me.

1

TROUBLED POLITICAL TIMES

The election that brought General Zachary Taylor to the presidency in a hotly contested three-way race did not occur in a vacuum. It was the product of a quarter century of important economic, social, and political changes that had significantly reshaped the United States and its politics. In the twenty-five years after the end of the War of 1812, the victorious nation enjoyed a period of spectacular population growth and economic development. With the end of attempts by the recalcitrant British and their American Indian allies to block American settlement in the trans-Appalachian region, which had been going on since the end of the Revolution, settlers poured into the new territories formerly closed to them. The number of states in the Union increased from the eighteen of 1815 to twenty-six by 1840—all but one in the West—with several more on the horizon. The nation's population, stimulated by growing immigration, grew from 7,240,000 people, as recorded in the U.S. Census of 1810, to just over 17 million in 1840.

Such growth was not limited to land acquisition and population explosion. The expansion of market-oriented agriculture in the Old Northwest and in the cotton lands of the South undergirded strong economic development under way, as did the rise of international trade with Europe and Asia out of the ports of Boston, New York, and New Orleans, among others. Another contributing factor was the growth of domestic commerce as a result of the completion of the Erie Canal and the full flourishing of the Mississippi River as a connector between New Orleans and the growing states of the upper West. The beginnings of the factory system in New England attracted a growing labor force from both domestic and foreign sources to the new textile mill towns. Many of the new immigrants were Roman Catholics from Ireland, who were met with hostility from the largely Protestant population of New England. All of this, precursor of so much more to come, added to the vigor of the economy and the size of the gross national product of the United States. As a result of all of these activities, the United States was becoming more diverse than it ever had been geographically, economically, and socially.[1]

There was a significant political dimension to these developments as well. In response to population growth and the complexity associated with economic development, new arrangements were made at the federal level to manage increasing numbers of national political conflicts. In the so-called Era of Good Feelings after the war's end, the national focus on politics decreased, although there remained many harsh confrontations at the state and local levels over a range of issues. For example, state governments reacted to popular demands for more democracy and debated the nature and location of financial assistance to the evolving economy. This local orientation began to change in the 1820s as new issues exploded onto the scene and as the presidential administrations of John Quincy Adams and then Andrew Jackson generated repeated battles over public policy at the national level. What was the role of the federal government in a so much larger, so much more diverse, nation? What should be the extent of popular participation in decisionmaking?

New national political parties began to emerge and drew support throughout the Union. They became part of the landscape in order to cope with the conditions roiling the political scene and to organize the fractious political divisions in the United States. Still in a rudimentary state in the 1820s, the Jacksonians and the National Republican followers of Adams battled in Congress and at the polls for dominance. There were occasional outbursts of sectional tensions as well. Many southerners believed that slave labor was critical to their agricultural enterprise. Others, mostly in the North, strongly challenged the continued existence of the institution in a democratic republic that had thrown off the shackles of the past. When the issue came to a boil in the Missouri crisis in 1819, it took great effort to calm the waters through compromise. As the United States grew territorially and experienced the beginning of what historians would later call the "market revolution," there was clearly much to deal with at the ballot box and in Congress and the

White House. These matters came to a head in a series of presidential elections beginning in the late 1820s and continuing into the 1840s that further defined the direction of post-1815 politics.[2]

THE PEOPLE SPEAK, 1840 AND 1844

The presidential election of 1840—the "hurrah campaign" of Whig candidate "Old Tippecanoe," the renowned Indian fighter General William Henry Harrison, against incumbent president Martin Van Buren, the builder and leader of the Jacksonians, now increasingly being labeled the Democratic Party—occurred amid a severe economic downturn. It proved to be a critical turning point in the nation's politics. Not only did Harrison defeat a sitting president, but he did so during (and as a result of) a major shift in the way elections were fought in terms of how the two national parties presented themselves and conducted their drive for office. Over previous decades, restrictive suffrage requirements had been loosened in many states under popular and political pressure to open up the voting arena to all adult white male citizens. New techniques seemed needed in order to mobilize and direct the mass of potential voters.[3]

As a result, in the election of 1840 both parties demonstrated heightened commitment to building campaign and get-out-the-vote organizations. This led to an increase in election noise and pageantry, or "the great commotion," in one historian's phrase, primarily because of a clamorous assault by the Whigs upon the Democrats, especially for championing the failed policies of President Van Buren during the economic collapse that began in 1837. Most particularly, the Whigs went after Van Buren himself, labeling him as "Martin Van Ruin," the "used-up man" of U.S. politics. He was, as U.S. Representative Charles Ogle of Pennsylvania described him, an elitist residing in the "regal splendor of the presidential palace," dining off a "gold plate," and using "silver service" paid for by the people, indifferent to the suffering of the American people caught in a destructive collapse brought on by his own (and his party's) outmoded, inadequate policies. The Whigs, in contrast, understood the nation's suffering and its needs in the emergency, as they were the true egalitarians interested in helping the people in distress. Their symbols, the log cabin where Harrison allegedly lived and the hard cider he allegedly drank, were held up in contrast to the Democrats' life of overfurnished poshness, including French champagne, hardly the people's drink.[4]

As the campaign developed, it seemed as if no holds were barred in U.S. elections. Never before had mobilization efforts been so widespread, organized, raucous, and defamatory. In earlier contests, noisy denunciations against one's opponents had certainly been present but not to the extent they were in 1840. The Whigs' particularly intense tone was one of vitriolic character assassination and demagogic calumny. It was a message widely spread by the party organization in a great number of rallies and parades and in the speeches and publications of Whig activists everywhere. And it worked. The first result of their efforts to bring down the president was a dramatic increase in turnout at the polls as more than 2.4 million voters from twenty-five states, 80 percent of those eligible to vote, came out to record their choice. It was the largest popular participation in a U.S. presidential contest to that point. (There was no popular vote in South Carolina, where the state legislature still chose the presidential electors.) In 1836, just over 1 million people had voted from the same twenty-five states, and the turnout of 57.8 percent of those eligible was close to the figure in other recent elections, which had hovered around 55 percent of those eligible to participate (see Table 1.1). Clearly, the Whig Party's vigorous efforts to get out the vote by raising a nationwide uproar against the failed incumbents had worked very well.[5]

Then there was the effect of that great rush to the polls when the votes were counted. Harrison won 19 states and 234 electoral votes to the president's 8 states and 60 electors. A third party, the antislavery Liberty Party, won no states and few popular votes. The story of the election was "Tippecanoe and Tyler, Too," whose rout of their opponents and successful takeover of Congress underscored the potency of the Whig Party's rousing tactics in getting out the vote and getting their political message across, which taught their leaders and their opponents that a new, more fervent, and better organized style of electoral politics was the pathway to the future in their contentious nation.[6]

As a result, the campaign of 1840 was not a one-shot affair. The pattern established in the Harrison election continued in the next presidential campaign four years later. Once again, intense confrontation between the parties was the new political order. Large armies of committed Whigs and Democrats again confronted each other at the polls over a broad political landscape. Partisan activists were busy in small towns, rural areas, and urban centers, mobilizing the faithful toward the polls come election day. Noisy parades, well-organized rallies, and fiery

Table 1.1. Percentage of Those Eligible to Vote Who Did So, 1828–1844 (Entire Nation)

Election Year	Percentage
1828	57.6
1832	55.4
1836	57.8
1840	80.2
1844	78.1

Source: *Historical Statistics of the United States Colonial Times to 1970* (Washington, D.C.: Government Printing Office, 1975).

speeches on behalf of the candidates—Henry Clay of Kentucky for the Whigs and James K. Polk of Tennessee for the Democrats—advanced the fortunes of the parties. Arguments were again pressed home in rhetoric infused by colorful imagery. Vehement assaults on the other side in partisan newspaper editorials and party-produced broadsides and pamphlets embodied the nationwide din. As these were read by individual voters or read out to receptive crowds at party-sponsored barbecues and rallies, a more populist written and spoken rhetoric than had been the national norm permeated the battle, intended to energize the masses. It worked, making this and future election campaigns ever more meaningful and central to the lives of many Americans. In 1840 and thereafter, electoral politics at the local, state, and national levels had become part hoopla, part entertainment, and part expression of intense dedication to partisan causes. And, once again, the turnout was impressive: 2.7 million voted in the 1844 contest, about 78 percent of those eligible, just below the record turnout four years before. Once again, the party organizations had been successful in their efforts to mobilize support.[7]

Elections were staged as populist uproars in order to bring out the large potential vote. But there was more. Behind the images, spectacle, and revelry of both the 1840 and 1844 campaigns lay divisive policy issues that shaped the rhetorical war between the parties. The language of politics had coarsened but retained its not-so-hidden substance. The social dynamics of life in the United States produced a plurality of different factions, many of them locally oriented, made up of people of diverse ethnic and religious backgrounds and varying economic concerns. They had different needs, and struggled against each other for mastery over the nation's broad landscape with little coordinated national perspective in their efforts.

When John Quincy Adams had become president in 1825, he and the so-called National Republicans who supported him came out of the tradition that pushed to increase the authority of the federal government as necessary and proper for the nation's well-being. Their articulation of that perspective and their efforts to enact legislation reflecting their beliefs were vigorously resisted by states' rights advocates such as Senator Martin Van Buren of New York. To Van Buren and his supporters, a powerful federal government posed dangers to state autonomy and personal liberty. Van Buren took the initiative to call upon Adams's many enemies to submerge the differences among them and coalesce behind the candidacy of the larger-than-life frontier Indian fighter and hero of the Battle of New Orleans, Andrew Jackson, on a platform calling for the primacy of state-centered authority in domestic affairs. He was successful. Jackson defeated Adams handily in 1828.[8]

Jackson's victory in 1828 did not end the battles between the contending groups. The years of his presidency stirred a whirlwind of continuing political excitement. In addition, Jackson's strong commitment to presidential authority, particularly his use of the veto, and the president's public pulpit against his enemies, stung the latter into moving toward a more organized coalition as well. In particular, his veto of rechartering the Bank of the United States caused a mighty political explosion against him. Similarly, when South Carolina attempted to nullify a tariff bill within its borders and the president threatened to lead a military expedition against the state, he created an even more intense political confrontation. At the center of all of this was Van Buren, who organized, planned, advised, and worked as hard as possible to guarantee the success of the Jackson administration. For his commitment and efforts, Van Buren, who served in Jackson's cabinet as secretary of state, and then at Jackson's request became vice president in 1832, attracted great hostility. The president's passing of his mantle to his distrusted and often despised associate in 1836 spurred his enemies to new efforts to bring the Jacksonians down. The differences that stirred up the policy battles were clearly not temporary; they had become a permanent element of the political landscape.[9]

Stimulated by the presidential activism, the resulting robust battles of these years and the efforts of political leaders to harness the conflicts through national political parties, which had become largely moribund during the recent past, reappeared on the scene. First the Jacksonian

Democrats, then the Whigs, reached out into the states and across sectional lines to develop a national focus and link different groups behind their causes. They found electoral success along the fault lines created by the persistent differences over economic and social policies, competing cultural values, tensions between different ethnic and religious groups, and ideological divisions over the reach of the federal government's power that had become the central forces in the decade-long confrontation between the activist Presidents Adams and Jackson, their associates, and their many friends and opponents throughout the country. By the early 1830s, both parties had established themselves on the political landscape as the foundation stones of what scholars refer to as the "second American party system," always ready to challenge, promote, resist, and seek victory at the polls.[10]

As these coalitions came to the center of the nation's political life, within both there often were internal disagreements over specific policies and priorities and which candidates would best represent their views. The needs of a particular locality or group pitted against those demanded by others and often as well the personal rivalries among leaders struggling to dominate party affairs generated heated conflicts. Different factions pressed their own choices in the run-up to each election. Sometimes the parties seemed to be too heterogeneous to stay together, and there were defections from each in the early years. For instance, many of Jackson's original states' rights supporters, but by no means all of them, deserted him in reaction to his claims of presidential power, including the right to subdue a recalcitrant state.

But the central thrust of each coalition was clear and persistently presented in legislative debates, election campaigns, and presidential messages. The Whigs, who took their name from the eighteenth-century English resisters to the growing power claimed by King George III, articulated a quite nationalist vision of government authority in the economic realm in particular, alongside their notions of congressional primacy in the federal arena. They believed in the virtue of high tariffs, the necessity of a national bank, and federal funding for local improvements such as the construction of roads and canals, the dredging of rivers, and the deepening and improvement of harbors, all designed to impel the nation's economic development. Many of them also wanted to use federal power to influence social norms and practices by defining who could be citizens and shaping the appropriate behavior of those citizens. Finally, they had originally come together against what they considered the excessive reach for more power by "King Andrew" Jackson, and they maintained a skeptical view of the presidency thereafter (at least when Democrats held the office).[11]

In contrast to the views expressed by Henry Clay and his Whig associates, their opponents, the Democrats (who were originally called Republicans in tribute to their announced commitment to the ideals of Thomas Jefferson, and then Democratic-Republicans), argued that the reach of federal power in economic policy should be much more restricted. They rejected most of the Whigs' demands for increased federal involvement in economic affairs, bitterly opposing a national bank, rejecting a high tariff, and eschewing the use of federal funds to assist local construction projects. The Democrats had different cultural perspectives as well, which usually emerged at the state level over school legislation and issues of inclusion in society, and in challenging their opponents' desire for government to regulate the personal behavior of its citizens. Finally, they firmly believed in the authority of the president over the other branches of the federal government.[12]

In these battles, the humbly born Jackson claimed to represent the people, and that the party he led sought equality (at least of opportunity) among all Americans. The president, Democrats claimed, was the "tribune of the people," their designated champion in their battles against the attempt to increase federal government power and thereby threaten the liberties of the masses of citizens. According to the Democrats, their opponents retained the elitist outlook inherited from their Federalist forebears. In contrast to the Jacksonians, they were not interested in helping all the people, but only the rich and well connected. The Whigs disagreed (and some of their newspapers even labeled their party the Democratic Whigs in response). The outcome of all this public posturing was that more people were now involved in politics than ever before, and each party's leaders worked assiduously to win their support.[13]

The frequent elections characteristic of the nation's political life, and the widespread activities in which the parties engaged in order to win and hold power, demanded effective leadership. As they emerged, the Whigs and the Jacksonian Democrats were organized and led by strong and astute activists, often newspaper editors such as Whigs Thurlow Weed and Horace Greeley, both from New York State, and Democrats Francis P. Blair of Maryland and Thomas Ritchie of Virginia. Many party leaders were also lawyers prominent at the local and state level who stepped in and worked hard to bring individuals and groups with similar values and interests together across state and regional lines to fight for their agreed-upon goals. As those eligible to vote became more numerous, state legislatures reacted to the pressure of populist currents and expanded the franchise in their states, and more voters became involved in what was taking place in the political world, these leaders of the party coalitions built the organizations required to run election campaigns, mobilize the voters, argue their cases, and elect their candidates.[14]

Campaign season was the highlight of the political year in its rousing excitement, along with the important messages that were conveyed by it, as the 1840 contest demonstrated. The voters responded well to the party drama and its underlying substance; as its relevance to their lives of what leaders proclaimed were "the grounds of differences between the contending parties" became clear, popular participation in campaign activities and at the polls on election day among those enfranchised increased greatly and, as noted, reached an unprecedented national level in the Harrison–Van Buren race. At the same time, some of those who remained not legally entitled to vote, such as women, became as politically involved as they could, both overtly and behind the scenes, in the campaign activities that defined so much of U.S. political life.[15]

In addition to the high turnout of voters and the impressive political participation of disenfranchised groups in election activities, the voters' expression of their strong loyalties to their parties came to characterize polling day. Americans raised in communities of partisan loyalists— their family, their clan, and their neighbors—came to maturity having internalized over time images of the deep differences between the national parties. They gladly cheered on their party as it made its case and vigorously challenged the opponents for their missteps, sourly deprecated their false claims, and shouted against their many inadequacies. Voters went to the polls secure in the knowledge that by choosing as they did, they were doing the right thing, that is, what was best for their country, for their friends and allies, and for themselves. That is what they had heard, learned, and believed.[16]

This widespread and deep partisan commitment did not occur immediately, but by the early 1840s the intense and continuing support of the growing electorate for the Whig and Democratic organizations had solidified. It underlay the major parties' domination of the nation's politics to an extent and in a manner never before known. Across the thirty states that constituted the Union by 1848, people proudly proclaimed themselves Whigs or Democrats, repeatedly acted on their identities when deciding how to vote or what to support in the legislative arena, and, individually and in groups, passed on their loyalty to future generations. The two parties had become firmly rooted in the nation's soil despite the suspicion of them left over from an earlier time that persistently lingered among critics of their claims, their activities, and particularly of the great power they now wielded in the nation's political life. Still, although not everyone was convinced of partisan virtue and the necessity of these organizations, substantially more than enough Americans were so convinced as to make them the powerful force they had become.[17]

Finally, as the parties took root and voters accepted them as the main engines driving the nation's politics, the Whigs and Democrats divided the electorate quite closely between them nationally as well as in many of the individual states. Each party's community of support was diverse but held certain basic characteristics. Each drew its votes from across the whole political landscape, winning backing from different groups in different places based on local conditions and inherited perspectives. The Whigs tended to appeal to the commercial-minded, those caught up in the expanding market economy both in the North and South, and were also strong among Americans of Anglo-Saxon Protestant backgrounds. Democrats were less committed, often quite hostile, to the commercial enterprises growing in society, and tended to attract many ethnic and religious groups such as Germans, Dutch, Irish, and Catholics along with other groups outside the mainstream Anglo-Saxon Americans. Each party drew some support from rich, middle class, and poor alike and, as a result, split the voter pool in almost equal halves between them. In the first half of the 1840s as the parties were coming to dominate the American scene, each had won one of the two presidential elections, the Whigs by a majority of about 150,000 in 1840, and the Democrats in a close race in 1844 when Polk received 1,340,000 votes nationwide and Henry Clay attracted 1,301,000 votes.[18]

There were similarly close margins that year in many crucial state contests. In Georgia, for example, the difference between the two parties in the 1844 presidential race was a mere 2,000 votes of the more than 85,000 cast in the state; in New Jersey in the same year, fewer than 1,000 votes of the more than 75,000 cast separated the two major contenders. Although not all state-level elections were that close, it was becoming clear that something of an equilibrium had been established between the two main parties. Either the Whigs or the Democrats could win a national election if all went well for them. All of this stiff competition intensified the need, political leaders recognized, to seek out every vote they could—to arouse, persuade, and then get their supporters to the polls on election day and ensure that they did what they were supposed to do once there.

CHALLENGING THE CONSENSUS

The Whigs and Democrats were never alone or unchallenged in their quest for power. Other political activists with distinct policy agendas sought office as well, fired by different ideological and policy impulses than those that shaped the warfare between the major parties. Political insurgency against the conventional wisdom espoused by the two national parties was constant in this period even as the Whigs and Democrats expanded their power over the nation. The 1830s and 1840s were years of social and intellectual ferment in the United States, with a culture of reform rooted in religious enthusiasm as well as secular influences growing quite active in parts of the North. Reform impulses were particularly strong among evangelical Christian groups in New England, in the "Burnt Over" District of upstate New York, and in the Western Reserve region along Lake Erie in Ohio. Such movements also appeared in some old radical democratic centers in rural New York and elsewhere. As they came together, they provided the raw material for attempts to seek the improvement of U.S. society to its fullest capacity. Reformers loudly and unremittingly condemned the different problems they saw around them, among them gender inequalities and the unacceptable practice of enslaving Africans by those in the South as well as perceived threats from immigration, non-Protestant religions (particularly Catholicism), and dissenting minority sects. All of these matters became nodes around which people came together to challenge what they saw as widespread complacency and indifference to these situations and to demand redress and the elimination of these unacceptable situations from their society.[19]

Reform pressure groups became particularly active at state and local political levels. Educational reformers such as Horace Mann in Massachusetts pressed for needed changes in the schools and educational policy in his state and elsewhere. Anti-immigrant nativist movements appeared in New York and in Pennsylvania, where Lewis Levin was elected to Congress from a Philadelphia constituency in 1844 on the Native American Party ticket. Agitation for temperance to limit the consumption of alcoholic beverages significantly roiled the waters in several states, particularly in New England, which under the leadership of Neal Dow passed the first such legislation, the "Maine Law," some years later. At the national level, women's rights groups led by Elizabeth Cady Stanton and her colleagues were increasingly active seeking suffrage legislation for women. They also strove to eliminate other gender inequalities rooted in U.S. society such as the fact that women could not own property or have custody rights of children, since both were considered chattel. Land reformers such as George Henry Evans pressed for laws to liberalize the distribution of federal property to would-be settlers and end other obsolete practices stemming from earlier generations that continued to limit land ownership.[20]

Sectional anger between North and South also flared up from time to time with great intensity and much loud, sharp-edged, highly challenging verbiage. Hostility to slavery had existed for a long time in the United States and had led to scattered efforts to abolish it. The American Antislavery Society, founded in 1833 by William Lloyd Garrison, brought antislavery groups together—to a degree—and focused and advanced the argument against its presence in the republic. The society moved from its original concentration on the moral suasion of individuals to do the right thing to active public proselytizing against the institution itself. The abolitionists' program of newspaper and pamphlet propaganda and relentless petitioning of Congress to act against the institution roiled the political waters and set off a powerful reaction among southerners strongly committed to their particular society and economy, rooted, as they were, in the extensive use of slave labor. In the late 1830s, southerners succeeded in having the House of Representatives impose a restrictive "gag rule" against what they and some northerners perceived as "inflammatory" petitions sent to Congress by northern reform groups condemning slavery and demanding its abolition, which threatened the peace and security of their section.[21]

Even as various political activists denounced the failure of the nation's complacent, unreceptive political leaders and the parties they led to respond to and ameliorate the issues raised by the reform movements, some of the challengers began to accept and argue that it was necessary for them to take another step: active involvement in electoral politics at the state and national levels was the key to achieving their aims. Since the existing parties were hopelessly unreceptive to them, some of the reformers began to move beyond proselytizing to form organized electoral coalitions to contest for power. Abolitionist and nativist parties, for example, the Liberty Party at the national level and the American Party at the state level, appeared in the early 1840s and united their usual tactics of public agitation, pressuring officials, and petitioning Congress with building electoral organizations to campaign and win at the polls in such receptive northern locations as the New England states, New York, Ohio, and Pennsylvania with their many electoral votes.[22]

Dissent against the prevailing two-party political stranglehold was not limited to northern reformers. Below the Mason-Dixon Line, a number of southern politicians led by the veteran cabinet member, senator, and U.S. Vice President John C. Calhoun of South Carolina sought to arouse their neighbors, arguing that contrary to the positions of the national parties, sectional differences were at the core of American life, and that northerners would always challenge southern interests and hamstring them if they could. Calhoun had lost faith in the willingness and ability of national parties to protect the South and its way of life. He and his colleagues believed their section faced great danger from northerners' growing hostility to slavery. They pressed, therefore, for ending the existing party distinctions among southerners, whom, they claimed, by dividing their strength into separate camps, politically weakened their section. Rather than relying on intersectional coalitions among the Whigs and Democrats, they demanded the organization of a sectional party that would bring together southern Whigs and southern Democrats to protect their region's social and economic systems from their increasingly active and dangerous enemies in the North. Only such a nonpartisan alliance among them, they argued, could guarantee their section's safety, prosperity, and future.[23]

These challengers made a mark on American life. They were influential among initially small, if intense, groups of sympathizers, and always hopeful about their prospects for additional support from others still to be convinced. But they were not, as yet, in the early 1840s, a major threat to the existing political world of national parties, the issues they championed, and the loyalty of party members to them. To be sure, some party activists complained about the sectionalists' presence and the difficulties their activities posed to the dominant parties. A Whig, Jonathan Nathan, wrote to New York party leader and future governor of that state Hamilton Fish, "It is a damnable fact that every new faction that springs up once a year subtracts largely from our [Whig] voters while the rascals on the other side [the Democrats] escape without even a blemish. This is true of abolition, Americanism, non-resistancism [*sic*], Fourierism, and Mormonism—a beautiful list of the bastard children of the Great Whig Party."[24]

Despite such grumbling and the occasional difficulties for one party or the other in the tug of war between different values and commitments, the challengers' advocacy was, in fact, largely displaced by the continuing attraction and great power of the main parties. Whatever their energy, eloquence, or the sanctity of their causes, reform efforts remained largely on the margins of electoral politics. Reform and abolitionist third parties did not do well at the polls in national races and made only occasional breakthroughs in local contests. The Liberty Party ran a presidential candidate and offered a national platform in both 1840 and 1844, for instance. In 1840, its presidential candidate, James Birney, received just more than 7,000 votes nationally, fewer than 1 percent of the total votes cast in the election. In 1844, Birney, who was again the party's candidate, improved to 62,000 votes, just more than 2 percent of the national total (see Table 1.2).

To be sure, a minor party could swing the balance of power in the close elections that so often characterized U.S. politics, as Liberty leaders claimed to do in 1844 when they won enough votes in New York State to deny its electoral votes to the Whigs and, therefore, a national victory for Clay. (That argument assumes the Liberty Party's supporters would vote for a major party candidate instead of staying home on election day if their own organization was not in the race—an unproven, unlikely assumption.) Given their poll numbers, they functioned most of the time more as protest movements than as competitive players able to win a share of political power.[25]

In the South, Calhoun's call for sectional political unity met substantial opposition from a majority of the region's political activists. Although, as many historians have argued, southern slaveowners were quite sensitive to real, imagined, or exaggerated attacks on their institution and their sectional self-consciousness was a fact of life, they had never cohered into a political force on that issue alone. As Calhoun well knew and constantly lamented, they continued to be divided along party lines for all of the usual reasons even as they were told that threats to their way of life were increasing to a dangerous level. Whatever their strong opposition to the antislavery agitation they read in northern newspapers and heard in congressional speeches, Calhoun's many opponents in his home section argued for the continued relevance of the party system, first because

John C. Calhoun, leader of those southerners who sought to unite the section politically as the only way to defend it from its enemies.

Table 1.2. Presidential Election of 1844

	Popular Vote	Electoral Vote
Polk (D)	1,339,368	170
Clay (W)	1,300,687	105
Birney (L)	62,197	0

Source: Svend Peterson, *A Statistical History of the American Presidential Elections* (New York: Frederick Ungar Publishing Co., 1963).

of the range of issues that, these southerners contended, crossed sectional lines, as well as the parties' relevance to the advancement and protection of southern interests. As a group of Georgia Democrats argued, after listing the principles and policies they stood for, "We look to the ascendancy of the democratic party of the Union alone for the maintenance of the foregoing doctrines [sectional and otherwise]." Therefore, should southern Democrats "drive from us men [their northern party colleagues] who are extending to us the hand of conciliation?"[26]

The answer was a clear and resounding no—among members of both parties. The argument that all must stand by the parties proved quite persuasive among their intended audiences. Whig and Democratic loyalists were generally successful in holding the political initiative and maintaining the nonsectional partisanship among their constituents everywhere across the South in all but one of the slave states, not unsurprisingly, John C. Calhoun's South Carolina. But even in that state, there were occasional if relatively feeble partisan attempts to build Whig opposition both to the Democrats and to the sectional unifiers who dominated the state's politics.[27]

In both North and South, then, the national parties were able to limit the influence of the reform challengers and largely control regional and sectional tensions. The political culture remained hostile or indifferent to advocacy groups that challenged the hegemony of the party system. As historian William Gienapp has written, "A decade of agitation by the abolitionists and proslavery partisans in the South failed to make slavery a vital, pressing concern in national politics." To be sure, antislavery sentiment existed beyond the abolitionist community to include many northern Whigs and a smaller group of northern Democrats despite their parties' usual public indifference to the issue. But even among those northerners who opposed the institution, the abolitionists and their demand for an immediate end to slavery in the United States proved too radical for their taste. Reform insurgency thus remained a minority impulse in U.S. politics, at times bothersome, as Nathan's comment to Hamilton Fish indicated, to political leaders seeking to mobilize popular electoral majorities on behalf of the mainstream issues and candidates they championed. But, despite such laments and occasional indications of headway, the dissenters did not get a great deal of traction among party regulars or most voters, certainly nowhere near as much as they had hoped.[28]

WHIG TRIUMPH AND FRUSTRATION

As the 1840s opened, despite Democratic confidence that having won three straight presidential elections in 1828, 1832, and 1836 the nation's majority party was firmly established and sure to win again, the Whigs emerged as the dominant force on the national landscape. Their handy win in the presidential and congressional elections of 1840 gave them control of the federal government for the first time since the organization of the two major parties. Whig leaders were overjoyed. They, now the confident ones, were convinced they were at the beginning of a steady course toward cementing their command of the United States over the fading Democrats. They expected to have their way, first by enacting the policies they had brought forward, and then by winning once again in 1844 and steadily thereafter, well into the future.[29]

But Whig political dominance was brief. The party split badly when its newly elected president, the aged William Henry Harrison (he was sixty-eight years old when he was sworn in—the oldest man to hold the office so far), unexpectedly died after only a month in office to be succeeded by Vice President John Tyler, a former senator from Virginia. The Whigs had originally come together as a broad-based anti-Jacksonian coalition made up of groups with different beliefs and commitments along with their common hostility to the sitting president's behavior, his moves to extend presidential power, and his use of the veto power as a weapon against Congress. Now Whig members of Congress, led by the party's great leader, Senator Henry Clay, tangled with Tyler, whose states' rights orientation to government power was unsympathetic to many of the mainstream Whig nationalist notions championed by Clay and his party allies, and Tyler was willing to use his veto power to prove it. Clay's legislative plans were, therefore, largely frustrated. Congress did pass, and President Tyler signed, a protective tariff bill in 1842, one of the keystone Whig policy commitments, but the president vetoed other Whig-

James K. Polk, whose policies during his single presidential term severely disrupted the nation's political landscape and threatened his party's continued success.

inspired bills that would have expanded federal government power. All but one member of Tyler's cabinet who were more in tune with Clay and the Whig mainstream than with the president resigned in protest. The party bickered openly and with great fervor. It seemed, to some, to be in danger of falling apart.[30]

Despite their bitter differences and Tyler's efforts to undercut those in Congress, the Whigs managed to recover and remember what they had in common in time to contest the election of 1844. Stimulated by what Michael Holt refers to as "the cohesive force of interparty conflict," that is, their determination to prevent the Democrats from regaining power, they moved beyond their conflict with Tyler by formally casting the president aside when their legislative caucus read him out of the party. Then, with the esteemed Clay as their presidential candidate, they went into the election with renewed confidence and high expectations for victory, to be followed, they envisioned, by the enactment at last of the parts of the Whig program that had been too long delayed by Tyler's intransigence.[31]

The election did not turn out the way Whig leaders expected. The Democrats won a hard-fought victory, albeit by an extremely narrow margin, behind their relatively unknown, much less experienced, and, in Whig eyes, unprepared candidate, a victory achieved despite the fact that he ran against one of the nation's foremost statesmen. "Who is James K. Polk?" the Whigs had sneeringly asked during the campaign (ignoring the fact that he had served as speaker of the House of Representatives for several terms and then as governor of Tennessee). Voters in the twenty-six states answered the question in a very close contest. About 79 percent of those eligible to do so went to the polls, just fewer than four years before. When the returns were in and counted, there was only a 1.5 percent difference between each party's national total—that is, fewer than 40,000 votes separated them in an electorate of 2.7 million (see Table 1.2). It was the closest contest for the nation's highest office in the years before the Civil War, but nevertheless a great disappointment, if not a debacle, for the overconfident Whig losers. The Democrats also won control of both houses of Congress.[32]

Polk's stunning victory left in its wake an elated Democratic Party and a bruised and distraught Whig coalition, especially as the triumphant Democrats, back in Congress behind Polk's vigorous leadership, successfully carried out an ambitious legislative program based on the promises and principles they had long advocated and enshrined in the party's platform. In 1844, that document emphasized the party's belief that the federal government was one of limited powers and that Democrats opposed a national bank, a protective tariff, and federal financing of local improvement projects. The document concluded with a call for further territorial expansion, specifically, "the reoccupation of Oregon and the reannexation of Texas." It was, of course, the statement of a program that the Whigs found inimical to all they stood for and that reversed whatever legislative achievements Clay and his allies had managed to get through Congress in the previous few years.[33]

In contrast to the previous decade, the 1840s were years of great territorial and population growth and economic development in the United States. The Polk administration, under its youthful and energetic leader (the forty-nine-year-old Polk was the youngest man to become president so far), took the lead in promoting such growth behind the policies the Whigs found so provoking as the Democrats challenged just about every point in the Whigs' belief system. To begin with, in the year and a half after the new president's inauguration, he followed standard Democratic policies in successfully reducing the regulative and promotional role of the federal government in economic affairs. Under Polk's stimulation, despite the howls from the opposition, the Democrats in Congress significantly lowered the tariff the Whigs had put in place only four years before and created an independent treasury designed to forestall the Clay party's clamor for a national bank and to divorce federal economic activities from any reliance on state and private banks.[34]

There was more to come. Again, against loud Whig opposition, Polk and his congressional allies aggressively pursued a program of territorial expansion long favored by mainstream Democrats and energetically advocated in these years by a group of politicians, journalists, and intellectuals called "Young America," writers and orators determined to expand American greatness across the continent. It began with the new president moving quickly to complete the annexation of the Republic of Texas, a controversial process that had begun under his predecessor, Tyler, who was also a committed expansionist.[35]

The Democrats had regained their footing and surged ahead at the expense of their opponents. No matter how close the presidential election, they were once more in power and used their position effectively to accomplish a great deal. Unsurprisingly, the Whigs were unrelentingly aghast at what was occurring. They believed that Polk's economic program was dangerously unsound, paving the way for future disaster for the nation as Jackson's and Van Buren's policies had done to it a decade earlier. They generally opposed Polk's territorial expansion policies as well. Their resistance had made it difficult to annex Texas when Tyler was president, and they had not changed their minds about such land acquisitions. The president's further territorial ambitions were, to them, too rash and divisive. They argued that any new territories would bring little advantage to the nation and the possibility of a great deal of difficulty to Whigs in the South, where there was more support for expansion generally, as well as with the government of Mexico, which still insisted on its claim to Texas.[36]

Whig leaders were, therefore, ever more determined to find the necessary means to overcome their enemies and end the Democratic Party's ruinous reign. As one historian has written, Polk's program and his accomplishment in getting it enacted by Congress "revived the competitive spirit of Whig voters" from their postelection doldrums. And as it did, the Whig Party's leaders acted on their renewed determination and sense of urgency. Their bitter resistance to the Democrats in power and tenacious resolve to crush them and their ideas at the polls, in the states, and in Congress became hallmarks of the years after 1844 and significantly further inflamed an already contentious political landscape.[37]

"THROWING ALL THE HONEST MEN OVERBOARD": THE DEMOCRATS CONFRONT EACH OTHER

Despite their successes against the Whigs, matters had not been all that smooth for the Democrats either during the Polk years. They had their own factional problems, which had erupted at their national convention in Baltimore in 1844 and led to the defeat for renomination of their titular leader, former president Martin Van Buren. The party's national convention had established a two-thirds rule in 1832—that is, a nominee had to receive two-thirds of the votes of convention delegates in order to be nominated, and those in attendance renewed this rule in 1844 on a very close vote. Its passage was seen as a blow aimed at Van Buren by his party enemies, and it was. He had the support of a majority of delegate votes going into the convention but could not add to them sufficiently to reach the necessary two-thirds. Other party hopefuls held on to their support, and still others sought to find a way out. To keep the party together, Van Buren's lieutenants finally withdrew his name and acquiesced to the subsequent naming of Polk as the party's candidate.

There was much rhetorical brawling among the convention delegates and in party newspapers as a result before things quieted down. Although resentment remained among some, party leaders were able to paper over their differences enough to run a strong campaign and regain national power. But things went awry once Polk was in the White House, despite his string of policy successes—most especially because of sharp Democratic disagreements at the outset over the president's appointments and territorial expansion policies.[38]

Much of the Democratic Party's problem originated in the continuing bitter divisions among internal factions in the state of New York, which drew in warring groups in other states as well as the leaders of the national party in Washington. New York Democrats had been battling among themselves for some time, originally over state issues such as banking policy and whether to borrow money in order to enlarge the state's canal system. An older group led by Van Buren and his first lieutenant, Silas Wright, held fast to traditional party antibank notions and financial discipline, refusing to increase state spending as other Democrats led by former governor William L. Marcy demanded. As a result, party relations attained an intense, bitter level of disagreement and increasing dysfunction. The rise and triumph of Polk and the latter's actions in office made things significantly worse between these factions. The Van Buren bloc—the so-called radicals, or Barnburners, as their opponents labeled them because they were willing to burn down the barn (the party) to get their way—had been loyal to Polk after he had been named the party's presidential nominee in 1844 and had actively worked on his behalf during the election campaign. They believed their support had been decisive in the close Democratic victory. But they thought the new president subsequently betrayed them on several fronts, ideologically and organizationally, particularly in his appointments to the cabinet and to other important federal positions. "Throwing all the honest men overboard" (that is, the friends of Van Buren), as one hostile Democrat characterized it, Polk favored instead the ex-president's Hunker party opponents—that is, according to the Van Buren supporters, people who hankered (hunkered) for office rather than stand by principle—and shut the Van Burenites out of their accustomed—and to them, rightful—place in the party and government. And Polk did so, insofar as the latter were concerned, in a particularly cumbersome, insulting, and demeaning manner, suggesting at best his indifference to their claims and at worst his hostility to their traditional role within the party.[39]

"My decided conviction, I am sorry to say," New York Democratic senator John Dix reported from Washington, "is that the administration here would not be unwilling to see the State of New York in the hands of the Whigs and that its influence is, to some extent, secretly to effect that object." Many in the Van Buren group accepted that dark notion of the Polk administration and became increasingly angry toward those who were now leading the party. Privately, they made their feelings plain in their correspondence with each other, and publicly, in their own newspapers throughout the state.[40]

Although their perceptions of Polk's actions as so hostile to them greatly exaggerated the reality of the situation, the president had stumbled from the first in his dealings with the potent Van Buren group. He had taken poor advice and had lacked sensitivity and subtlety in his interactions with the former leader of their party as he had constructed his government. He subsequently compounded his missteps by the way he handled the pending annexation of Texas—Van Buren's hesitation about acquiring that area had been a large factor in his defeat for renomination in Baltimore. Most Democrats were ardent territorial expansionists, willing even to acquire areas in which slavery existed. Many of them had supported Tyler in his efforts to bring Texas into the Union and looked forward to the United States spreading its wings to the Pacific Ocean as well. They agreed with Polk's sentiment in his inaugural address that "our system may be safely extended to the utmost bounds of our territorial limits."[41]

Others among them, particularly those around Van Buren, continued to be more uncertain, or cautious, about such dreams, fearing the disruptive consequences both in foreign affairs and on the domestic scene of an aggressive and too precipitate territorial policy. In office, Polk ignored such doubts as he moved quickly to complete the process of annexation Tyler had begun, choosing a method that, Van Burenites believed, favored southern interests and violating an agreement the new president had made with them. This did not end Polk's troubles. As he carried out other parts of his agenda, he met further resistance from fellow party members. Democrats in other northern states joined some of Van Buren's New York supporters to express outrage at the South's overreaching influence and the president's willingness to allow slavery to expand into new areas while, as they saw it, moving more slowly to secure "rightful" U.S. claims to free territories in the West. (Within a year they would become even more incensed as Polk ignored the conviction of his idol, Andrew Jackson, "that we not submit to be negotiated out of our territorial rights" in Oregon; Polk negotiated, and then compromised, with the nation's traditional enemy, Great Britain. He agreed to accept a reduction in our expansive boundary claims in slave-free Oregon despite his earlier public statements—and assurances to all concerned—that he would never compromise them.)[42]

Still other Democrats who were not part of the Van Buren or expansionist groups joined in the rising complaints against the president for other policy reasons and out of frustration at his challenging the leader of their party. Like the Hunkers in New York, these usually loyal Democrats were no longer as committed to financially chaste, anti–federal interventionism in economic affairs, traditional Jacksonianism. They were particularly incensed, therefore, by the president's resistance to and then veto of a bill to have the federal government finance river and harbor improvements, which had been supported by the Whigs and, significantly, many of Polk's congressional party colleagues. The president's action led to a backlash against him in mid-1846 from some otherwise loyal Democratic legislators, particularly in the rapidly developing western states, where such federal aid was considered imperative to their well-being despite their party's normal resistance to that kind of expenditure.[43]

The Polk administration had significantly roiled the political waters, accomplishing much as it did so but also threatening the plans and hopes of many of its Democratic colleagues. The party dissenters were convinced Polk was acting first as someone who, consciously or not, was jeopardizing Democratic unity and weakening the party by his refusal to live up to the promises he had made to Van Buren about appointments and Texas policy; second, as someone primarily behaving in narrow sectarian terms, a slaveholder president with a sectional orientation, some said, which led him to follow policies unacceptable to other sections of the Union; and third, as someone overly rigid in his refusal to listen to the needs of loyal Democrats on matters of great importance to them, an insensitivity that threatened not only their interests and electoral fortunes but their continued place in their party's hierarchy as well.[44]

The Democratic dissenters still wanted to support their party and its programs (they generally voted for Polk's legislative initiatives in 1846 as the committed party loyalists they considered themselves). But their anger against the president continued to grow. Given all that had transpired after Polk took office, particularly in regard to Texas and Oregon, the old antislavery charge against the heirs of Thomas Jefferson and

Andrew Jackson that the Democratic Party was controlled by its pro-slavery southern wing now seemed especially pertinent to many of the president's critics. Tyler's last secretary of state, the ever agitative John C. Calhoun, had framed the argument for annexation in sectional, pro-slavery terms. He suggested that the acquisition of Texas was important because it would protect slavery against the South's enemies at home and abroad, that is, the abolitionists and the British government, which many believed also wanted to acquire Texas for its own purposes, includ-ing pushing its hostility to slavery on the southwestern border of the United States. The way Polk seemed to pick up on Calhoun's formula-tion as he moved to complete annexation in his first days in office clearly showed, to his uneasy critics, his similar primary devotion to southern interests.[45]

The idea of such southern control of their party's affairs had long been denied by loyal Democrats—certainly by Van Buren as well as by many of his closest supporters. Now, as the Polk administration dealt with the nation's territorial interests, some of them were no longer as sure as they had been that there was not an unacceptable southern bias to their party under the slaveholding president from Tennessee. As they saw it, there were too many indications of southern Democrats' aggres-siveness to gain power, attempts at dictating policy to others, and deter-mination to have their own way in national affairs even at the expense of their party colleagues. The Democratic dissenters also realized that their party's prosouthern image was bound to hurt them among some northern voters who normally could be expected to support them. As New York Barnburner leader Silas Wright had put it early on, "The Texas treaty is made upon a record which is sure to destroy any man from a free state who will go for it."[46]

THE UNITED STATES AT WAR, AT HOME AND ABROAD

All of the simmering contentiousness among Democrats boiled to the surface in the year and a half after Polk's inauguration. The factional conflicts and charges of bad faith filled the columns of some Democratic Party newspapers as they became increasingly hostile to the president's behavior, usually expressed in the most angry language, adding addi-tional noise to the cacophony the Whigs were raising against Polk and his policies. Polk had gotten his way in most of the policies he had put forward since he assumed office: a lower tariff, an independent treasury, and the sustaining of his veto of the river and harbor improvement bill. But to some observers the Democratic portion of the political landscape seemed more combustible by mid-1846 than it had been, increasingly broken into a swirl of angry party groups seeking redress, redirection, and revenge against others with whom they usually had been allied in the pursuit of agreed-upon ends.[47]

To be sure, neither party factionalism nor the repeated expression of political frustration by those defeated in the policy wars were unusual in these years on the contested terrain of U.S. politics. There was always a certain amount of turmoil among activists in both parties. As noted, internal differences over candidates and policy priorities were regular features of the life of Whigs and Democrats in each political season. But party leaders worked very hard to preserve their organizations' unity in order to maintain the momentum and power in the battles with their opponents. Despite the noise and continuous pressure from the dissenters, they were largely successful. Party lines held in Congress, at the polls, and within each organization for all but a relatively small part of the time.[48]

Still, there was enough dissent to worry each party's leaders. There appeared to be an increased intensity of forces within both parties and between them in the mid-1840s that would directly affect the strategic situation. Certainly the Texas controversy and what followed had given new life to bitter suspicions. Polk's provocative policy toward Mexico, beginning with his ordering U.S. troops into a disputed strip of land near the Rio Grande River, and the consequent outbreak of war between the two countries in spring 1846, heightened the contention by further infuriating the Whigs and some of the Democrats already unhappy with the policy direction and behavior of the Polk administration.[49]

The war's outbreak, when troops from each country exchanged gunfire in the disputed border zone the Polk administration claimed was part of the United States (a claim the angry Mexicans did not accept), confirmed the prediction of the president's opponents that such a conflict would inevitably occur given Polk's foreign policy excesses. The beginning of armed conflict was the unavoidable consequence of his threatening behavior toward the Mexicans, placing the army in a position where there was likely to be resistance to its presence. Further, to the antislavery advocates, both Whigs and Democrats, and among the nonpartisan reformers as well, Polk's provocative initiatives toward the nation's southern neighbor in order to secure more territory for a slave state confirmed their belief that Polk was overbearingly southern in his orientation, and determined, therefore, to bring more slave territory into the Union.[50]

Although there was wide initial popular support in the United States for the conflict with Mexico, much of it dissipated quickly, largely but not entirely along political lines. Whigs and some unhappy Democrats did not hold back their criticisms even though the nation was at war. They made their opposition to Polk's expansionist foreign policy clear and moved to rouse others to join them in resisting what was going on as U.S. army troops moved deeper into Mexico. Whigs never let up, thereafter, in this assault on the war and Polk's misbehavior. "We look in vain," one of their pamphlet writers declared, "for anything like honesty of purpose in the origin or prosecution of this war." To Henry Clay, the war was "wrong, dishonorable, and dangerous"; it "was begun without any necessity, and in folly, and is conducted without wisdom."[51]

As he had done before in the confrontations between the parties, Clay led the way in framing and articulating the widespread Whig opposition, bringing it to a head in a major speech he made to a cheering partisan crowd in Lexington, Kentucky, in November 1847. He assaulted all that Polk had wreaked in his policies in the Southwest and laid out the baneful consequences to the nation still to come if the Democrats continued in office. Whig newspapers and other dissenters were quick to pick up on his lead. A number of other party members joined Clay in speaking out in harsh terms against "Mr. Polk's War." Among them two members of Congress, Alexander Stephens of Georgia and Abraham Lincoln of Illinois, were particularly harsh and uncompromising in their speeches. As a first-term member, Lincoln first came to national attention on the floor of the House of Representatives through his angry verbal assaults against Polk's Mexican policy, particularly the president's false assertion that Mexican actions along the border had started it. (Lincoln introduced a provocative resolution demanding that the president indicate on just what spot the fighting had broken out.) The nation's leader, Lincoln concluded, was a "bewildered, confounded, and miserably perplexed" man.[52]

Other Whigs joined in denouncing the president, some of them less strident than Lincoln but just as determined in their opposition. On the other side of the political spectrum, most of the anti-Polk Democrats were more circumspect, or at least ambivalent, about the situation. Many publicly supported the war (and meant it); some criticized what they saw

Abraham Lincoln, first-year Illinois U.S. representative, early supporter of Taylor, and vigorous campaigner for the Whig ticket.

as Polk's ineffectiveness in conducting it. Unlike the Whigs, the bulk of them stayed silent about the conflict's morality and about delving into the question of just how the conflict had begun.[53]

In this fervent, contentious political atmosphere no one lost sight of all the elections still to come. Political leaders were already focusing on the midterm contests for congressional and state offices in 1846 and 1847 and the presidential election the following year. Polk and his substantial bloc of party supporters continued on their course, asserting and acting on their case for Democratic control. The anti-Polk groups of all political stripes continued to fight back and turn up the temperature in challenging the confident president and his supporters. Their anger was palpable and their frustrations deep—and repeatedly expressed.[54]

But what could they hope to accomplish as long as the bulk of the Democratic Party remained whole behind Polk? Even with an electorate closely divided between the two parties and the opportunity that presented in the abstract, what did the challengers from both of the major parties have in common that could bring them together to thwart the president? Neither of the challenging groups, the Whigs generally nor the unhappy Democratic blocs, had as yet worked that out by summer 1846 or were even sure that working together against the president was desirable. The Democratic dissenters still looked to regain what they considered their natural places in their party's councils despite their setbacks since 1844. The Whigs, despite their anger and frustration and determination to thwart the president and his allies, remained uncertain and divided among themselves as to the most effective means of regaining power. As the midterm elections loomed, the nation was clearly going through troubled political times, but despite the intense opposition to his policies, the president still seemed to have the upper hand.[55]

Lacking among the administration's opponents was some kind of centerpiece, if there was one to be found, that could draw together all of the dissenters, Whigs and Democrats as well as the reformers of various persuasions, in a way that would allow them to overcome the difficulties of their situation—their numerical weaknesses along with their usual political differences and long-standing antagonisms—and thus halt the triumphant march of the southerner Polk and his sectional and partisan allies. Unexpectedly, an attempt to overcome that lack of an acceptable framework for cooperation, and thus meet their aims, was about to be introduced on the floor of the House of Representatives as the congressional session wound down in the first days of August 1846.

2

"A NORTHERN NO!"

A sharp upsurge in sectional tensions during the second half of Polk's term brought the political unrest of the mid-1840s to a head and gave the opposition to President Polk an opportunity to challenge the administration and its allies despite their strength among party members and in Congress.[1] As the first session of the 29th Congress was drawing to a close, the simmering hostility against the president and the South was about to become something more than fervent words expressed in speeches, pamphlets, and editorials. Despite the triumphs of a mostly productive legislative session for the Polk administration and the ruling Democrats, the tensions that existed in their ranks now led to an eruption that threatened to adversely affect the chances of further electoral and legislative victories for the party similar to the ones it had enjoyed up to now.

As the national legislature moved toward its last actions of the session with final adjournment only days away, the president sent a message to Capitol Hill requesting passage of an appropriation bill to provide funds for negotiations with Mexico that would culminate in a treaty expected to include U.S. acquisition of a significant patch of territory, if not all that enthusiasts for such expansion desired. (Some of the Democratic expansionists pushed for the United States to obtain all of Mexico.) Expansion had been the linchpin of Polk's war aims; triumphant U.S. troops already controlled large areas of northern Mexico, including the provinces of New Mexico and California as well as Mexico City and its approaches. As noted, most Democrats remained enthusiastically supportive of the administration's territorial efforts.[2]

Divisions about the issue remained between the parties, not unexpectedly, although a number of the Whigs continued to be somewhat more ambivalent in their approach and ambiguous in their public expressions as the war moved toward U.S. victory. There had been support for the annexation of Texas and now hope for territorial gains in the Southwest among some—but not all—of the Whig Party's southern bloc, who did not want to be charged at election time with being opposed to adding more slave territory. However, these expansionist supporters remained a minority voice in party councils. The Whig Party leadership echoed Henry Clay and came out strongly behind a policy of "no territory"—that there should be no additions to the nation's land mass as a result of the war—a policy most party newspapers, members of Congress, and other activists supported.[3]

On the evening of August 8, 1846, as both houses convened for an unusual nighttime session, David Wilmot, a Pennsylvania first-term Democrat, rose to offer an amendment to the pending appropriation bill. Wilmot had been a strong supporter of the administration and its policies throughout the session, including Polk's lower tariff proposal, although he came from a state containing significant protectionist sentiment. He was the only Pennsylvania Democratic representative to support the president's lower tariff bill. Now, contrary to his previous behavior, he challenged Polk, moving an amendment that had originated in discussions in recent days between frustrated northern Whigs and angry northern Democrats (including several who were close to former president Van Buren), none of them used to working together for legislative purposes but all of them hostile to slavery generally and worked up about what they saw as Polk's prosouthern, proslavery, territorial policy. (To be sure, the motives of the groups, soon to be labeled the provisoists, were not entirely altruistic; for example, many of them articulated exclusionary racial attitudes when they spoke out. They followed Wilmot's argument that the new territories should be open only to white settlers, who did not, they strongly suggested, want to live and work alongside black slaves.)[4]

Wilmot's proposed amendment read that "as an express and fundamental condition to the acquisition of any territory from the Republic of Mexico by the United States by virtue of any treaty which may be negotiated between them, and to the use of the Executive of the moneys herein appropriated, neither slavery nor involuntary servitude shall ever exist in any part of said territory, except for crime, whereof the party shall first be duly convicted." With little time for debate before the session ended *sine die*, the amendment passed a sparsely filled House on a largely sectional vote by those present. It went immediately to the Senate but did not come to a vote there as time ran out on the session amid confusion while it was being debated and before it could be voted on. But the failure to pass what the president called this "mischievous and foolish amendment" by the upper house of Congress did not end the issue.[5]

As noted, commitment to the partisan imperative had been effective previously in holding antislavery advocates at bay. There were indications, however, that conditions might be changing. The Wilmot Proviso was clearly a challenge to the president's policies, behavior, and alleged tilt in favor of the South and slavery. Its introduction suggested that new energy was feeding the rising anger as the antislavery impulse extended beyond the original hostile group of reformers into the ranks of party regulars. Both disaffected Democrats and northern Whigs apparently were not only prepared to keep up their challenge to the South's successes—or, perhaps, excesses—but some of them now argued that they should ignore party lines and work together to accomplish their goals, which they recognized as the all but unheard of idea it was in this partisan political nation.[6]

A model of what might be done already existed. In New Hampshire, where there was more of an antislavery perspective and resistance to further addition of slave territories to the United States than in most northern states, antislavery Democratic U.S. Representative John Parker Hale had refused to vote for the annexation of Texas or support the Mexican-American War and thus his party leader, the president. As a result, he was denied renomination to his congressional seat by a hostile state Democratic establishment tolerant of the South and the Polk administration's prosouthern policies. Hale and other New Hampshire Democrats who shared his view then entered into a coalition with antislavery Whigs and members of the Liberty Party in his home state, which proved powerful enough in the New Hampshire legislature to elect him to the U.S. Senate in 1846.[7]

Hale's election, coupled with other northern Democrats' support for the Wilmot Proviso, made it clear that the sectional genie had, for now,

David Wilmot, author of the provocative legislative amendment barring slavery in the Mexican cession.

been let out of the bottle. Sectional tensions had increased palpably in Washington and beyond during the Polk administration, raising challenges to the normal ways of U.S. politics. The question of slavery's further extension beyond its current boundaries had been reopened by the annexation of Texas, intensified by the war with Mexico and U.S. acquisition of territory by conquest, and come to a head with the introduction of the Wilmot Proviso. The amendment was clearly a reaction among the dissenting political groups against the president and his southern party allies that went beyond anything previously experienced. This strategy might be strong enough, some observers now suggested, to alter the landscape on which the approaching U.S. elections would take place.[8]

Despite the fact that Democrats had initially taken the public lead on the Wilmot Proviso, many northern Whigs came out in support of it as well. They had long grappled with finding an alternative policy the public would accept, as their proposed "no territory" option was not attracting much support outside of Whig ranks. Some of them favored the proviso as a useful—perhaps last gasp—means of blocking the plans of Polk and his southern Democratic allies. Working with the dissident Democrats gave them a chance of frustrating their political enemies. Otherwise there was little hope they could accomplish their goals given the congressional political arithmetic that favored the Polk administration.[9]

Whether such an alliance could be successfully constructed beyond the particular situation existing in New Hampshire remained unclear. Whigs, Democrats, Liberty Party supporters, and the other reformers present were not natural allies. They continued to disagree with, even loath, each other most of the time. They had almost no experience (outside of New Hampshire) in working together for any reason, nor, heretofore, any appetite to do so. There was too much that separated them in the past, and that had not changed. The only thing clear as Congress adjourned in summer 1846 was that suddenly there might be the outlines of an antisouthern political constituency—ideological and behavioral—among northern members of Congress and their supporters, even if it was still not very well organized for action. There was no indication as yet of how large this bloc might be and how much staying power it might have, but the presence of such a coalition, whatever the uncertainties, might be more than enough to advance to another level of resistance.

But such hopes still lacked sufficient force. After Congress had adjourned, despite its potential, the proviso did not immediately change the course of U.S. politics outside of Congress. There was no immediate

John P. Hale, senator from New Hampshire who was elected by an antislavery coalition in his home state and then nominated for the presidency by the Liberty Party in 1848.

rush to support or attack Wilmot's foray against southern interests—or to see it as the beginning of a serious challenge to the prevailing political culture. Although some political activists in both parties supported the amendment, others strongly opposed its "threatening mandate of Federal legislation"; many ignored it or wished "the agitation of the Slavery question" would "cease." These reactions echoed the familiar attitudes so often expressed by political leaders and their followers in the 1840s when confronted by sectional agitation and attempts at confrontation.[10]

The political storm raised by David Wilmot in summer 1846 remained at the outset, therefore, largely a battle confined to Washington and some attentive activists in a number of states. Its ultimate outcome, and how sustained its force might become in the face of strong competing pressures and other activists contesting it, remained unknown. Whatever the success of expansion of the constituency, for the moment, to encompass a larger sympathetic audience beyond the existing group of abolitionist and antislavery resistors to Polk's policies—and to the southern defense of slavery and its leaders' recent aggressiveness in seeking to have their section's way in national affairs—no one could be sure how far it would go and what impact it would have in the arena of U.S. politics gearing up for the impending presidential contest.

"ENDEAVORING TO LIMIT THE EVILS OF SLAVERY"

What brought together an organized political movement in time for the presidential election of 1848 was the outcome of the war with Mexico, along with the continuing travails, frustration, and anger of the Van Buren Democrats and other dissenters in the last part of 1846 and throughout 1847. The political turmoil associated with the Polk administration continued when the 29th Congress reconvened in its second session at the end of 1846. By then several states had held local and congressional elections that resulted in substantial gains for the Whigs, including a shocking victory in the race for the governorship of New York, where the Whig candidate defeated the great Democratic leader, close Van Buren friend and ally, and, to many, the party's putative presidential candidate in 1848, Silas Wright. Wright was highly popular among party leaders and their followers and had won a smashing victory in the gubernatorial contest in 1844. Since then, however, he had lost much support for a range of reasons but was still expected to win reelection in 1846.[11]

When the results of all of the elections to the 30th Congress were finally in, a quite large Democratic majority in the House of Representatives had become a narrow Whig lead. The Whigs now held 116 seats to the Democrats' 108, with 4 scattered among minority parties. It was a severe setback for the president's party. Polk's policies, the angry challenges to his administration, and internal Democratic divisions had all, apparently, taken their toll on the party's usual voter support.[12]

Their midterm electoral losses were only the beginning of the Democrats' woes. Soon after Congress reconvened in December 1846, a radical Democratic representative, Preston King of New York, reintroduced the Wilmot Proviso in the House of Representatives. Again it passed that body but not the Senate. More critically, it set off another round of angry North-South confrontation, bitter debate, and sectional voting. A few members of the House had backed off somewhat over the congressional break in their willingness to challenge Polk and his favorites. Preston King, his Van Burenite New York colleagues, and other allies, had not. His action and their determination proved only the beginning of a long battle to shape the direction of Congress and public regarding the newly acquired territories and the question of slavery's expansion into them.[13]

At the same time, a great deal was happening outside of Congress to invigorate the controversy even further. Throughout 1847 the New York Democratic Party was tearing itself apart. King's allies among the Van Buren Democrats and their Hunker enemies battled over whether the state party would adopt the Wilmot Proviso as a clause in its party platform. The Barnburners argued that New York Democrats had always "believed in the wisdom, humanity, and constitutionality of the policy of endeavoring to limit the evils of slavery by protecting the unsettled territories of the United States against its introduction while they are under a territorial government." In short, the proviso was nothing new, and they wanted it enshrined in their party's public document. The Hunkers resisted with equal fervor and dismissed the Barnburners' demands as hostile to President Polk and threatening to the party's nationwide unity. Their battle reached a crescendo at the Democratic State Convention in Syracuse in September 1847, which was a disaster for the party. Both factions were present and ready to fight for their demands. In that fight, the Barnburners lost out. Their Hunker opponents controlled the agenda of the meeting and the nominations for state offices and used their control to deny renomination to several incumbents because they were prominent Barnburners. Not unexpectedly, they flatly refused to adopt the Wilmot Proviso as part of their state platform as the Barnburners demanded.[14]

The Barnburners, stung by their complete dismissal, refused to retreat from their position and from then on were in revolt against their fellow Democrats in the state, the latter's alleged subservience to the Polk administration, and their alleged complicity in the defeat (and recent sudden death) of Silas Wright. At the same time, in their meetings and the conventions that followed the Syracuse defeat, members of the Van Buren bloc reiterated their loyalty to the national party and its traditional policy stances to which they had been committed for so long. They made it clear that they were not trying to revolt against their longtime political home but rather to force it to return to its true pathway. They wanted its leaders to recognize what now had to be done in the face of the missteps of the Polk administration.[15]

One major question that loomed over the intraparty battle was who would represent New York's Democrats at the upcoming national convention. The Barnburners considered themselves the true Democratic Party of New York and expected national party leaders to recognize them as such and seat their delegates and no others when the time came. Their Hunker opponents made the same argument to Democrats in other states about themselves. Unable to find common ground, each bloc proceeded, in separate meetings, to select a full slate of thirty-six delegates to the national convention, refused to recognize the claims of the other side, denounced each other vigorously on the floor of the meetings and through their newspapers, and continued to fight over the appropriateness of the Wilmot Proviso as a party plank. The Democratic Party of the largest state of the Union had fallen into a sorry condition at the outset of a presidential election year. Given New York's recent electoral history, nothing could be worse for the national party and its prospects.[16]

In the meantime, in other states, antislavery proponents were also wrestling with the question of their next step. Whig supporters of the proviso, particularly those in Massachusetts and Ohio, engaged in confrontations comparable in fervor and potential divisiveness to the Democrats in New York. At the center of these intraparty conflicts was the specific question of whether the anti–slavery extension sentiments so many of them expressed would become an essential, that is, official, part of their state's Whig creed and, presumably, of the national party itself by being included as planks in the party's platforms at each level.[17]

These efforts initially had limited or no impact on most of their colleagues, even those among them who claimed to be hostile to slavery.

Party regulars were, therefore, able to beat back the attempts made at state conventions in 1846 and 1847 to adopt the Wilmot Proviso as a party commitment, leaving in their wake a disgruntled group of antiextension activists led by Charles Sumner, Henry Wilson, John Gorham Palfrey, and their fellow "Conscience Whigs" in Massachusetts, and a similarly unhappy group led by U.S. Representative Joshua Giddings from the Western Reserve area in northeastern Ohio, who was a longtime activist against slavery.[18]

As a result of their defeated hopes, some members of the Ohio group began to consider forsaking the old parties as hopeless and focusing their efforts instead on building an anti–slavery extension coalition of the disaffected groups of Whigs and Democrats, despite the difficulties such efforts would inevitably incur, to continue combating the aggressions of the southerners in the upcoming presidential election. Their efforts, not unexpectedly, did not initially succeed, since the idea of coalition with their partisan enemies continued to be resisted by most of Ohio's Whigs, even those among them who supported the proviso.[19]

The original organized political abolitionist group, the Liberty Party, was also considering how to proceed in the face of the uproar over Polk's expansionist policies and Wilmot's initiative to prevent the further extension of slavery, but not, as Liberty Party members had long demanded, to abolish it everywhere in the Union. Salmon P. Chase, a leading Liberty stalwart in Ohio, took the initiative among the so-called coalitionists among his party supporters, leading them in a similar search for combined action against the extension of slavery, ignoring, for the moment, the long-standing deep chasm between members of different parties and the highly unusual nature of what they were trying to effect.[20]

Like other such efforts, Chase's idea was not universally supported among his usual colleagues. To many of them, political coalition on the basis of the nonextension of slavery, not its abolition, gave away too much of what they believed in, even if they could overcome their misgivings and really trust their potential free-territory allies. As a result of disagreement over its ultimate ends, the Liberty Party split. It made two separate nominations for president. Many of the original core group of the party seceded in late spring 1847 and nominated Gerrit Smith as their choice for president; they prepared to contest the upcoming election on an abolitionist platform under a new name, the Liberty League. Several months later a second group, desiring to build a broader constituency, nominated New Hampshire's Senator Hale to run on the Liberty Party ticket. But that did not attract many others in the antislavery camp, and Hale himself made it clear he was quite hesitant about his nomination and about staying in the race.[21]

Chase persisted in his quest for willing coalition partners among sympathetic Democrats, Whigs, and others. He continued to argue it was the only effective means they had to strengthen the nation's antislavery politics and attain their objectives. But the outcome of his efforts continued to be uncertain. There was talk and much maneuvering among the antislavery leaders in reaction, but few signs of widespread success for his endeavor. At the end of 1847, a great deal remained up in the air in the antiextensionist camp, with a disabling lack of clarity about how they should proceed. In order to reach any agreement, there were still many divisions to overcome.[22]

THE SOUTHERN REACTION TO WILMOT

The upsurge in sectional political activity was not confined to the North in the wake of the introduction of the Wilmot Proviso. Southerners were certainly not pleased by the latest northern assault on their beliefs, and their leaders reacted angrily in newspaper editorials, speeches in their legislatures, and presentations to aroused crowds in public meetings against what they saw as an unconscionable, dangerous, and uncalled-for threat to their way of life. Those leaders who had already made efforts to unite their section in the face of persistent northern hostility believed that the increased antiextension activity among northerners gave them another opportunity to awaken their fellow southerners to their plight and bring them to their political senses at last. This was about, they pointed out, the most critical of all issues for southerners. Once again, they reminded everyone that slavery was an essential part of southern life and that attacks on it went to the heart of what defined the South as a society and made its economy prosperous.[23]

As a result, when Congress reconvened in December 1846, Calhoun, who had recently returned to the Senate to oppose the war with Mexico and any acquisition of territory as a result of it, introduced a series of resolutions arguing that the new territories nevertheless were the common property of all of the states, and ordaining, therefore, that citizens of any state had the unhindered right under the Constitution to take their property (certainly including slaves) into those territories. Congress could make no laws, he underscored, foreclosing that right. At the same time,

Calhoun also began discussing with his allies what additional political tactics they should adopt in the face of expansionism—especially whom they should support in the forthcoming presidential election.[24]

Calhoun's resolutions did not pass the Senate, nor did they receive the warm reception in his home section he wished to see. Despite their consensus about the importance of slavery to their society, southerners continued to disagree about how to defend themselves if it became necessary. Neither most southern Democrats nor southern Whigs were much impressed by Calhoun's proposals or his arguments on behalf of them. Whig hostility to and distrust of the South Carolinian was of long standing—he had once joined with them against Andrew Jackson but had subsequently deserted them. Whig leaders were determined to maintain their party's intersectional unity against Calhoun's attempt to erect a sectional barrier. Democrats also continued to resist his ideas by celebrating the importance of party unity and underscoring more fulsomely than ever the positive behavior of their northern colleagues. Northerners were, southern party loyalists argued, "rallying to the rescue of the Constitution." That is, they were opposing the Wilmot Proviso and coming out instead in favor of extending the existing Missouri Compromise line to the Pacific Coast and opening up the area south of it to slavery. Their section could have no better friends and allies.[25]

Calhoun and his supporters continued to be unconvinced about their safety at the hands of any northerners, including northern Democrats, and did not stop pushing their notions despite the lukewarm responses they were receiving so far from their sectional colleagues. Sympathizers took up the South Carolinian's initiative in several southern state legislatures and in a number of party conventions that passed resolutions opposing the Wilmot Proviso and asserted southern rights in the territories. But most of them did not go beyond that, at the outset, to adopt the kind of rigid, uncompromising stance Calhoun favored. A major exception was Alabama, where Calhoun's initiative took on particular force when the Democratic State Convention in early 1848 instructed its delegates to the upcoming national convention not to vote for anyone for the presidential nomination who had not declared himself in favor of congressional protection of slavery in the territories.[26]

This so-called Alabama Platform received much notice in the press and at public meetings, and was copied, in various forms, in other parts of the South. At the same time, some state leaders followed Calhoun's lead and began thinking about finding an independent candidate for president, untied to either party, who could be counted on to place the defense of southern interests at the forefront of his political agenda. As the editor of the Charleston *Mercury* put it, in the familiar terms of the Calhounites, "our safety in the Slaveholding States consists alone in CON-FIDENCE IN EACH OTHER, AND UNION AMONG OURSELVES." It was but a step from such sentiments to a movement calling for Calhoun to receive an independent nomination for the presidency, a proposal advanced by several popular meetings throughout the South, coupled with the passage at some of them of a southern rights platform on which he would run. The South Carolinian, his backers believed, seemed willing to be considered for the role they envisaged for him.[27]

All of this activity produced a great deal of noise, much heat, and to some southerners, clear indications of an increased threat to the smooth course of politics in their region. The party loyalists need not have worried at this point. Despite their anger against Wilmot and the other northerners involved with him, southern politicians remained divided over their tactics beyond denouncing malevolent northerners and crying out against the way their section was being unjustly attacked. Calhoun's arguments for an end to party distinctions still received little support in the allegedly endangered region. As one of his allies unhappily noted, "too large a portion" of their sectional colleagues has "not yet abandoned forever party predilections." Like their northern counterparts, a majority of southern political leaders continued to argue for the relevance of the Democratic and Whig Parties in their lives and the ability and willingness of those parties not to harm southern interests. So long as their constituents believed that, the sectional uproar could be contained. They rejected, as so many of them always had, "the ULTRA, uncompromising policy of Mr. Calhoun."[28]

THE CENTER HOLDS—FOR THE MOMENT

The result of this preliminary thrust and counterthrust in the politics of the impending national election was, as noted, a mixed bag. Much had crystallized as the Polk administration's policies had taken hold. In both North and South, sectional challenges to the existing norms of politics seemed to have gained some momentum in late 1846 and throughout 1847. North of the Mason-Dixon Line, those opposed to the further territorial extension of slavery had become more visible, more forceful, and, to their opponents, more threatening than they had been at any earlier time. They had articulated "a northern no" to the recent course of the president, his administration, and his southern allies. In the South, actions defending the institution of slavery and the rights of slaveholders within the Union had also become more prominent—the proponents of such strategies were certainly more vocal than they had been in some time, if still not in command there. The effectiveness of these efforts was not clear, but to many observers, the United States, as the Polk administration wound down, was going through a troubled, or at least an unsettled, political time.

Still, as much as the furor unleashed by events since 1845 dominated the minds of many of the politically involved in both the North and South, not everyone caught up in the political world accepted the sectional thrust embodied in the Wilmot Proviso or the drive for southern unity. The U.S. political mainstream remained committed to the two national parties, their themes and symbols, and the interests each of them pushed forward. Both parties continued to resist the sectional impulse and largely keep their political ships in their normal channels as they prepared for the upcoming presidential election. They were used to managing and/or ignoring sectional factions when they appeared and they brought their experience into play in response to the Wilmot Proviso and its aftermath.

Northern Democrats led the way in their constantly reiterated denunciation of sectional agitation. We are against the Wilmot Proviso, one editor wrote, as "mischievous" and "wholly irrelevant." We "prefer the simple support of the Democratic cause, divested of all new and disorganizing tests." They should not "surrender national questions and measures for a new and a sectional issue." Others of both parties joined in, echoing similar sentiments. They saw maintaining their party's unity throughout the country as their paramount need and the articulation of their traditional, nonsectional, divisions as their most effective weapon to accomplish that. That commitment to cross-sectional unity among like-minded individuals was important to them as they moved into the presidential election year.[29]

A critical question remained. Would their political world maintain the antisectional balance and direction that usually defined it to the degree desired by most party leaders? The sectionalists on each side had articulated a set of reciprocal political demands. Those in the forefront of the sectional attacks and responses—the New York Barnburners, the Hale coalition in New Hampshire, the mostly Whig and Liberty dissidents from Massachusetts and Ohio in the North, and their opposite in John C. Calhoun and his group of southern naysayers—showed little indication that they were going to back off from their positions or their determination to shift, fundamentally, the direction of the political world. These challengers to the political status quo had reason, they now believed, for optimism. If not the political establishment, perhaps the American people were now moving toward their way of thinking. To the sectionalists, more people seemed aroused by the current confrontation than had previously been the case, and many of them appeared to be angrier than ever before. Most critical of all, the territorial situation that had led to the growing tension remained unresolved as a new presidential election year opened.

"THE SORE-HEADED LEADERS IN THE STATE OF NEW YORK"—AND SOME OTHERS—NOMINATE A PRESIDENT

The peace treaty with Mexico ceding the vast domain of California and New Mexico to the United States arrived in Washington in February 1848. Although negotiator Nicholas Trist, a U.S. State Department official, did not win from the defeated enemy all of the territory President Polk had desired, the president submitted the treaty to the Senate, which proceeded to ratify it over continued Whig objections to adding so much territory to the Union and the publicly expressed unhappiness of extreme expansionist Democrats who agreed with the president that it did not add enough. Congressional acceptance of the treaty was the end of a foreign affairs episode, the Mexican-American War, but it left open difficult questions that had been disturbing the domestic political landscape since summer 1846. Would slavery be excluded from or permitted in the new areas acquired from Mexico? This question would now become enmeshed with the impending campaign to elect a president.[1]

The treaty and the complications that accompanied it arrived as both the Whigs and Democrats were gearing up for their national conventions to choose their tickets and articulate the issues on which they intended to run in the fall. The leaders of both parties began with the obvious belief that their party could win if they nominated the right candidate, publicly laid out the most compelling solutions to current issues, and organized their efforts so as to get as many of their usual supporters as possible to the polls. But conventions often were difficult territory for party leaders as blocs of activists representing different groups in a pluralist nation struggled to dominate their party's affairs. Choosing the candidates who would make up their tickets was particularly tense and conflict-prone. Who among them was the right candidate for the purpose of public support? Putting the wish to maximize their appeal and get out the vote first in choosing their nominee could, and often did, clash with the expectations and demands of the different blocs seeking their share of power and prioritization of their particular policies.

The result was a great deal of internal party sparring along with feverish maneuvering among the leaders in different states as aspirants with powerful claims to consideration were put forward. Such normal jousting had, of course, been magnified by the tensions unleashed during the Polk administration and the frustrations felt by the Whigs because of their recent problems. Finally, the fact that the electorate had proved so closely divided between the Whigs and Democrats in the most recent presidential election added to the pressures, the mix of problems to be faced, and the decisions to be made at these meetings. Everyone wanted to win and, at the same time, wanted to believe that their particular favorite for the nomination and their particular policy priorities were the keys to victory for their party.[2]

THE PARTIES PLAN AND PREPARE

The Democrats' thinking about the upcoming contest began with James K. Polk's announcement at the time of his nomination that he would not be a candidate for reelection, in an apparent attempt to calm his party after the divisive events at the 1844 convention and in hopes of placating the various leaders who had expected to benefit from Van Buren's fall but had not. Some party leaders close to Polk had since unsuccessfully tried to get him to change his mind. Whatever the reasons were for his early refusal, by 1848 the president was more than resolute in his position. He had had enough of Washington and the persistent nerve-wracking complexities of national political warfare, which had made him an object of loathing and had so cruelly worn him down despite his comparative youth. (He would die just weeks after leaving office.)[3]

There were several candidates ready to move into Polk's place. They had been put forward by local meetings or suggested by editors of friendly party newspapers (in the absence of primaries, which were instituted at a later date). Those named were men of national reputation who had proven themselves loyal, committed Democrats over a long period. They included Polk's secretary of state, James Buchanan of Pennsylvania, a fifty-seven-year-old former minister to Russia with a long domestic career résumé as a U.S. representative and senator. He had been first elected to Congress a few years after the end of the War of 1812 and had remained politically active since. Second was an equally experienced former soldier in that war, then a practicing lawyer, the territorial governor of Michigan for many years, then U.S. secretary of war, minister to France, and now senator, Lewis Cass, the sixty-six-year-old chair of the Senate Military Affairs Committee. He had been born in New Hampshire but was primarily associated with the rapidly growing Old Northwest states. He had moved to Ohio early in his life and spent many years there and in Michigan. He was now considered the West's leading political figure. He had been a candidate for the nomination in 1844, actually outpacing Martin Van Buren's total delegate support in the balloting just before the convention swung to James K. Polk. Finally, Levi Woodbury, another native of New Hampshire, born in 1789, who stayed in his native state to become first its governor and then one of its U.S. senators, rounded out the leading candidates. He later became secretary of the navy and secretary of the treasury under Jackson and Van Buren, respectively, and was now an associate justice of the U.S. Supreme Court.[4]

In addition to these front-runners, several others were mentioned in the early going, including Polk's vice president, George Dallas, like Buchanan an experienced politician from Pennsylvania and the latter's bitter rival for control of the party in their home state, and Robert J. Walker, once a U.S. senator from Mississippi and for the past four years U.S. secretary of the treasury. Walker had been an avid promoter of Texas annexation during the Tyler administration and the architect of the lower tariff passed by the Democratic Congress in 1846. In a special place as a potential candidate was the ever hopeful Martin Van Buren, who, like Cass, was in his late sixties. His political biography was extraordinary as a longtime activist who had had a great deal to do with the establishment of the Democratic Party in the 1820s and who then had successfully worked to unite it as a national force. He had never been far from the seats of power. He had held several offices in New York State, including governor for a short time, had been an important member of the U.S. Senate in the 1820s, had then served in Jackson's cabinet as secretary of state and as "Old Hickory's" vice president before twice becoming his party's candidate for chief executive, successfully in 1836, then losing in 1840, and finally being rejected for renomination at the national convention in 1844. Angered by what had happened to his party and to himself and his friends under Polk, he was thought by some close observers to be considering another run in order to regain control of the Jacksonian party from those who had, he and his followers believed, torn it from its roots and debased it.[5]

No one was sure how the nomination battle would be resolved. To many party leaders, the current situation among the Democrats was, as U.S. Representative Stephen A. Douglas from Illinois wrote in April, a "glorious state of confusion."[6] But all of the frenetic activity on behalf of different candidates after they had been identified as potential nominees was, of course, now part of the established reality of the run-up to the national convention. Each camp had high hopes for their man and worked hard to achieve them. Friends of the candidates worked assiduously to round up delegate support for their favorites. Each of the plausible nominees began with significant support in his home state and surrounding areas. But cheerleading and local support was only the beginning of the task each faced. In the year or more preceding the national convention, advocates of the potential nominees kept busy establishing newspapers and building state-level organizations on behalf of their candidates. They rounded up endorsements from party leaders and commitments from delegates and worked with activists to influence the preferences stated in local party meetings and at state conventions; some of them tried to woo delegates already committed to others to their side.[7]

The outcome of their activities depended on a great many things: local and regional loyalties, personal appeal, policy preferences, and the matters that had gone on during Polk's presidency. Furthermore, despite what they believed to be the successes of the administration in both domestic and foreign affairs, many of the Democratic leaders realized they were more in trouble with the voters than they cared to be at the outset of a presidential campaign. Their state and congressional election losses in 1846 weighed heavily on them. They did do somewhat better in the contests held in 1847, but the electorate's message seemed obvious. Despite Polk's achievements, there remained much opposition to Democratic policies from the still potent Whigs as well as a great deal of frustration within the president's party itself because of his refusal to support their particular issues, all of which could impact the choices made by the delegates to the party's national meeting.[8]

Nor could Democrats ignore the sectional tensions among them. Whatever the motives of the supporters of the Wilmot Proviso, some of whom were accused of simply seeking revenge against Polk, not truly caring about the slavery issue, they were forcing others to face, however hesitantly and unwillingly, the ills of slavery in their society. Critically, the division in the New York Democrats continued to fester as the campaign season got under way. Publicly, Martin Van Buren was in semi-retirement at his home in the Hudson Valley, but remained involved behind the scenes as his close lieutenants led by Benjamin F. Butler, including his politically experienced and aggressive son John, were making his feelings known.[9]

The New York Democrats continued to indicate loudly and relentlessly that they would not get along with each other even in the face of the upcoming election. As 1847 approached its end, the outraged Barnburners came together in a mass meeting at Herkimer in upstate New York to protest the hostile actions against them by the Hunkers at the regular party convention in Syracuse the month before. Their anger was palpable, and they made sure that everyone knew where they now stood, that reconciliation among the New York blocs was impossible. Therefore, they reiterated, the national party had to recognize those men they had chosen, and not those of the Hunkers, as the sole official delegates from New York, and be seated as such in Baltimore.[10]

They had more to say at the Herkimer meeting beyond making clear which group of Democrats was really, in their view, the true New York party. They invited David Wilmot to join them, and he did so, speaking alongside the Barnburner leaders as they denounced any further extension of slavery. They asserted with much conviction that they would not support anyone, candidate or party, that was not antiextension. They made it clear, above all, that they wanted the language of the proviso included in the Democratic national platform.[11]

The Barnburners' convening of the Herkimer meeting and their loud fulminations and nonnegotiable demands once there aroused the usual anger from their state party colleagues. To these Hunkers, the meeting of the dissidents was "the nearest approach to the Hartford Convention," a particularly offensive characterization given that long ago meeting's still extremely negative image in the minds of most Americans. The Hunkers had little sympathy for the Barnburners' many complaints and their subsequent actions. Most critically, the Hunker attitude toward the proviso and its supporters remained unyieldingly hostile. It was, their leading editor wrote, "a mere cover, in all its phases, to divide and distract the Democratic Party of the North, to destroy its nationality, and

... give the Whigs a victory in the presidential canvass." Expressing that sentiment, although it was widely shared among New York Democrats, did not resolve anything. The Barnburners were making it as clear as they could that they did not intend to back down from their positions or their intentions of representing the state at the national convention.[12]

Mainstream Democrats in other states had also been debating how they should handle the issue raised by the rebellious Wilmot's and the Barnburners' foray into antislavery politics. Most of them had no intention of supporting the proviso. They feared its potential to distract them and their supporters from focusing their primary attention on traditional concerns. These party stalwarts wanted to engage in the normal tussles of partisan warfare. They did not want new issues such as the proviso to come into play and alter the political landscape, threaten their unity, and upset their electoral calculations. The most recalcitrant traditionalists among them argued that the party should, as one editor had put it earlier, do its best to ignore "this pretended question of free soil." And all of them knew full well—and were obviously concerned—that southerners were reported to be "furious about the proviso" and would not accept any limitations on their right to take their slaves into the territories.[13]

If, however, the party had to face the issue, a number of suggestions was offered of ways around the proviso and thus out of the difficulties it posed. James Buchanan, for example, proposed extending the Missouri Compromise line of 1820 (running east to west along 36° 30' north latitude) from its current endpoint on the Missouri-Nebraska border westward through the new territorial acquisitions all the way to the Pacific Coast, allowing slavery to be introduced south of the line but barring it to the north. Many southern Democrats favored this approach because it opened up great possibilities for them in the Mexican cession and, at the same time, got their party out of the dilemma posed by the extension issue.[14]

But, of course, John C. Calhoun did not agree; he saw extending the Missouri line as an unacceptable maneuver that limited southerners in their constitutional right to go anywhere in federal territory (i.e., north of the Missouri line) if they wished to. As one of his supporters, Senator Albert Brown of Mississippi, put it, "I shall not admit, as some southern men have done, a right in the people of the Territory to exclude me and my constituents from a full participation in the use and occupancy of these Territories." The idea was "monstrous," to him. Critically, a number of other Democrats in the South, not usually Calhoun supporters but

John Van Buren, Democratic dissident, leader of the Barnburners, and a major figure in the Free Soil campaign.

sensitive to the South Carolinian's influence among some of their own followers, joined his protest. He and they were opposed to a pending bill in Congress to organize the Oregon Territory without slavery. This bill got entangled in the uproar over extensionism, and President Polk hesitated about it but ultimately signed it when it finally passed, because, as he indicated, the new territory lay well north of the Missouri divide.[15]

Calhoun's notion of the constitutional propriety of allowing slavery in all federal territories had few enough supporters. And his hopes for a presidential run that would significantly reorient political matters in the United States had not gotten far, leading him to indicate his lack of interest in pursuing that ambition any further. Nevertheless, some of the dissenters around him still wanted to stand clear of the major parties. But what was their alternative? Calhoun's concerned followers would have to find another political pathway of achieving their purpose of protecting the rights of slaveholders if they could.[16]

Other Democrats opposed the extension of the Missouri line as well, but for a different reason. They feared that such a solution would rouse parts of the northern electorate against their party since it potentially opened vast new areas to slavery, and could possibly lead, therefore, to the party losing votes on polling day from those whom they could usually count on or at least hope to attract. The Democrats could not afford the defection of such potential supporters in the closely competitive states in the Northeast. The existence of that possibility led, therefore, to an intense search by party leaders for still other ways of resolving the issue before it bit too deeply into the presidential race.[17]

In 1847, Vice President George Dallas had offered a different solution to the party's dilemma: "The very best thing that can be done when all is said on this subject that may be said," he argued, "will be to let it alone entirely—leaving the people of the territory to be acquired the business of settling the matter for themselves." This was an early call for what later would be labeled *popular sovereignty* by its supporters and *squatter sovereignty* by those who were less enthusiastic. Senator Daniel Dickinson of New York, a Hunker leader, picked up the idea and introduced a popular sovereignty resolution in the Senate in December 1847. Lewis Cass publicly adopted this approach as well and made it one of the cornerstones of his drive for the presidential nomination. His 1847 letter to a Tennessee politician, A. O. P. Nicholson, spelled out his commitment against accepting any jurisdiction by Congress in the matter, leaving the decision about practicing slavery to the resident population of a territory.

When the idea was published in party newspapers, it received a great deal of support from other Democrats in both the North and South. It was, one Georgia party editor wrote, "entirely satisfactory to the southern portion of the Union."[18]

As the Democrats met and discussed their positions in their various local and state meetings, it became clear that the state parties were not going to support the Wilmot Proviso at the national convention. It would not be, they insisted, part of the platform they adopted. The leading candidates for the nomination all strongly opposed it as official party doctrine as did a great many of the rank-and-file Democrats. Most of the northern state conventions called upon to name delegates to the national meeting of the party and to suggest platform planks they wished to be considered there underscored their belief that the whole matter was an unwelcome intrusion into normal political affairs, and refused, therefore, to accept Wilmot's idea or language as part of their party's creed. Northern Democrats "have evinced a disposition not to surrender national questions and measures for a new and a sectional issue." And, one editor concluded, "the proviso is one of them." They did so even though they knew that there was provisoism among some insistent party members in their states.[19]

Still, as they sought a formula to get the sectional issue off the political table, party leaders also tried hard to calm down the anger and bring the various factions together, pleading for tolerance among those agitated whatever the outcome of the debates over Wilmot's initiative. Their weapon was an appeal to party loyalty and the common ideals that bound them together, reminding the New York dissidents, for example, that the opposition to the proviso expressed by so many northern Democrats was not "treason to our political faith" and should neither be condemned nor held against those who disagreed with the New Yorkers. Rather, everyone should recognize that they could still work together on behalf of the issues that had always defined them and that remained central to their supporters.[20]

ROUGH AND READY

The Whig National Convention was scheduled to meet in early June in Philadelphia. As did its Jacksonian enemies, the party could also look to a roster of veteran, middle-aged, and older party leaders as attractive potential nominees. Each was, like his Democratic counterparts, an experienced officeholder at both the state and national levels. Also, as with the Democratic hopefuls, each had a reasonable level of support to begin with and hope for more. The most preeminent, former House speaker and secretary of state Henry Clay, now seventy-one years old, led from his position as the Whigs' long-recognized leader, best articulator of their creed, and oft-chosen (in 1824 and 1832) and most recent (in 1844) presidential nominee.

Others included the always hopeful eminent statesman from Massachusetts, Daniel Webster, in his mid-sixties, who had made his reputation in his many years in both the U.S. House and Senate and as secretary of state under President Harrison at the beginning of the 1840s. He had long hoped for (and expected) his party's nomination but had previously always been disappointed. He was joined by two other currently sitting senators, the sixty-six-year-old John J. Crittenden of Kentucky, Clay's longtime colleague in that state's politics and a well-regarded party leader nationally (in addition to his Senate service he had briefly served as the nation's attorney general under President Harrison), and former governor Thomas P. Corwin of Ohio, the youngest of the candidates at age fifty-four, who had made his mark recently in dramatic speeches on the Senate floor as a fierce opponent of the war with Mexico. Finally, Supreme Court Justice John McLean, sixty-three years old, also from Ohio, rounded out the group. He was a familiar political figure. He had, over the years, served as postmaster general as well as on the Court, and was a perennial favorite for the nomination among some party leaders, particularly in the western states. There was something to be said for each of them: each had the experience to be a national leader, had served in Washington, and was well versed in the nation's current concerns. And each believed that he had enough party support to be favored in Philadelphia.[21]

But, as Whig leaders had been thinking hard about their candidate, along with what would be their most effective strategy in the upcoming campaign, a number of them, including Clay's close ally Crittenden, reminded their colleagues that the party opposing the Democrats did not normally have enough strength to win a national election. (They had, after all, lost four out of the five contests since 1828.) This was, therefore, not the time for overoptimism in their ranks or for normal factional behavior by party members. To raise their electoral totals, the Whigs, they argued, had to reach outside their current roster of available candidates

John J. Crittenden, veteran Whig leader and longtime Clay associate who abandoned Clay, coming out in favor of Taylor instead before the party's national convention.

and find someone who had particularly strong appeal to the voters. As one writer put it, "The enemy was in possession of the Capitol—under whom could a change be effected?"[22]

If the party needed a fresh face with wide appeal who could attract more than Whig votes, that was not the oft-defeated Clay, who "cannot be elected," or any of the other veteran Whigs, no matter how stalwart they were. Their best bet was, as in 1840, a military hero, the arguers continued, "sufficiently adventurous to tickle the masses," such as one of the two outstanding leaders in the Mexican-American War: the professional soldiers Winfield Scott and Zachary Taylor. Both of them were, indeed, fresh faces with wide appeal beyond political insiders and their followers. Each had won major battles against U.S. enemies and much acclaim, Taylor at Palo Alto, Monterey, and Buena Vista, and Scott on the march to Mexico City, battles that had established U.S. dominance and led to ending the war. Their victories echoed the exploits of the earlier military heroes George Washington, Andrew Jackson, and William Henry Harrison. Although the Whigs had vehemently opposed Polk's policies toward Mexico and the ensuing war that had brought both generals to public attention and admiration, both Scott and Taylor were thought more sympathetic to the Whigs than to the sitting president, who had, in their eyes, treated neither of them well, and with whom each had clashed. Their promoters believed that they could carry their own states, Louisiana by Taylor, Virginia by Scott, plus the normal Whig voter base elsewhere, and, most critically, attract enough other voters not usually with them to lead their party to victory.[23]

A small group of Whig members of Congress, soon dubbed the Young Indians by their colleagues, picked up the notion of choosing a military man from outside its normal ranks, and concluded that the Virginia-born, sixty-four-year-old Taylor, "Old Rough and Ready," officially a resident of Louisiana where he owned a plantation, fit the bill best. His virtues as a vigorous and successful leader in his chosen profession were manifest, while to the chagrin of Winfield Scott's supporters, that politically unsophisticated general had publicly stumbled several times, including writing an anti-immigrant letter seeking nativist support for his candidacy, which many Whigs feared would be used by the Democrats to pull immigrants to the polls to vote against them. He made a number of other gaffes that Democrats were quick to claim made him look silly and certainly most unpresidential. In contrast, Taylor's supporters argued, Old Rough and Ready remained above reproach.[24]

Five of the six members of Congress originally behind the push for Taylor were from the South; the other was Connecticut's Truman Smith, who had managed the party's campaign efforts in 1846 and 1847; he was, like his southern colleagues, desperate to nominate someone who could return the Whigs to national power. They were joined in late 1847 when Congress convened by a newly elected U.S. representative from Illinois, Abraham Lincoln. As with the others already working on behalf of Taylor, Lincoln, long a devoted follower of Henry Clay, nevertheless did not believe he was the one that could bring a Whig victory. With great reluctance, he had come to agree that the party had to go outside its usual ranks. He was satisfied that the party could win with the general, whereas "we cannot elect any other Whig."[25]

The congressional Young Indians, along with similar activist groups in Louisiana and Kentucky, began working on Taylor's behalf among party members in Washington and in various states as the Whigs began convening to select delegates to the national convention. Lobbying their colleagues and setting up Rough and Ready Clubs to promote his candidacy in different parts of the Union, they sought to build a popular groundswell in his favor. They did their work well. The involvement of these shrewd political operatives greatly strengthened Taylor's position among other party loyalists. Daniel Webster made a speaking tour of several southern states in 1847 on behalf of his own hoped-for candidacy, but found that his supporters were numerically overwhelmed at his appearances by the presence of many more enthusiasts for Taylor, who made their position clear to the embarrassed statesman.[26]

The political attraction of Taylor for Whigs appeared in other ways as well. The bitter tensions that had arisen between the general and the Polk administration over the way the war should be fought, which had become public while he was winning his victories in Mexico, gave them even more reason to find him compatible as their leader against the hated president and his party. Any enemy of Polk had much to commend him. At the same time, Taylor held still another attraction in the eyes of some Whig leaders. As a Louisiana resident and a slaveowner, he would be particularly appealing to the party's southern bloc as being one of them, and, perhaps, his proponents hoped, he would be seen that way by other southerners normally outside of their party ranks as well. This affiliation prompted a reaction against him, however, from northern Whigs with strong antislavery convictions, who had grown increasingly sensitive about who should lead their party with the rise of the territorial

Truman Smith, U.S. representative from Connecticut,
Whig Party campaign manager, and early
enthusiast for Zachary Taylor's nomination.

issue and the failure of the Wilmot Proviso to get through Congress. One observer had warned Crittenden in mid-1847 that Ohio Whigs were declaring that "they will go for no slave State man." That attitude would remain a crucial reality thereafter.[27]

Not all Whig leaders were convinced by the arguments for a military hero. Most preferred to stand by their great leader, Clay. As one of them put it, "If the Whigs succeed at all, it must be on the merits of their own principles, maintained by their own votes. Other expectations will prove illusory." These Clay loyalists were determined to provide him one more opportunity to win the presidency. He deserved it given his long service to the Whig cause, because he was the embodiment of all they stood for, and—ignoring the fears of the Young Indians and others—because, they argued, he could win. He had barely been defeated four years before, and the party had done better in elections since. Among his supporters, Horace Greeley, the influential editor of the New York *Tribune*, stood out. He was a longtime associate of Thurlow Weed and William Henry Seward in the leadership that dominated New York State's Whig politics. Now, rejecting the Taylor boom, he strongly stood behind Clay as the best embodiment of the Whig creed they had all long fought to establish in the United States. He was not alone in such convictions among other party loyalists.[28]

A number of the other candidates continued to attract some support as well, including the somewhat tarnished Scott. But none of them was able to arouse the level of backing Clay and Taylor had amassed in the preliminaries to the party convention. Some quickly dropped by the way-side. The supporters of Scott and Webster continued to stick it out in the hope that they could overcome the leaders' advantages and, as the front-runners fell or stalemated each other, expect that the convention delegates would turn to their favorite instead.[29]

Both leading candidates had their liabilities as well as assets. Clay, for example, in addition to being a shopworn loser to many, and despite holding the most solid Whig credentials, had made missteps in his major address to a crowd in Lexington, Kentucky, the previous November. In addition to denouncing the war with Mexico and assailing the president for his policies and for overstepping his powers (a favorite Whig theme), Clay had turned to discussing slavery and made remarks that, to many southern Whigs, seemed less supportive of the institution than he should be. His remarks were careful, not confrontational, but he said that he had "ever regarded slavery as a great evil, a wrong." He went on to argue that its future was up to the people in the states in which it existed, not to anyone else. Sensitive southern Whigs found the word *evil* a bid for northern Whig support, an action sectionalists believed made him dangerous to their well-being. Whatever else he had said, they simply did not trust Clay to protect them from the threats they detected against their way of life, nor did they think many Whig voters in their section would either. Thus he was potentially a political liability.[30]

As for Taylor, his opponents pointed out that unlike the other generals who had earlier been elected president, he had no civic experience, no familiarity with the way U.S. politics and government operated. He had never voted. He had been a career professional soldier (unlike Washington, Jackson, and Harrison, who had risen out of the ranks of the state militia and volunteers), appointed to the army in 1808. He had spent most of his life at a succession of tiny army posts on the frontier commanding small groups of soldiers, hardly good preparation for running a country. His career worked against him in another way. Some Whigs continued to be quite hesitant about nominating a military man, an act they considered contrary to their party's position on the war. And, although he was attractive to southern Whigs, his slaveowning offended northern antislavery Whigs more and more, continuing to prompt sharply expressed hostility from some of them and suggestions that they could not support a party ticket with him at the head of it. He was "a Slave owner—a Slave breeder," one antislavery Whig pamphleteer wrote, "and the candidate and warrior of the promoters of the Extension of slavery."[31]

Taylor proved to be a maddening candidate in the run-up to the Whig National Convention. His general popularity among the American people was so strong that throughout 1847 non-Whig meetings had also pushed his candidacy forward, and, in his responses to their warm words in his favor, he seemed to encourage them. There was not a nomination tendered, whatever the source, Taylor seemed able to refuse. When he responded to the outpouring of support, the general apparently had difficulty admitting he was a Whig. He saw himself, it appeared, as a candidate who was above parties, as a nonpartisan people's representative, free of what he argued were the limiting shackles of partisanship and glad of it. He proved it by accepting nominations from a meeting of an anti-immigrant Native American Party and from a Democratic meeting as well. And he wrote letters (too many letters, some frustrated Whig leaders thought) reiterating his independence from normal political institutions, which obviously did not appeal to staunch Whigs. If he "keeps writing letters," one observer wrote, "Clay will be nominated."[32]

Taylor's no-party, really antiparty, stance and apparent naiveté about the norms of the nation's political process were not what most traditional Whigs had in mind for their presidential candidate, and appalled many of them, increasing their initial hesitancy about putting him at the head of their ticket whatever his supposed electability. Given their supporters' long-standing commitment to certain policies, would his candidacy hurt efforts to mobilize the party's base to come out on election day? The participation at the polls of the Whig faithful, too, was needed if the party was to win. And, if elected, could he be counted upon to act as a Whig while in office? Given his behavior to this point, no one could be sure.[33]

These negative reactions to Taylor obviously troubled his backers and led them to take the initiative to repair the damage. In response to the growing wariness toward him from too many who were needed if they were to triumph, Taylor's backers prevailed on him in April to sign a letter drafted within their ranks and addressed to his brother-in-law John Allison that sought to calm the apprehensions his behavior had raised. In it, Taylor made what one historian called a "tortured accommodation to party." He was, he said, "a Whig but not an Ultra Whig." So far as his actions as president were concerned, he would act "independent of party domination." At the same time, he would not be the kind of unacceptably (to the Whigs) aggressive executive that Democratic presidents Jackson and Polk had been. He believed Congress should lead the way in domestic policy and, as president, he would exercise his veto power rarely against declared congressional preferences even when he disagreed with them. When they read the letter, hesitant Whigs were supposed to be reassured and recognize Taylor's position as a far cry from the excessive executive behavior they had always deplored. It was supposed to echo one of the critical themes that had brought the Whigs together in the first place fifteen years before.[34]

The letter to Allison did calm many of the qualms Whigs had expressed about their prospective candidate. Many of them wanted to believe that "the letter breathes the true Whig spirit," whether it was written by Taylor or not. As a result, more and more of the activists came to support Taylor with increasing enthusiasm. Still, as their national convention approached, division and confusion clearly remained in Whig ranks about the outcome, with both Clay and Taylor attracting solid blocs of delegates to the national convention along with often angry opposition as well. Despite the speculation in party newspapers, no one seemed to have an accurate count of which candidate was ahead and what, in fact, would be the best course for the party to adopt.[35]

CASS IS THE MAN

The fifth Democratic National Convention convened in the Universalist Church in Baltimore on May 22, 1848, with former House speaker Andrew Stevenson of Virginia as permanent chair. The streets were filled with enthusiastic and noisy supporters of the candidates. Some of the crowd got inside the church and added to the din there. There were 290 delegates accredited to the assemblage, apportioned on the basis of each state's electoral votes. The delegates had been chosen earlier by state party meetings. (Some states split individual delegate votes among several party loyalists, allowing them to share in the excitement of the convention.) The Calhoun-influenced Democrats of South Carolina were an exception to these rules and practices. They had refused to name a slate of delegates to a convention their leaders (i.e., Calhoun) opposed and preferred that they boycott. But the credentials committee of the national convention got around that by allowing the single South Carolinian in attendance, James Commander, to cast all nine of his state's votes.[36]

That same committee also had to deal with the two competing delegations from New York, the thirty-six member Hunker group selected at the state convention in September from which the Barnburners had departed and a second set of thirty-six delegates named by the Barnburners in a meeting in Utica in February. Despite the continuation of their angry rebellion, that meeting had given everyone some hope because it had appeared to be more conciliatory than the Van Burenites had been in the fall. In contrast to their inflexible behavior at Herkimer, in preparing for their appearance at the national convention they seemed more willing to accept the need for party loyalty and not insist on specific tests (i.e., the Wilmot Proviso) being included in the national platform. But they still adamantly held to their claim to be the legitimate Democrats representing their state and their demand, therefore, that they had to be the only ones from New York seated by the national party. Martin Van Buren had written a widely circulated statement that came to be called the Barnburner Manifesto, then issued by the Democratic caucus in the New York State Legislature, that spelled out their claims and their strategy, denouncing slavery extension once more and strongly asserting the Barnburners' rights to be seated at the convention.[37]

The credentials committee and then the full convention, to which the matter was referred, tried to find grounds for compromise. But the committee also had a demand of its own—that the convention receive the assurances of both of the contending groups that, if admitted, they would accept the actions of the convention and support its nominee. The Hunkers agreed to the stipulation, but the Barnburners stuck by their guns and refused. Faced with the continuing division and the hardening of positions among the New Yorkers, the credentials committee therefore recommended to the convention that the Hunker delegation be the only one seated. The full convention, still looking for a solution that would, the delegates hoped, bring peace and party unity to their meeting, refused to accept the committee's proposal and forced the issue to come before the entire assembly for resolution. There, after a stormy debate lasting several days, with much booing, cheering, name-calling, and just plain shouting from the packed galleries, during which the New York Democrats' dirty linen was exposed to all, the body judiciously suggested that the state's delegates be split equally between the two sides. (That motion barely passed—by a vote of 126 to 124.)[38]

Neither the Hunkers nor the Barnburners agreed to that compromise—neither would budge as to who were the real representatives of their state, and the convention had to proceed without New York's vote in the proceedings, although both remained in attendance. Traditional politicians were not happy with their failure to bridge the party's divisions. "Indeed," a southerner wrote, "it is hard to tell whether Mr. Calhoun or the sore-headed leaders in the State of New York are most bent on making mischief for the national democracy in revenge for the action of the Baltimore Convention of 1844." But there was little anyone could do about it. Feelings had gotten out of control in the New York matter, and it was now clearly beyond the capacity of the delegates present to repair the rift.[39]

The convention continued its organizational efforts despite the rebuff from New York. The delegates adopted once again, after some debate, the rule in place in 1836 and 1844 that, to be nominated by the party, a presidential candidate must receive two-thirds of the convention's votes. The rule had caused them much trouble in 1844 and its shadow had lain over the party since; it continued to have an impact now with the Barnburners continually being reminded, and reminding themselves, of what they had lost four years before because of the requirement. The rule's proponents saw it as a useful tool to underscore the wide support for their candidate and preserve the rights of candidates against any possible steamrolling by a majority bloc at the meeting.[40]

While all of this crucial organizing activity was going on, the advocates for the various candidates continued to try to round up the necessary votes for their man. Each of the main candidates, Buchanan, Woodbury, and Cass, had come into the convention with substantial blocs of supporters chosen in state party meetings over the previous months. The first ballot cast, on May 23, showed that Cass was outdistancing the rest, but remained well short of the number needed: he received 125 votes, Buchanan had 55, and Woodbury had 53, with 18 others scattered. Almost all of the delegations voted as a unit supporting the choice of their majority. Cass won the five states of the Old Northwest, his home territory, where his popularity was extremely high. He won the votes from five more in the Southwest, along with Virginia and three from New England. Buchanan and Woodbury's votes largely were confined to their home states and some of their nearest neighbors. Each drew occasional stray votes largely based on internal state rivalries and other such difficulties. The convention took three more ballots before the battle finally ended on the fourth roll call with Cass receiving 179 votes of the 250 cast, more than enough for the nomination. In the style of the time, the convention then moved to make his nomination unanimous as a sign of their collegial unity and partisan determination.[41]

As the result was announced, whatever sense of elation may have been present was dampened when the thirty-six Barnburners, who had quietly sat through it all to this point, following the advice given them by Martin Van Buren before the convention, defiantly left the meeting hall in protest at the way they had been treated by the assembled delegates and of the nomination that the party had made. The radicalized New Yorkers, by now all but totally alienated from their former allies, had objections to most of the Democrats' potential candidates because of various matters, but critically because of the party and its nominee's lack of commitment against any further extension of slavery. Cass, in particular, remained totally unacceptable to the Van Buren group. They remained convinced that he was their enemy and was less committed to the party's traditional policies than he claimed to be. The Hunkers, who had also not taken part in the proceedings to that point, had no such reservations or were determined to go along come what may, and, therefore, in contrast to their state rivals, indicated on the following day that they would support the party's nominee.[42]

The convention reassembled that evening when six men were put forward as candidates for vice president. At other times the delegates might have turned to New York State to find someone to balance the ticket and sooth the anger of the defeated. But that was now clearly impossible.

Instead, they took a cue from their Whig rivals. It had been suggested to President Polk some time before that "we must have one military hero on our ticket," and the convention now found one in fifty-seven-year-old former U.S. representative General William O. Butler of Kentucky. He had served in the War of 1812, recently run for governor of his home state, and successfully commanded volunteer troops in Mexico. He won on the second ballot over John Quitman of Mississippi, another Mexican-American War commander and a strong advocate of southern rights.[43]

After the nominations were completed the convention turned the next morning to considering the party's platform. The completed document, unsurprisingly, repeated themes familiar from previous platforms and from the repeated iteration of them by Democratic orators and editors in earlier campaigns going back to Thomas Jefferson and the great days of Andrew Jackson. These paeans to past glories were reinforced by the writers of the document adding words celebrating the many beneficent actions taken under the most recent Democratic president, James K. Polk, and in his resisting succumbing to the pressures on him. The keynote was pure and unshakable Democratic outlook: "The federal government is one of limited powers," the drafters wrote. It should not establish a national bank, it should practice rigid economy, and it should follow a low tariff policy—all of this to demonstrate contrast to the Whigs with their roots in the excessive national power ideas of the earlier Federalist Party.[44]

At the conclusion of their litany of traditional Democratic beliefs, the drafters appended a pointed condemnation of the abolitionists and any attempt by Congress to interfere with questions of slavery. "Congress has no power under the Constitution," the platform read, "to interfere with or control the domestic institutions of the several States." Further, it continued, any attempt "to induce Congress to interfere with questions of slavery," that is, the goal of the supporters of the Wilmot Proviso, "are calculated to lead to the most alarming and dangerous consequences."[45]

This clear-cut disclaimer was not enough for some of the more prickly and zealous southerners present. William Yancey of Alabama offered an amendment to the platform that the party adopt even stronger language than it had against any attempt to limit slavery in the territories. Further, he argued—and moved—the federal government had a positive responsibility to promote and protect slavery in the new territories rather than leave such to the people in a locality to decide. The motion failed by a

William Lowndes Yancey, U.S. representative from Alabama and Democratic author of the proslavery Alabama Platform.

very wide margin, 216 to 36, whereupon an angry Yancey, along with a number of other southerners of like mind, also marched out of the convention.[46]

The Democrats came out of their meeting, as all parties must, with their leaders exuding confidence in what they had accomplished. They had chosen their candidates wisely and had put forward their most effective and vote-winning issues. They believed that their troops, having been aroused, would return home to organize their battle to elect their ticket. Despite Barnburner doubts, Lewis Cass was a down-the-line Jacksonian Democrat, "a perfect embodiment of progressive democracy," and a vigorous, determined territorial expansionist. His service to the country over a long career and his commitment to the traditional ideals of the party all added up to, as they saw it, a strong ticket for them. With a united party behind him, and running against any one of the normal range of potential Whig candidates, his chances, they argued, appeared excellent. His great strength in the growing western states of the Mississippi Valley, both north and south, in addition to the support from traditional Democratic strongholds elsewhere, presaged a decisive victory for himself and his party.[47]

There were a number of problems to be sure, whatever boost the Democrats believed they had received from their meeting. When he returned home, Yancey determinedly continued his efforts to challenge the party for its inadequacies and failures when it came to protecting the constitutional rights of slaveowners. Despite his efforts and party members' fears that his actions would hurt the ticket, his position received far less support from his sectional colleagues than he had expected. Only a few Democratic meetings in the slave states after the national convention went along with Yancey's initiative. Most southern Democrats held steadfast. Nevertheless, to those analyzing possibilities and counting votes, the fear always remained close to the surface that a threat to their party's well-being remained unsettled.[48]

On the other side of the party, the anger and alienation of Van Buren and his colleagues had reached the point of mutiny against their traditional political home. In addition to their outrageous treatment at the convention, their long-standing identification of Cass as the leader of the anti–Van Buren element in the party and one of the main figures largely responsible for Van Buren's failure to be renominated four years before made it impossible for them to reconsider their position and support him. They also reiterated their opposition to his policy stances, first because he was against the Wilmot Proviso, second for what they considered his retreat from several long-revered Jacksonian economic policies, and third his belligerent, and, to them, dangerously militant, expansionism.[49]

What all of this would add up to in the campaign and in the election remained to be seen, but, given what was happening to the Democratic Party, the Van Burenites were about to do something politically earth-shaking. They had reached the point where they were ready to overthrow all they had been part of in order to challenge those who had caused the decline of their party and were responsible for its current behavior. As the editor of a Barnburner newspaper put it, what is the remedy for such erring party behavior as was now before them? It "consists in deserting a party, rending asunder all its ties, and planting ourselves upon those just and true principles upon which all republics must be based. A new party is formed, the republic is saved."[50]

"ANYTHING BUT A WHIG"

The Whigs came together in Philadelphia on June 7, 1848, in a meeting hall called the Chinese Museum. As with the Democratic National Convention in Baltimore, the city was crowded outside of the venue with party supporters ready to parade and cheer for their candidates and determined to pressure the official delegates to act in their favor. Inside were the same overfilled galleries and raucous reactions to speeches and decisions taken as had characterized their opponents' recent meeting. There were 279 delegates accredited to the gathering, although there were many more than that actually in attendance on the floor. (Each state could cast ballots equal to the number of their U.S. representatives and senators. But they could select more than that number to attend the meeting.) South Carolina had only two delegates present of the nine allotted to it. Several other states lacked one or two as well. Unlike the Democrats, the Whigs would decide the nomination by a simple majority, not two-thirds, of the votes of the delegates.[51]

With former governor James Morehead of North Carolina as the permanent chair, there were the usual preliminaries and backstage maneuvering as the different sides sought some advantage for themselves in the proceedings, along with the usual rumors of plots being hatched and alliances formed to push one or another candidate forward. There was some talk by Clay supporters of introducing a motion that nobody was eligible for the party's nomination unless he was pledged to Whig principles, an obvious swipe at the reticent Taylor. This and other delaying initiatives did not get far. The fact that Taylor's supporters dominated the official officers of the meeting elected by the delegates allowed them to overcome whatever barriers others sought to put in their path to victory.[52]

Voting for the presidential nominee began on June 8 with the party's disagreement about candidates still much in evidence. Two ballots were taken on the first evening. Taylor led from the beginning, receiving 111 votes to Clay's 97 on the first ballot, with both men far outdistancing their surviving rivals, Webster and Scott. Taylor's major support on this ballot came from southern Whigs, and Clay's from several of the northern and border states including New York, Pennsylvania, Maryland, and Kentucky. Unfortunately for Clay, his home state of Kentucky's votes were split with Taylor, an indication of the latter's appeal. It took two additional ballots the next day before a majority voted for the general, although Taylor's totals grew as each successive count was taken, with delegates from all parts of the country now coming over to support him. On the final ballot, he received 171 votes, a clear majority, with Scott now in second place with 60 votes. (Clay had dropped to 35.)[53]

Throughout all of the exciting proceedings on the convention floor, many of the anti-Taylor Whigs were clearly restless and growing more so with each vote. Their angry feelings burst out as the other delegates acted to anoint their nominee. Many of the general's opponents refused to join in the enthusiastic floor celebrations when Taylor's victory was announced, and several antislavery party members from New England rose and passionately expressed their bitter reactions against the party's folly in nominating a slaveholder to lead them.[54]

At the same time, in addition to the sectional impulses in play in the voting early on, Taylor's refusal to come out in favor of the party's traditional issues obviously continued to rankle many of those present and reinforce the belief of the skeptical party members that this clear denial of their heritage and long-standing commitments was the wrong way for the Whig Party to proceed. The Philadelphia convention had ignored them, however, and nominated someone who was, in the sharp, direct, and accurate words of one Taylor opponent, "anything but a Whig."[55]

The vice presidential nomination was also the subject of intraparty tension. Fourteen names were put in nomination, with Abbott Lawrence of Massachusetts, a former U.S. representative, considered the front-runner in the period leading up to the convention. But his position, too, was constrained by the kind of anger that had erupted from time to time as the Taylor bandwagon reached its destination. Those concerned about the denial of Whig principles inherent in Taylor's nomination, or the fact that their candidate was a southern slaveowner, opposed Lawrence, a Taylor supporter before the meeting and a prominent cotton manufacturer considered close to the South and its way of life—a "Cotton Whig" in the parlance of Massachusetts politics. These delegates threw their support instead to forty-eight-year-old Millard Fillmore of New York, well known among activists as a strong party loyalist who had spent his long political life as a state official, U.S. representative, and, recently, his party's candidate for governor of his home state. The contest between these two was quickly settled. After a close first ballot Fillmore won on the next.[56]

The nominations largely concluded the convention's official business. Unlike in 1844, the assembled Whigs did not draft and debate a platform despite demands from the floor that the delegates formally assert party doctrine. It was not that the old issues were dead but that their leaders' nonpartisan strategy continued in play. The party would not win on their usual policies, as they could not with the usual candidates. Further, new issues that had come up that might have helped them—the party's hostility to the war with Mexico and its resistance to further territorial expansion—were now unfortunately moot because of the peace treaty. At the same time, Taylor's Allison letter, if not saying all that many wanted, had returned them to what many considered the party's long-held basics: the importance of presidential character, leadership ability, and awareness of the danger of overreaching executive power. Most Whigs seemed content with that representation of themselves as the proceedings came to an end. At a mass ratification meeting held outside the convention hall on the evening of the nominations, the assembled crowd agreed to endorse a statement of where it stood in lieu of the absent platform, a document that was all about Taylor, assuring everyone that he was a first-rate candidate, asserting that he was also a Whig, and calling on all party members to work on his behalf.[57]

Of course, regardless of the mass meeting's statement and positive atmosphere, few attentive voters would have any doubt by November as to what the Whigs believed about the partisan conflicts of the past two decades. Despite their lack of an official platform and their emphasis on their candidate, they could not escape their record. Democrats would prove more than ready to denounce the Whigs' failure to tell the world what they believed in, and then they would help the voters' understanding of what was really in play in the battle between the two parties. They would be relentless in spreading the word in detail in their campaign that, whoever was their candidate, the Whigs remained the party of Henry Clay, Daniel Webster, and the ultranationalist, John Quincy Adams, a party with which voters were familiar, espousing the same old debased notions, high tariffs, and the rest, whatever new public face they had tried to assume at their convention.[58]

"A GREAT CRISIS HAS ARRIVED": THE EMERGENCE OF THE FREE SOILERS

There was, as could be predicted, a great deal of dissatisfaction about both parties' presidential nominations as the delegates returned home, and much denunciation of what had happened—or not happened—at each convention. Most political leaders had naturally wanted to forestall any further internal confrontation within their parties. That quickly proved impossible. A group of disgruntled people refused to accept the Baltimore and Philadelphia results along with the defeat there of the Van Buren bloc and of Clay. They believed both of them deserved better for all they had done throughout their long careers. There was even some talk among several of the frustrated Whigs of having Clay run for president as an independent candidate. But the defeated leader, as depressed and angry as he was, refused to go along, even though the Whig Party with Taylor at its head had been "butchered at Philadelphia" and was now "a putrid corpse" in the words of one of its most prominent (and unhappy) editors. Nevertheless, despite their hero's disclaimers, there continued to be occasional eruptions from Clay's frustrated supporters as the campaign got under way.[59]

Beyond the brief Clay boom, there was more energy among others who were similarly determined to revolt because of the way the parties had dealt with the issues raised by the Wilmot Proviso. Neither convention had adopted the proviso's language or spirit as part of its commitment and public appeal. Clearly, neither major party was interested in bringing the slavery extension question before the electorate. The Democrats had finessed the issue by supporting an approach seemingly democratic in form, but one that left open the possibility of additional slave territory in the West; the Whigs had simply bypassed the matter. These maneuvers, whatever their political utility to some, were clearly not acceptable to dissidents in either party.[60]

The question for these frustrated activists was whether they could find an effective way to achieve their purpose within the current political order. The Barnburners had made their position clear when they were denied their expected place at the Democratic National Convention and then walked out of their party home. As they did so, they publicly reiterated their determination never to support Cass and a party dominated by those resistant to guaranteeing free soil in the territories. Nor did they intend to go away. But what could they do instead? And would anyone join them in their protest against political business as usual?[61]

The dissident antislavery Whigs helped them find an answer. Even before they left Philadelphia, several of the convention delegates, led by Henry Wilson of Massachusetts, met to denounce what had happened and call for a meeting of like-minded friends to consider their options. Although the response of the antislavery Whigs present in Philadelphia to Wilson's immediate postconvention meeting was not as large as he and his like-minded colleagues hoped, they did begin to make some progress. Out of their initial efforts came further consultations and several more meetings, including a large one in Columbus, Ohio, on June 21, the "free-territory" conclave, with Whigs, Liberty Party members, and Democrats in attendance. The assembled delegates argued that "a great crisis has arrived" in the country's history, passed resolutions denouncing the major parties, and called for further action by all who agreed with them. Specifically, they wanted all opponents of the extension of slavery to gather in convention in Buffalo, New York, in early August to consider their next steps. The majority of those at the Columbus meeting, loyal Whigs and Democrats though most of them were, had reached the point of challenging all that they had previously been committed to politically as they now refused to go along with their parties, which had strayed so badly.[62]

The day after the Columbus meeting, the Barnburners gathered their supporters once more in Utica, New York. They were joined by a few sympathetic Democrats from other states and a smattering of New York Whigs. And there the assemblage crossed a political Rubicon. Denouncing Cass, slavery extension, and the way the Democrats had treated that issue at their convention, those assembled announced that they would put their own candidates for president and vice president into the field. After a certain amount of pushing and pulling over different possibilities (including someone suggesting Zachary Taylor as their standard-bearer), they unanimously nominated an at first reluctant Martin Van

Buren for the presidency and pro–Wilmot Proviso senator Henry Dodge of Wisconsin for vice president. (Dodge, however, when he learned of the action taken by the meeting, followed the example of so many other reluctant northern antislavery Democrats and refused to join in the developing revolt and accept the nomination of a splinter party.)[63]

Finally, a large body of the restive antislavery Whigs, most of them from Massachusetts, stimulated by the many protest meetings throughout that state and elsewhere since the nomination of Taylor, assembled in Worcester the following week to add their voices to the laments about what had occurred in Baltimore and Philadelphia and to articulate as well their determination to take action about it. They, too, suggested that those who believed as they did should attend the proposed August meeting in Buffalo.[64]

In these meetings, the groups in revolt were trying to leap past years of differences among them and come together as the champions of policies to prevent the further spread of slavery on U.S. soil. As they held meetings in their states to select delegates to Buffalo, they continued to find that not all of those they expected to be with them, in fact, agreed with their plans. Despite the rumblings of protest and the serious issues the dissenters were pointing out, not all of their neighbors were convinced that as much of importance was at stake as claimed by the antislavery groups, nor that much would happen because of any strategy the latter would devise. This was a good sign to some. Both the mainstream Whig and Democratic leadership wanted to believe that this lack of a large-scale surge in favor of plans to continue the protest meant that after tempers had cooled and everyone had a chance to settle down, the angry dissenters would come back to their political homes and support the candidates chosen.[65]

The party leaders were wrong. In early summer, the mood of the protesters was not conciliatory, and, as a result, an anti–slavery extension coalition was well on its way toward some kind of realization. Out of the factional uproar among Democrats and the bitter recriminations from antislavery activists among the Whigs, much energy had arisen and more was on its way. The leaders of the various dissenting groups stayed defiant and, more critically, continued to move toward establishing a third party to contest for power in the impending election. Dissenting Democrats, Conscience Whigs, and longtime opponents of slavery, particularly those members of the Liberty Party led by Salmon P. Chase who were willing to consider coalition with other groups, saw an opportunity to reorder the nation's political dynamics toward focusing on "the great political question of the country," that is, restricting the spread of slavery into the new western territories.[66]

The difficulty of melding the various constituencies into a single movement remained obvious to all those who were trying to do just that. The potential for crippling disagreements was as high as ever, and the tensions created by that possibility remained close to the surface. Antislavery activists continued to hesitate to trust each other despite their common antipathy to any further growth of slave territory. They had always disagreed over their primary focus, the extent of their concerns, and the tactics they should pursue. The abolitionists among them were a minority; the majority of those in revolt took a more moderate position about the future of slavery, arguing that there was little they could do about the institution where it already existed. Further, despite Chase's urging, some hard-line abolitionists still resisted any political coalition with more moderate antislavery factions. They continued to stand behind the Liberty League and its nomination of Gerrit Smith as its candidate for president.[67]

Nevertheless, the will to come together remained strong among the dissenters of all stripes despite their long-standing hostility toward each other. "Friends," a Whig member of Congress said at the Buffalo meeting, "we must unite . . . and take up the glove where the South throw [sic] it down." And his Whig friends present followed his advice. Each bloc's skepticism about the others with whom they were negotiating never disappeared. But it was overcome sufficiently to allow the political coalition to move forward. It was, after all, as one Free Soiler wrote, "part of the work of earnest antislavery men to forget party memories and prejudices for the sake of the cause."[68]

As all of this activity intensified, other groups of possible supporters not usually part of the two-party system were attracted to what was going on and became involved as well. Women's rights advocates had convened in Seneca Falls, New York, that June in a dramatic national meeting to air their grievances about their status and role in society and to energetically press their demands for legal equality. Many of the attendees were antislavery activists as well, including the former slave and great orator Frederick Douglass, and like him some of the male reformers who were present and who were close to the meeting's organizers went to Buffalo afterward to consider seriously something that had never been attractive

Salmon P. Chase, Ohio Liberty Party leader and strong advocate for a cross-party Free Soil coalition.

to most of them, joining with professional politicians and others long immersed in the compromises and limited intentions of electoral politics to further their purpose. They included representatives of free black groups intent on pushing the envelope of racial equality as far as possible. Most of these free blacks, along with the women involved, could not vote in a presidential election, but they could contribute their ideas, energy, organizing skills, and long experience in advocacy politics outside the polling place to those coming together in Buffalo.[69]

"VAN BUREN AND FREE SOIL, ADAMS AND LIBERTY"

All of this drama, and the political tumult that accompanied it, culminated in the last national party convention of a highly unusual political year, the Free Soilers' meeting in upstate New York in early August. Buffalo was a comparatively convenient place to reach, via the Great Lakes from the west, up the Hudson River and along the Erie Canal from the east and south, or by railroad from several different starting points, so that the meeting drew a large crowd. On August 9, an audience estimated to be as many as 20,000 politically involved men and women who were hostile to slavery from every free state, three of the border slave states, and the District of Columbia convened to challenge their society's values, or indifference, and the norms of conventional politics in the United States.[70]

At this motley assembly of former political enemies and various reform advocates all went well despite the attendees' different antecedents, memories, priorities, and ongoing disagreements over many things. Leaders from the major centers of free soil action—New York, Massachusetts, and Ohio—dominated the proceedings. Much preliminary planning had gone on among them. On the first morning, a large assemblage convened under an immense tent in a public park and got down to business with Massachusetts Conscience Whig Charles Francis Adams as chair. This assembly's primary occupation over the next several days consisted largely of listening to a great many speeches, from morning to night, on behalf of their cause, including from Frederick Douglass and other free blacks active in the antislavery movement. A smaller Committee of Conference, as it was initially labeled, selected by the attendees (more than 460 delegates in all) made up of an equal number of delegates from each state and congressional district represented at the meeting, and divided equally among the three main factions present, met separately in a local church with Salmon P. Chase as chair to draft a platform, nominate candidates, and then report its actions for approval back to the mass meeting outside.[71]

The resulting platform was the work of a subcommittee led by Benjamin F. Butler, the Barnburner leader and former law partner of Martin Van Buren, and dominated by Butler and Chase. The drafters took a clear, if middle, ground on slavery, forswearing abolitionism in favor of provisoism, that is, no further expansion of the institution into the new western territories. That moratorium could only be accomplished "by an act of Congress." At the same time, the drafters recognized that the federal government had no power over slavery in the states where it already existed. Nor did the platform mention several other matters that had long been objects of the antislavery groups' anger: the existence of slavery in the District of Columbia, where the federal government did have the authority to end it, and the extra seats in Congress (and the additional political power they had as a result) allotted to the slave states by the Three-Fifths Clause of the Constitution. Nor did the drafters of the platform, not surprisingly, have anything to say about racial equality or women's suffrage. Nevertheless, despite its shortcomings in the eyes of some of those present, it was certainly an advance over the action—and inaction—of the earlier Whig and Democratic National Conventions.[72]

The platform also contained commitments to a number of other things that were part of the usual political dialogue of the major parties, such as advocating federal financing of river and harbor improvements (a Whig standard) and a tariff for revenue only (a Democratic favorite), as well as issues raised by various reform groups, including cheap postage and a more liberal federal policy toward land distribution that favored settlers. Despite these other items signaling the acceptance of many reformers' policy agendas, there was no question about the central thrust of the new party. The platform summed it up in its conclusion, in its famous declaration that they intended to march together on behalf of "Free Soil, Free Speech, Free Labor, and Free Men." The working committee, now called the Committee of Conferees, and then the mass meeting in the park, adopted the document by acclamation.[73]

When it came time to nominate a presidential candidate, despite the continuing reservations of the abolitionists and the Whig antislavery activists present, the participants were able to overcome their apparent dilemma. Here in Buffalo was an opportunity beyond anything the antislavery movement had been able to accomplish before on the national scene—a moment of possibility to challenge the hated institution to some effect. But, as some of those assembled pointed out, at what cost? Martin Van Buren's record was hardly commendable for many of those assembled, given his previous indifference toward slavery, his often demonstrated hostility to abolitionists, and his pre-Texas down-the-line support for southern political demands through the years. The obvious wariness about him and consequent hesitation of so many of those gathered at Buffalo were palpable. The former president was an imperfect candidate for their movement. But then, what could they do; who would be better? The answer seemed clear to those who had brought the assemblage so far: "Mr. Van Buren has some sins to answer to," Chase wrote to John P. Hale. But if he is true to free soil now—and he seems to be—then "much in the past may be overlooked."[74]

Chase was not alone in his stance. Despite Van Buren's problematic record on the South and slavery, naming him made sense to many of the experienced politicians present given what he brought to the new party. The Barnburners were the largest element in the emerging coalition and the best organized for the kind of political race they were about to enter. Given Van Buren's long experience in electoral politics and his present attitude about the matters of mutual concern that had brought them together, he was clearly the best chance the new party had to shake things up on the U.S. political landscape—perhaps even enabling them to win.[75]

Despite all who favored him as the convention moved toward nominating its ticket, the ex-president continued to face opposition, primarily from the supporters of John P. Hale (already nominated for president by the Liberty Party National Convention the previous year) as well as from others who favored Charles Francis Adams and Joshua Giddings, Ohio's staunchly antislavery members of Congress. All of these names were brought forward. (John McLean was briefly mentioned as well, but his name was quickly withdrawn.) Van Buren received 244 votes to Hale's 181 (or 183 depending on the source) on a straw vote—the only ballot needed in the Committee of Conferees—with the rest scattered among the others named. Hale's supporters then withdrew his name and the committee members made Van Buren's nomination unanimous.[76]

The party's vice presidential nomination went to Adams, ironically the son of one of Van Buren's most enduring political enemies, the recently deceased John Quincy Adams. Despite his antecedents, however, the choice was a logical move given the younger Adams's vigorous opposition to slavery and southern arrogance. In terms of old political identities, the committee had come up with a balanced ticket, a Whig and a Democrat. Given the reality of the situation, it was as good as any named was likely to be in uniting the disparate elements present in Buffalo and putting the dissenters' best effort forward. Whatever tensions and uncertainties remained, the others present in the meeting largely agreed with the decision.[77]

When the choices of their agent, the Committee of Conferees, were reported to the waiting masses in the park, there was widespread acclamation for what the committee had done—enough to seem to conquer the still lingering doubts and hesitations. The moment of unity dramatically culminated with Liberty Party stalwart Joshua Leavitt, previously no friend of Van Buren or the norms of U.S. politics, emotionally moving that the nominations be made unanimous—which, with a shout, they were. The leaders of this coalition of differences—except on the main point of resistance to the further extension of slavery—had accomplished an astounding political feat. The Free Soil Party was on its way, parading under its waving banners calling for "Van Buren and Free Soil, Adams and Liberty."[78]

REACTIONS

The Free Soilers left Buffalo in an exuberant mood, imbued with the sense that they were making history—convinced, in the words of one historian, "that God had called them to serve in a near apocalyptic struggle."[79] They had advanced well beyond most people's original expectations of what they could accomplish. Out of all the raw material present, an anti–slavery extension party of greater breadth than ever before had become a reality with an enthusiastic group of supporters prepared to fight on its behalf unto election day. The Free Soilers believed their success had wounded the major parties by their real threat to shift the course of political conflict in the United States. Coupled with the internal conflict raging within the old parties, Free Soil leaders also believed that the latter were now in great danger. Clay's supporters among the Whigs, for example, continued to be distinctly angry at the outcome in Philadelphia, and they were not alone among party members in their continuing resistance to what had happened at the party's national convention.[80]

At first, several prominent Whigs, including Clay himself, made it clear that their anger had important consequences for the party. They would neither fall in behind the nominee nor take any active part in his campaign. "I think," Henry Clay summed up, "that the Philadelphia convention has placed the Whig Party in a humiliating condition." He would not run himself, but would not publicly support Taylor either— nor did he to the end of the campaign. Horace Greeley, who had referred angrily after the convention to "the putrid corpse of the party butchered at Philadelphia," waffled about what to do for two months before he finally and reluctantly put the names of Taylor and Fillmore on the New York *Tribune*'s masthead.[81]

Democrats, too, continued to worry about the wrath of the disaffected among them and, like the Whig leaders, wondered how many of their adherents, now that there were three parties in the field and the dissenters had the direct opportunity to emphasize sectional matters ahead of all other questions, would desert Cass and go for Van Buren in the North or support Taylor in the South. And, as did the Whig leaders, they realized that as always there was little margin for such defections in a close contest if they hoped to win in November. As a result, party newspapers were filled with denunciations of Van Buren and his supporters for their apostasy, revealing their fears about the likelihood of defections of needed Democratic voters.[82]

But the Free Soil activity and its underlying impulses had not swept the entire field of political attention, commitment, and behavior, certainly not as much as the most optimistic among them wanted to believe. Shrewd observers realized that there were, not unexpectedly, forces at work to limit partisan defections, promote traditional levels of unity, and prevent rifts from developing into unbridgeable chasms in the old parties. Party members were used to the kind of sharp internal battles that preceded each election campaign, and accustomed as well to party members coming together again as they prepared to face their enemies. They expected that to happen now despite the energy exhibited by the supporters of the Free Soil revolt. And the partisan bonding began to occur, however grudgingly. We did not want Taylor, one Whig editor wrote, but for those of us who participated in the convention that nominated him, "we are bound by every principle which governs political parties to adopt the nominations and sustain them at the polls." What, after all, "could be worse for the country than the Democratic measures and Democratic men? What can be lost by supporting Taylor?"[83]

Even after the establishment of the Free Soil Party, many of those opposed to slavery among the Whigs stayed away from it. As noted, Van

Buren's candidacy at the head of an antislavery coalition provoked a great deal of disbelief and open hostility among many of those who had long fought against the institution and who could not now get past their image of Van Buren as having been a pliant southern tool throughout his political career. Abraham Lincoln, for example, worked assiduously on behalf of Taylor and to prevent other Whigs from defecting to the Free Soilers. Somewhat less enthusiastically, but ultimately clearly enough, so did William Henry Seward and Daniel Webster, both of whom campaigned for the Whig ticket throughout the campaign. All were opponents of southern demands for the further extension of slavery, but none proved willing to become Free Soilers because, as Horace Greeley put it, their "party fidelity" dictated otherwise—as Whigs, they had to keep the Democrats and their policies out of power—and that continued to be the most important consideration for them. Not all succumbed all at once, but over the weeks after the conventions ended, among many of those originally reluctant to support Taylor or attracted to the Free Soil effort, their partisan feelings came to the fore and they made up their minds to fall in behind the Whig presidential nominee even if his name was not Clay.[84]

Democrats had similar hesitations about defecting. There was no immediate surge to the Free Soilers from many of those Jacksonians who opposed slavery. They may have trusted Van Buren somewhat more than did the Whigs but did not desert the Cass ticket. A young Vermont antislavery Democrat found that even though many of his contemporaries in the party were "indignant" about the failures of their leaders to confront the slavery issue, when it came to leaving the party and supporting Free Soil, nearly all "began to make excuse[s]" as to why they would not do so. They, too, fell into line behind their party's nominees as a course preferable to schism, a Whig victory, and the threat it posed to other Democratic issues that remained important to them. Some may have hesitated about their choice but most did not. Prominent longtime political friends of Van Buren such as Senator Thomas Hart Benton of Missouri and former governor Marcus Morton of Massachusetts as well as the ex-president's close colleague for twenty years, prominent Jacksonian editor Francis P. Blair, refused to join the new movement, declaring instead their loyalty to the Democrats and to their most important priority: preventing the Whigs from attaining power. So did "Long John" Wentworth, the U.S. representative from Illinois who had spoken forcefully in support of the Wilmot Proviso in the House of Representatives, but now also made it clear that he and those who believed as he did should "strive to lick Taylor first," and warned that they would not be able to do so if party members strayed from their normal home on election day. None of these men supported Cass with any great enthusiasm but remained loyal to the party nevertheless.[85]

New York's John Dix, a loyal Van Burenite, painfully articulated what was running through the minds of such men who were hostile to slavery and angry at the Democratic Party but unable to swallow what was now happening. "That he [referring to himself], a Democrat of the old school," Dix wrote, "should find himself associated with gentlemen of the Whig Party, from whom he differed on almost every point, whose political principles he had always opposed, and with whom he could never agree on questions of taxation, public works, finance, constitutional interpretation, and State and national policy, was a painful and distressing surprise. He was willing, if it must be so, to go with his own section of the Democratic Party, even when deeming their [sic] course not the wisest. But when it came to alliance with Whigs and abolitionists, he lost all heart in the movement." Dix, faced with conflicting pressures, finally overcame his unhappiness and hesitations about defecting from his political home and came to the side of his close friends and allies the Barnburners. He actually ran for governor of New York on the Free Soil ticket. But many others politically like him would not, and did not, succumb. Dix's stated conundrum affected these others and led to different decisions as each faced the necessity of choosing what he would do in the campaign and on election day.[86]

Several motives influenced those who chose to stay with the old parties despite their commitment against slavery, including the personal ambition of some of them. Nevertheless, whatever else was in play, at the bottom remained the loyalty to the two-party system of so many of those involved, their particular place in that system as either Whigs or Democrats, and their primary desire that their party and its policies triumph. They accepted the constantly reiterated warning that Democratic defections to Van Buren's candidacy would open the doors for their opponents to gain power and thus thwart what they wanted to accomplish at all levels. Unhappy Democrats were constantly warned, as one example of the pressure on them, that they must not defect but rather "sacrifice their private griefs upon the altar of the common good."[87]

This was certainly not an unexpected attitude from either Whigs or Democrats given the strength of party commitment in this era. Some of the Whigs, in particular, tried to escape the dilemma by arguing and trying to persuade others that the Free Soil Party was not necessary, that their antislavery beliefs would advance within the traditional party system. Taylor, they said, would prove to be friendly, or at least accepting in some manner, to the Wilmot Proviso. Benjamin Wade, a prominent Ohio opponent of slavery, wrote, "I believe the free states safer with Old Zach and a free territory Congress than with a miserable doughface [i.e., a northern Democrat] with a Congress of like mind at his hands." For one good reason, the attitudes of the two presidential candidates toward the veto power was critical in this argument. Whigs were told that Taylor would not use the power, so that when Congress passed the Wilmot Proviso it would become law. However, Cass undoubtedly would veto such a bill. By which candidate, Whig loyalists asked, would opponents of slavery extension be better served?[88]

On the other side of the slavery divide, among the independent southerners hostile to the two major parties, most remained convinced that there was nothing to be gained for their section and its interests by supporting either major party candidate. That was Calhoun's position. He made it clear that he would support neither Taylor nor Cass. To be sure, a number of his supporters, as well as some usually partisan Democrats rarely sympathetic to Calhoun's outlook, did fall in behind southern slaveowner Taylor, who presumably shared their values in a way no northern candidate could. These Taylor Democrats, as they were called, worked to convince Democrats to support a hybrid Taylor–William O. Butler ticket, thereby eliminating the northerners present on the two major parties' slates.[89]

In contrast, other party stalwarts in their section (including in South Carolina) worked hard to keep their fellow Democrats in line behind their party's official nominee, whatever their hesitations. Stephen A. Douglas, traveling in the South after the Democratic National Convention, sent optimistic reports to Lewis Cass that things were looking good for the Democratic nominee except in South Carolina. But even there, things were going well. Although Calhoun remained publicly aloof, even some of his close colleagues spoke in favor of the regular Democratic ticket despite their strong reservations. Beyond the Calhoun group, the loyalists among southern Democrats had no such reservations and showed it. When Yancey returned home after walking out of the Baltimore convention, he continued to be frustrated by the response to his ideas in his home state. He had to report to Calhoun that he and his friends could not carry the day on behalf of federal guarantees for slavery in the territories. They found themselves hamstrung because there was too much support for Cass in Alabama. Democrats were "determined to vote for the regular ticket" and would not do anything to threaten the party's chances. Here, too, Cass's position as a loyal advocate of traditional Jacksonianism and his perspective on the territories and against the Wilmot Proviso worked in his favor among those party loyalists who might be feeling the pressure to bolt.[90]

In other southern states as well, there was the same resistance from loyal Democrats to Yancey's ideas and demands. The Georgia Democratic State Convention resolved "that the people of the South do not ask of Congress to establish the institution of slavery in any of the Territory that may be acquired by the United States. They simply require that the inhabitants of each territory shall be left free to determine for themselves whether the institution of slavery shall or shall not form a part of their social system." Cass and other supporters could not have said it better. The whole political hullabaloo around the South's position and what southerners should do was summed up well by Jefferson Davis, Taylor's former son-in law, who remained close to him, in a speech in Mississippi in September. He spoke of Taylor's many virtues, but, because he was running on the Whig ticket, Davis "would be obliged to vote for Cass and Butler."[91]

Finally, in the North, the free blacks and other reformers sympathetic to what had happened in Buffalo faced resistance from some of their allies to supporting the Free Soil ticket given the party's failure to confront the critical issues of slavery where it already existed, racial equality, and the political and social rights of women. At a "national negro convention," they unhappily debated what their appropriate action should be. Despite their frustration, they finally reluctantly resolved to recommend that the Free Soilers be supported by their peers. They still insisted on a higher standard about the central issues of the movement—which they never received. Frederick Douglass's newspaper, the *Free Star*, after some hesitation, put Van Buren's name on its masthead, admitting that Douglass and others were compromising their beliefs but were willing to do so because the Free Soilers, even with Van Buren as their leader, advanced all previous movements against slavery despite the party's obvious limitations.[92]

By mid-August, the parties had chosen their candidates and completed their initial moves, were doing their best to maintain the enthusiasm the conventions had engendered, counter internal threats to their unity, tamp down complaints and unrest that could grow out of hand, and prepare themselves for the strenuous months ahead. Except for Old Rough and Ready Taylor, the nominees of the three parties were familiar names in the nation's political circles. Each of the presidential and vice presidential candidates represented the traditional political culture of their time, that is, party leaders went with the well-known players of many of the battles of the recent past—"old actors upon the political boards," as Benjamin Butler put it at Buffalo.[93]

There had been some exceptions in previous elections, but presidential politics was clearly a mature man's game regardless of the impulses emanating from the intellectuals and editors known as Young America. Nevertheless, the enthusiasm and vigor of younger men working their way up in the political world were also present in the mix, political activists cutting their teeth in their efforts on behalf of Cass, Taylor, and Van Buren. In activists such as Abraham Lincoln, Stephen A. Douglas, and John Van Buren, the next generation of the nation's political leaders was showing itself. Critically, they would be on the front lines as the campaign got under way.[94]

All three candidates formally accepted the nominations tendered to them by committees formed by the conventions shortly after their parties' meetings had adjourned, Cass resigning from his seat in the Senate as he did so, and began their preparations for the campaign to follow. Taylor's acceptance was delayed a bit when the letter officially informing him of his nomination was not picked up for a time at his local post office by the candidate's associates. Ultimately, the misunderstanding was straightened out to the relief of the anxious Whig Executive Committee in Washington.[95]

Unsurprisingly, each of the candidates' responses reiterated their commitment to the particular cause they now led and expressed their eagerness to get on with the task of winning the contest. They were ready for the strenuous months of battle about to begin. With their acceptances, the initial stage of the election of 1848 had ended. The party leaders and political activists had done their work to bring forth their party's best candidate. The next question—and the only important one—was how the rank and file of the contending coalitions would react to all that had happened—for whom would they vote? The first step in finding that out would be in the coming weeks as the campaigns of the three parties began their crusades for victory.

"THE WORK TO BE DONE"
THE PARTIES ORGANIZE

Organize in the counties, in the Precincts, in the towns.
Warn the Committees, scatter the documents, get out the stump
speakers, hold meetings, talk to your neighbors.[1]

The three parties entered the campaign season with high
expectations for the success of their causes despite the
obvious problems each faced. Democrats, one of their
editors reported, were "becoming more spirited and ani-
mated every day" thanks to what he suggested was their
successful convention in Baltimore. His letters from
party colleagues, he went on, "show an improving and
more buoyant feeling" among them than had been true
in recent months.[2] Leaders of the other parties received
similar assurances from their local sources throughout
the country. Much of what they heard may have been
wishful thinking, but party leaders tried to build on the
optimism and make the expressions of confidence a reality. The crucial point for all of them was to ensure that the
positive, active, "buoyant feeling" would remain in force
and continue to grow steadily until election day and that
their supporters would enthusiastically come to the polls
in the largest number possible and, when there, do their
partisan duty. This was always important to accomplish,
but particularly so in 1848, as conflicted voters might not
vote at all because they were unable or unwilling to choose
between the alternative thrown into play by the sectional
impulse: for Southern Democrats, slaveholding Whig
Taylor or their old party; for antislavery Northern Whigs
and Democrats, the Free Soilers or their old party.[3]

The key was the same as in any contest: effective

organization everywhere. "UNIVERSAL AND SYSTEMATIC ORGANIZATION must be had in EVERY town." Such "is the first duty of a Party," Thurlow Weed's Albany *Evening Journal* exhorted its Whig readers in August. "It is also," the editor continued, "the best guaranty for success." Not as many potential voters would necessarily turn out on their own unless they were prodded to do so during the campaign and on election day. Some would, but the rest needed to be urged again and again and shown what was necessary for them to do and why. Remember, another party editor continued, "the great name of TAYLOR, though it is a tower of strength, is not of itself potent enough to command success."[4]

The Democrats and Free Soilers agreed with this imperative—and also proceeded to follow Weed's credo as they moved forward. They, too, vigorously confronted their main concern that the voters had to be energized and then kept enthusiastic through a long campaign season by the constant activities of party agents. "The work to be done is an organization which shall bring every voter to the polls," the editor of the main Democratic paper in Tennessee, the *Nashville Union*, told his readers. "Can we effect this organization? is the question which we now propound to our Democratic friends. If we can, the State is safe. IF NOT, IT IS LOST. That is the whole story." Free Soil editors agreed as well, arguing that "we must at least equal" the opponents' organization. "We must have in every ward, town, and village a Free Soil league." They did not want to find themselves out-organized by their opponents. There was too much at stake to lose an election because something important had not been done by party workers.[5]

There was a complicated and busy electoral calendar to master. There were multiple elections in 1848 in addition to the race for president. Many congressional seats were contested, as were a number of governorships and state legislative seats. The Democrats and Whigs offered candidates in all but a few of these races. The Free Soilers ran hopefuls for office in fewer contests than the old parties did, but their efforts were nevertheless considerable given the newness of their organization. They put candidates forward wherever they thought they had a chance, including fighting for votes in a number of the border slave states. They ran candidates for governor in ten of the fourteen races scheduled and put up fifty-nine candidates for the U.S. House of Representatives in districts where they believed there was a chance for their party.[6]

Presidential balloting would take place everywhere on the same day, Tuesday, November 7, for the first time in the nation's history as ordained by recent congressional legislation. (Before that, each state could opt for its preferred date and did. In 1844, voting for the presidency occurred on nine different days between early October and December 1.) In the absence of congressional legislation affecting nonpresidential elections, many of the state-level and congressional races, including those for governor in a number of key states such as Pennsylvania, Ohio, Tennessee, and North Carolina would be held on other days, particularly in August and October, as had long been the practice in those states. So in 1848, beyond the main event, other contests would still have been settled by the time voters came out to choose a president. Whenever they took place, however, it was understood by all of those involved in the campaign that each of these contests was critically important to party success and therefore demanded the same kind of organizational attention from party leaders they paid to the presidential contest.[7]

"WHIG CLUBS SHOULD BE FORMED IN EVERY TOWN"

The construction of a campaign was neither haphazard nor accomplished through a well-oiled electoral machine. Its reality in this era lay somewhere in between. The first step in getting their campaign under way was for party leaders to convene state-level meetings to ratify the national conventions' presidential and vice presidential nominations. Even as these leaders did so, followed soon after by the candidates accepting their nominations, party supporters were at work building or reviving the partisan networks and structures experience had taught them were needed to mobilize support in their area. They relied on organizational templates derived from previous state and local elections originating in New York and elsewhere in the 1820s and 1830s under the leadership of Martin Van Buren and his colleagues, then coming onto the national scene in the 1840 and 1844 presidential races. By 1848 the basic elements of these organizations had been largely designed as a result of those earlier contests. But the actual organizations built in each election had never been permanent, and they effectively disappeared after the battle was over. They had to be constructed anew in each election cycle.[8]

These structures were highly decentralized. At the national level, the Democratic National Convention in Baltimore established a national committee (for the first time designed to be permanent) made up of a single representative from each state and chaired by the veteran editor and Jacksonian stalwart Benjamin Hallett of Massachusetts. He was assisted by an executive group of three experienced officeholders and editors who were based in Washington to oversee the party's efforts. A Whig Executive Committee, chaired by Young Indian and experienced campaign manager U.S. Representative Truman Smith, performed the same function for the Taylor forces. The Free Soilers did not formally establish a similar setup, but "Prince John" Van Buren, a skilled political veteran of many contests and apt pupil of his father, acted as unofficial chair of what one historian has called the party's "haphazard organization."[9]

The national committees did not have a great deal of power besides that of general guidance and coordination, constant exhortation of those leading the campaigns locally, establishment of national campaign newspapers, and fund-raising as best they could. But they did not command many of those working in the campaign, beyond their immediate headquarters, as to what they should do on their own turf. In these decentralized coalitions, each party primarily relied on state leaders and committees as well as U.S. senators and representatives and local committees in the various civic jurisdictions, towns, villages, urban wards, and counties within each state, along with the efforts of editors, as many volunteers as could be brought in, and officeholders at those levels, to organize and run things. "Whig clubs should be formed in every town," a Massachusetts editor summed up for all those involved in political activity that summer and fall, "and sound documents and campaign papers be extensively circulated." The Georgia Democratic State Convention, said another editor, will "effect a complete organization of the party and impart to it that energy and confidence which is the sure harbinger of victory." Those were the keys to meeting their parties' needs.[10]

The authority of these campaign organizations derived from their predecessors' experience and previous success in doing what most of those involved realized needed to be done. They varied in effectiveness from state to state. Some organizations were acknowledged for their proficiency from early on; others proved less capable of accomplishing all that was necessary and were therefore the subject of much complaining from candidates and national leaders about their alleged ineffectiveness. But whatever their skill level and ability, these many party committees were the driving engines of the electoral universe in 1848.[11]

The committees' function was clear-cut: to identify and mobilize their parties' available personnel and other resources to get out their message as to what was at stake everywhere they had candidates. "Agitate! Discuss!! Debate!!!" they demanded; workers should never stop beating the partisan drums loudly on their behalf and, most of all, labor unstintingly to keep the voters aroused to fever pitch. The committees began by compiling poll lists of their likely supporters in their neighborhoods. "No Town or Ward should be without a perfect POLL LIST. There can be no efficient Organization without such a list." Local leaders knew who their supporters were and any changes that occurred from year to year. The lists might not always be perfect, but they were as close as human knowledge about the constituents could make them.[12]

The lists were used to keep in touch with a party's likely supporters throughout the weeks until election day. The workers spread their party's message to the voters by distributing newspapers, pamphlets, and other printed material as widely as they could (including having their party's members of Congress using their right to free postage to send copies of their speeches and other useful documents back to their home states and districts), and, in every way possible, keeping in touch with the voters from whom they expected support. In short, party organizations set out "to arouse the popular mind, awake the dormant attention, and to exhibit the dangers of apathy to the people at large," and they continued to do so right up to election day. The country "is in danger," they repeated over and over, "and strong arms and stout hearts must defend it" on the hustings and at the polls.[13]

The production and distribution of propaganda was the key initial element of organizational activity. "Documents of the right sort must be made to pass around like hotcakes, going into every hole and corner where there is the least possibility of making a convert to our faith." One of the first things the Democratic National Committee and the Whig Executive Committee did was to establish flagship party newspapers in Washington and New York, the *Campaign* and the *Recruit* for the Democrats and the *Grape Shot* for the Whigs. They were published weekly throughout the fall, joining a roster of regular partisan daily newspapers already in the field, including the Democrats' Washington *Union* and, in the same city, the Whigs' *National Intelligencer*. There was also the antislavery *National Era* at the national level, along with many others published in major cities and each state's capital such as the Richmond *Whig*, the Illinois *State Journal*, the Albany *Argus*, the New York *Tribune*, the Philadelphia *Pennsylvanian*, and the Barnburners' New York *Evening Post* and *Albany Atlas*. Most of these periodicals were published daily, and they were often supplemented by special campaign editions issued weekly. As a result of the vast expansion of the nation's communications networks—roads, canals, the telegraph, and the development of the U.S. Post Office—the national and state committees and the partisan editors of the sheets themselves could send out each edition of these publications in great numbers throughout the country.[14]

There was a great deal to read to prepare for election day. With few exceptions, these newspapers contained little hard news about the events of the day in the world outside the cocoon of the current campaign. Editors placed the names of their party's nominees in large print on their paper's mastheads, printed lists of the forthcoming rallies, meetings, and appearances of speakers, published documents such as party platforms, and, most of all, filled their columns with exhortation, opinions of their own, and reprints of editorials from other newspapers that in all ways celebrated their candidates and deprecated the other side. Much of this material ran originally in the main newspapers of each party, then circulated from one level to another as the messages were picked up and reprinted elsewhere, such as in local publications in county seats.[15]

In addition to newspapers and franked copies of congressional speeches, the party committees relied on pamphlets they had commissioned and produced guides such as *The Democratic Textbook* to help local activists in their efforts. The latter volume, issued for the first time in 1848, contained a great deal of useful information to disseminate, such as arguments in favor of Democratic policies, charges to make against the Whigs, and favorable descriptions of the party's candidates, among other matter. The many pamphlets published, sometimes as little as a page or two but usually about eight to sixteen crowded pages, added to the parties' information banks for speeches and editorial material. Their titles, for example, "The Windings and Turnings of Martin Van Buren" or "General Taylor and the Wilmot Proviso" or "Facts for Those Who Would Understand Them: General Cass's Position on the Slavery Question," among many others, suggested the nature of the ammunition they provided to party activists, who drew on them extensively as they prepared their editorials or composed stump speeches or answered the questions of supporters (or challenges from their opponents) at rallies.[16]

The presidential candidates were the subjects of campaign biographies commissioned by their parties usually from loyal newspaper editors, such as *The People's Life of General Zachary Taylor, the Hero of Palo Alto, Monterey, and Buena Vista,* and *Life of General Lewis Cass.* These volumes were obviously not designed to relate a full life of the candidate, including both the highs and lows. Rather, they served the political

*Democratic campaign banner with likenesses of
Cass and Butler used at rallies and parades.*

purpose of leaving little doubt as to who was the best candidate running in 1848, painting dramatic portraits of great men of sturdy character who, unlike their opponents, had the common touch in dealing with the American people as well as devotion and commitment to their needs, combined with great personal ability appropriate for the office they sought. Cass, for example, was a man of "enlarged experience—of extensive attainments—honest in his principles—pure in his private life—amiable in his manners," and so on. Taylor and Van Buren were painted with similar compelling attributes.[17]

"WITH THE TRUTH ON MY SIDE": CAMPAIGNING FOR VICTORY

Newspaper editorials, pamphlets, copies of speeches, and other printed materials provided the raw material on which each party drew to focus its campaign. These were often available in languages other than English, German in particular, given the parties' sensitivity about the foreign language speakers among them who were also voters. The material, in whatever language, was taken up and presented in the numerous meetings local leaders organized everywhere they could, in town halls, taverns, town squares, and private homes. Campaign season was filled with such gatherings until the last moments before election day. "Hold frequent meetings," one editor exhorted. His followers obeyed.[18]

As a result, few days passed without events being held on behalf of the cause. Each of them had a similar structure. In rural areas, they usually met on market day or at another time when people were free and likely to come into town. In urban centers they were often held on weekends but might be convened on other days as well, often at night after people had finished work. The committees found speakers to address the party's assembled supporters at the barbecues, open-air rallies, and other large and small gatherings they had set up, and organized debates between local and state candidates and their surrogates at the same venues. The Whig committees organized get-out-the-vote clubs, and the existing Rough and Ready and Palo Alto clubs expanded in number to trumpet Taylor's virtues, joined as the campaign began by Fillmore Ranger clubs. Democrats and Free Soilers followed with their own variations on this theme.[19]

The raucous qualities of U.S. elections were well-established by 1848. Whatever the size of the gatherings, they were noisy and vitriolic as party loyalists cheered mightily while those supporting the other side shouted hostile questions, challenged assertions, made rude remarks, and added to, if not the clarity of the proceedings, their intensity. In preparation for such an occasion with a local or guest speaker, the party committees posted announcements inviting the public to come, prepared the site with a speaker's platform in place, chairs available for the committee members and distinguished guests, and a clear space where the listeners stood. There were often farmers' wagons in the background on which people sat as well. The women of the community prepared some kind of refreshment for the speakers and party officials, sometimes for the assembled crowd as well. Many of those who had come to hear the speaker often brought food (and drink of varying alcoholic content) of their own. The committees organized marching bands to appear at their meetings, adding to the noise as they paraded through the towns preceding groups of loyalists carrying banners containing images of the candidates, party slogans, and propaganda on them, all for the purpose of calling out the faithful and imbuing them with the desired sense of devotion to the cause.[20]

When the audience had assembled, the band quieted and a local officeholder or member of the town or county party committee called the gathering to order, then spent some time in rousing the crowd with his oratory on behalf of the party, its principles, and its candidates. He then introduced the speaker of the day, who proceeded, often for several hours, to lay out the case for his favored party and against its opponents. His speech was usually interrupted by many shouts of approval and perhaps by as many negative remarks. Finally, with much cheering from the faithful and newly convinced, the event ended with reminders to everyone to come out to vote without fail and to get their neighbors to do so as well.[21]

Smaller meetings were much less elaborate, with a number of people standing around a farm wagon or someone's front porch, on which the speaker stood. They were often in someone's home with the speaker addressing whatever number showed up. But whatever their size and venue, these events were dedicated to the same purpose. There was an entertainment value to these meetings that everyone involved recognized. In the absence of other attractions, they provided a certain amount of diversion beyond the political for those attending. The United States was largely a rural nation, and as one historian has written, "rural life was hard and monotonous. . . . Political events provided a welcome respite from drudgery and social isolation." But their main purpose remained clear: informing and arousing, not only entertaining, the voters. State and local committees worked particularly assiduously to bring well-known speakers to their area to address their meetings. Because presidential candidates did not usually publicly campaign in this era, prominent party leaders such as Daniel Webster or Polk's vice president George Dallas, known for their oratorical skills, were much in demand to speak in place of the candidates. Often these leaders were overwhelmed by the number of requests they received to go somewhere and fight for the cause. William Seward energetically campaigned for General Taylor in Ohio, Pennsylvania, and Massachusetts in addition to his home state of New York, provoking his wife's anger because he was away from his family too much.[22]

The parties' younger members spoke at home or away as needed. For example, the devoted Taylor Whig from Illinois, Abraham Lincoln, already noted in national party circles for his many fierce attacks on the floor of Congress on President Polk and against the Mexican-American War, traveled to Massachusetts immediately after the Whig National Convention to deliver a series of twelve speeches over eleven days to party ratification meetings in the eastern part of the state. Actually, he gave pretty much the same speech twelve times—on behalf of Taylor and Fillmore and the Whig cause in general—sharing, at one point, the same platform at a great Whig rally in Boston's Tremont's Temple with the much better-known William Seward.[23]

The Democrats and Free Soilers fielded similarly gifted orators on their own behalf. In addition to chairing the Free Soil campaign, John Van Buren was much in demand as a speaker for the party. His oratorical as well as his political skills were widely known and appreciated by his colleagues. The Free Soil Convention had excitedly resolved that he should campaign wherever he was needed: "Let him stump the world" was their wish, echoed by local and state Free Soil leaders faced with a most difficult task. He was joined in the party's front lines by the much in demand Salmon P. Chase, David Wilmot, and Charles Sumner, among others.[24]

For the Democrats, older party leaders such as Thomas Hart Benton and rising younger stars such as Stephen A. Douglas were called upon constantly by their peers, and responded as their partisan culture demanded of them. Douglas, for example, traveled to a number of southern states to speak to party meetings on behalf of Cass and Butler. He would have done even more, but he fell ill and had to call a halt to his efforts. All of these leading speakers were joined in their efforts by other friendly U.S. senators and representatives as well as state and local officeholders.[25]

To accomplish their goal of reaching as many supporters as possible, party leaders sought assistance wherever they could, even at times challenging well-established social understandings and practices. Continuing the precedent set at the Buffalo convention, for example, Free Soil meetings included African Americans, some of whom were called upon to speak for Van Buren and Adams. At that time, it was considered very scandalous for women to address the public, but newspapers took notice of their presence at what were once all but exclusively male campaign events (heretofore considered too indelicate for the opposite sex). Women who were members of reform movements were more used to being involved in such public ways than were female partisans of the major parties, but the latter now became more involved in their party's campaigns. For the first time the Democrats, who had always been so critical of the reformers allowing women to participate in public activities beyond their traditional roles, proved willing to enlist them to help organize their rallies—and attend them as well. In 1848, as Elizabeth Varon suggests, the Democrats "chose . . . to harness women's partisanship rather than criticize it." They were late in doing so. The Whigs had brought women into some of their activities as far back as 1840, and continued to invite them from then on.[26]

As with the African Americans, women's participation in party activities was not central, systematic, widespread, or the beginning of a major shift away from the basic masculinity and whiteness of U.S. politics. The role of these outsiders (as the white male majority considered them) was circumscribed. They "mainly watched and cheered," some of them formed partisan clubs, and a small number "made substantial contributions with their pen and voice." But, however limited their presence was compared to future elections, their greater presence in the campaign activities in 1848 was a shift, nevertheless. Some outsiders in the political world were now becoming more a part of the raucous scene than they had ever been before.[27]

In his memoirs, George W. Julian provides a striking recollection of his efforts on behalf of Van Buren and Adams. The thirty-one-year-old native of Indiana was an upcoming Whig loyalist who became a Free Soiler in 1848 and, traveling around on a borrowed horse, spoke on behalf of his new cause in the eastern part of his home state." Having a

*Whig campaign banner with
likenesses of Taylor and Fillmore.*

first-class pair of lungs and much physical endurance," he later recalled, "I frequently spoke as often as three times a day, and generally from two to three hours at each meeting. I spoke at crossroads, in barns, in post-houses, in sawmills, in any place in which a few or many people would hear me. . . . With the truth on my side, I was delighted to find myself perfectly able, single-handed, to fight my battle . . . on the stump." Having spoken for as long as six to nine hours a day for weeks before the election, he rightly concluded the campaign of 1848 "was unspeakably relentless, vitriolic, and exhausting." Julian was not alone in his exertions and experiences. Others of all parties could have offered similar descriptions of their own activities.[28]

The parties needed to raise money in order to pay for printing, transportation, catering of food and drink at party rallies, and visiting speakers' housing and sustenance. All of them principally relied on their leaders to show the way. They assessed members of the state and local committees for their share of what was needed, appealed to their well-to-do supporters in local communities, approached Boston and New York merchants, bankers, and businessmen to contribute as much as they could, dunned party members who held official positions—clerks, court officers, postal workers, land surveyors, and the like—for a portion of their salaries, and called upon the candidates themselves to give as much as they could spare. The amounts they needed (and raised) were not large by modern standards—one estimate suggests that it took close to $50,000 to elect a president by midcentury. Lesser amounts were needed—but similarly vital—for the other offices being contested. Whatever the total, the funds were crucial to the parties' efforts and often more difficult to find than the fund-raisers hoped they would be despite their relentless and best efforts.[29]

Although their personal characteristics were sometimes referred to, usually by the opposition, presidential candidates did not get the kind of scrutiny of their physical appearance or their personal behavior that was to become familiar at a later time. Whatever characteristics they might have as good family men, social companions, and dignified public figures (or not), these attributes generally did not come up even in the heat of an intense campaign. As for their physical appearance, although each of the candidates inspired loyalty in the electorate, none of those running in 1848 was chosen by his party because of his well-turned-out appearance, commanding physique, or attractive disposition. Van Buren was known for his fine wardrobe and amiable social graces, but he, once a

Free Soil campaign banner with likenesses of Van Buren and Adams.

redheaded dandy, was now heavyset and bald. Cass was also a large man who apparently lived well, wore a wig, and was described by a contemporary as a "dull, phlegmatic, lymphatic, lazy man . . . [without] an atom of magnetism in his nature." Taylor was short in stature and bowlegged. He "looked less commanding afoot," his biographer has written, "than when astride his charger." He seemed most comfortable in well-worn, even shabby, unfashionable clothes, including an old straw hat.[30]

But all of this was largely irrelevant. The role of the presidential candidates in the 1840s was to be neither seen nor heard but principally talked about—and caricatured—by others. They remained at home receiving individuals and groups of supporters, making a few remarks to them, consulting with their associates over strategy, writing letters (usually not for publication) to party leaders, and rarely appeared in public, leaving their surrogates to campaign for them. Cass, on his return to Detroit from Washington after his nomination, did attend party rallies in the cities in which he stopped en route, usually to receive the accolades of party dignitaries but rarely to speak. After he got home, he remained there for the duration of the campaign. Taylor also mostly stayed home at his plantation in Louisiana. He did make a number of trips around the state by invitation, but not officially as a presidential candidate. Rather, he went solely, it was said, to receive honors from his admirers for his exploits in Mexico.[31]

Candidates for the other offices did personally campaign in a style that had evolved over many years. Most of them were on the road for many days, extensively stumping their locality or state on their own behalf, moving from village to village throughout their district, often engaging in arranged debates with their opponents, and meeting the voters repeatedly in as many different venues, from mass rallies to smaller gatherings, as they could—wherever there were people present whom they could cajole and persuade to join them and voters of like mind in their communities on election day.

No one forgot that all of this organizational work had as its main purpose to maximize, to the greatest degree possible, their party's attractiveness and the number of its voters who would turn out in November (or another time). As the editor of an Illinois Democratic newspaper said to his readers, his party's activities were designed to get people to "vote the Democratic ticket, and nothing but the Democratic ticket, at all elections." Workers for the party should therefore "never fail to attend the polls, talk to your neighbors, circulate the papers."[32]

Party leaders kept repeating to themselves from the beginning to the end of the campaign the familiar mantra that the better were their organizational efforts, the more success they were likely to have on election day. And the busy process usually worked to the leaders' satisfaction. Sometimes the parties' activities exceeded the bounds of good order. Meetings became more than tumultuous as partisan combativeness descended into physical confrontation, including fistfights, an occasional knifing, and other violence—for example, when provoked Democrats burned down a Rough and Ready clubhouse in New Orleans.[33]

Whatever the shortcomings of these often incomplete and sometimes haphazard organizational structures, complained about from the beginning to the end of the battle by insiders who were never satisfied, who believed that not enough was being done, that something was being ignored or missed or forgotten, the party organizations did successfully bring the voters and their families, as well as hangers on, out to their rallies and other events in large numbers during the campaign months and successfully involved them in the process leading toward election day.

ON THE EVE

As the campaign drew to a close and the last torchlight parade of the faithful, exciting mass rally and rousing stump speech had occurred, party leaders hoped all that could be done through "perfect organizations" had been accomplished, that their party's message had been received by its intended audience, and that their candidates' attractiveness had been understood and internalized by highly enthusiastic voters. As they entered November, the leaders hoped that everyone's blood was racing. Agents of the contenders for power had rallied "the lukewarm" and encouraged "the timid" into a state of spirited face-to-face confrontation that would soon enough pay off for them.[34]

Even with only a little time left to go before the polls opened, there were always some things left to do. Party workers did not let up, bringing their labors to a climax by spending the last days before polling day itself completing and checking their lists of voters and distributing already prepared ballots containing only their candidates' names that had been printed for their voters by the local newspaper. The voters took these with them to the polling place and used them there. (At this time, there were no government-provided official ballots listing all the candidates in the race. These were truly partisanly organized contests to the last moment.) On the crucial Tuesday itself, they worked hard to ensure that their supporters turned out, continuing to remind everyone what was at stake, arranging transportation to the polls as needed for the elderly or ill, constantly checking their lists of voters to make sure every one of their supporters was participating, handing out more ballots as needed, and never letting their guard down or their enthusiasm flag throughout the day.

To the end, party officials and their associates never forgot the obvious—that every vote was needed and had to be secured if humanly (and politically) possible. The rest of the story—the test of their success—would follow when the sheriff or another local official opened the polls early the morning of Tuesday, November 7, closely observed by party agents already on the scene who then remained as poll watchers throughout the day until the last voters had deposited their ballots.[35]

"THERE NEVER WAS AN ELECTION . . . OF GREATER IMPORTANCE"
THE PARTIES DEFINE WHAT IS AT STAKE

Faced with unhappy postconvention grumbling and, even more important, continuing expressions of distrust and anger from many of their Whig colleagues about what had occurred in Philadelphia, Zachary Taylor's advisors drafted and prevailed on him to sign and send a second letter to his brother-in-law John Allison in early September. The candidate reaffirmed his commitment to the Whig Party, which, he claimed, should never have been in doubt. He had been misunderstood or misrepresented. He did not hold an "equivocal attitude" toward the parties in the race—he was a Whig. He explained that what he had meant earlier was that he was not a partisan in a "straitened and sectarian sense" who would act as some of his recent predecessors had done while in office. He was not a divider aiming to confound those who disagreed with him. "I am not engaged to lay violent hands indiscriminately upon public officers, good or bad, who may differ in opinion with me"—as Taylor's intended Whig audience understood Andrew Jackson and Martin Van Buren had done with their spoils system. "I am not expected to force Congress by the coercion of the veto to pass laws to suit me," he continued (unlike the Democrats, Jackson and Polk, and the renegade Tyler, who had been quick to do so). "And I understand," he summed up, "that this is good Whig doctrine."[1]

Being against the "spoils system" and the overreach of presidential vetoes was certainly "good Whig doctrine," if not quite the whole of it. No matter. What Taylor said in the latest letter to John Allison served his and the Whigs' purpose. Having indicted, without directly mentioning them, the Democrats' leading lights, Presidents Jackson, Van Buren, and Polk, for their deleterious, overly partisan actions while in office, the letter's message was obvious and the language indisputable as to where the Whig Party's candidate stood. It certainly proved enough to delight most Whig editors and other party loyalists, ensuring them that they were in good hands. It was clear, as one of them wrote, that "Gen. Taylor is a Whig, and devoted to the principles of that party." That was what they wanted to hear.[2]

By the time that second Allison letter appeared, campaigners for all of the presidential candidates had been blasting away at each other for some time. Extensive campaign activities began in early summer and intensified after the last of the three national conventions had completed its work. As their organizations got up and running, party leaders turned to fulfilling the primary purpose of those institutions—to provide the means through which each party's argument, as embodied in the publications, speeches, meetings, and public spectacles they produced, reached the electorate. Taylor's new letter gave the presidential campaign its final impetus to move into the highest gear possible as everyone settled into the grooves of hard campaigning. "The pace indeed was speeding up," one of Taylor's biographers has written.[3]

ASSESSING THE ELECTORAL LANDSCAPE

When George Julian got up to speak to a crowd of potential Free Soil voters in central Indiana, or Abraham Lincoln addressed loyal Whigs in Massachusetts, or Stephen Douglas aroused a Democratic meeting in the southern states that fall, there was a great deal of partisan substance to their speeches. Each party argued that it had a distinct message to present to the voters, one its leaders had carefully thought out and developed as they considered the political landscape, their own strengths and weaknesses, and the situation of the other parties in the election. Everyone was conscious of the existing electoral calculus: the extreme closeness between the two major parties in the 1844 presidential race. Several key states, including New York, Georgia, and Ohio, had been electorally too close to call—they could go to either party. Most of all, although several states were almost certainly out of the reach of one or the other party, the presence of the Free Soilers and the restlessness of the Calhoun and Yancey supporters in the South could materially disrupt the usual pattern of party leaders' calculations in important areas. The electoral potency of the revolt against the further extension of slavery and the reaction in defense of southern rights was not because of the numbers of its supporters, but rather the fact that the political world was so closely divided in many places where people went to the polls. Even relatively small defections from the major parties to the Free Soilers, or from Democratic crossovers to the southerner Taylor, or the refusal of others to vote at all could therefore seriously affect the polling outcome in several states in both the North and South. Under the right conditions, these dissenters from the main parties and those who abstained could decide elections no matter how large the party loyalist voter pool was on election day.[4]

These calculations shaped the messages the parties presented as they sought to rally support. First and foremost, Whig and Democratic leaders (and Free Soilers as well) set out to convince voters how much was at stake in the contest in terms of the principles for which the parties stood, the different policy choices each offered, and the potential results, therefore, of victory or defeat. "The battle is to decide great issues" was the keynote, and "to fail will be to lose all that is valuable in a free government."[5] To back up that admonition, party leaders offered campaign arguments covering many and varied grounds, old and new. As they mobilized their arguments against their opponents, these embodied the several different factors that were clearly in play as in all elections, that is, the existing record along with the new matters that had become part of the electoral calculus.

The arguments were neither complex nor particularly sophisticated. Whatever underlying meanings, intentions, or ambiguities they may have contained, the messages were clear enough to their intended audiences in the well-defined and understood political world Americans inhabited. They were designed to be pointed, direct, simple, and evocative, intended to link voters' hopes, fears, and experiences with one or another of the parties running and do so in an understandable—not to mention rousing—manner. To accomplish this end, each of the two major parties proceeded to focus on three different areas as the campaign unfolded. First was the appeal, ability, and character of the presidential candidates. Party leaders believed they had much to gain either by exalting or, alternatively, denigrating the capabilities, honesty, and plans of the nominees chosen. Second were the sectional issues recently raised to a high pitch. Neither Whigs nor Democrats wanted the slavery extension issue to become prominent enough to dominate the election. (The Free

Soilers obviously disagreed.) Most of them did not believe that it would. But party strategists were well aware that sectional tensions were now part of the complex of issues in the political arena and that they had to deal with them in some fashion as they dealt with the other issues they confronted, those that already existed, or those that arose during the course of a campaign.[6]

Finally, the ongoing relevance of the traditional policy issues that had long divided Whigs from Democrats was always on their minds and, the party leaders believed, the minds of most of the voters as well. As noted earlier, the parties' records and differences on these long-standing matters were well known (despite the failure of the Whigs to produce a platform at their national convention), and party leaders used that knowledge when they believed it was beneficial to them as they fashioned their arguments against their electoral enemies. Finally, their messages were not so much designed to persuade people to change their minds and switch parties—even though some Whig leaders hoped to do just that at the outset of the campaign—as to energize the party's loyal supporters and bring them enthusiastically to the polls.[7]

As they sought to gain an advantage over their opponents, Whig and Democratic leaders used all three approaches at different times, in various ways, and in different places as their electoral needs and strategic calculations dictated they should. They constantly sought to find ammunition in their opponents' alleged missteps, failures of leadership, or lack of character at some moment or on some important issue. To be sure, there were always boundaries limiting what each could say. Those were set by the old parties' long-standing and well-known policy positions, along with those that had now been introduced by the Free Soilers. Any deviations from or backtracking on their previously stated positions for electoral advantage would provide their opponents the opportunity to pounce on them and denounce their deviousness and attempted gulling of the electorate—charges no party leaders wished to have lodged against them. Whatever each said, therefore, remained within those boundaries, framed within language that was often harsh and prosecutorial against the other side, a discourse of confrontation. And, of course, looming above all was the question of how to handle the complications introduced by the quite different emphases of the Van Buren coalition in the arguments they presented.[8]

*Stephen A. Douglas, Illinois Democratic leader and
tireless campaigner for Cass and Butler until he fell ill.*

"TAYLOR, THIS SECOND WASHINGTON"

Whig leaders began their campaign by following the arguments of Taylor's original supporters that he was their greatest asset because of his stature in the public view as a proven leader and someone unmarked by what they argued were the destructive vicissitudes of partisan politics—the proverbial Washington outsider. They quickly brought up how he had demonstrated his noble qualities to his country as the head of the U.S. Army in northern Mexico, winning widespread acclaim for his accomplishments. Since then, he had added to his luster and his attractiveness to all Americans. The Whig leaders continued to believe and argue, therefore, that with him as their candidate they had a good chance of winning some Democrats to their side. The war, one of their editors wrote, had "relaxed the strictness of adhesion to old party lines. . . . The bonds of mere partisanship had been loosened." Whether that was wishful thinking, Whigs certainly believed as they opened fire on the Democrats that they would benefit from this new political possibility.[9]

To capitalize on the opportunity this supposed loosening of traditional political bonds presented, the Whigs reverted to a tactic they had employed in the past: the antipartisan argument. That is, they assailed the excessive power of political parties and their insistence on unquestioning loyalty to them as a major defect in the political system. It was time for a major shift in understanding and behavior. They kept returning to the argument that Taylor was above the narrow perspectives, shams, and connivances of sectarian partisan warfare. He had demonstrated that he was not a politician but rather an independent leader free of the restraints "ultra" partisanship imposed on lesser men. He was committed to the welfare of all Americans, not only those who belonged to the party that had made him its candidate, and he would not overstep his constitutional powers as he carried out his policies. The Whigs had "nominated a man who makes one pledge, the only pledge a president should make—the only pledge Washington would make—to administer the government according to the Constitution." Party leaders particularly liked and readily adopted the comparison of their candidate with the premier founding father and greatest hero in U.S. history. "Taylor, this second Washington [who had been critical of partisan political divisions and organized factions in his Farewell Address], would bring the Government back to the purer principles and better policy of the first."[10]

According to the Whigs, Taylor's attributes at all levels were manifest and superior to the usual run of partisan candidates. One Whig pamphlet writer laid it out in *Sketch of the Life of General Zachary Taylor, the People's Candidate for the Presidency*. Published not inadvertently on July 4, 1848, the pamphlet spent a great deal of space describing the illustriousness of Taylor's military career and his many talents as a leader, particularly when facing the Mexican Army, despite of the efforts of the Polk administration "to destroy . . . [him] in the estimation of the country" regardless of his great victories and exemplary service. His name "is pure and untarnished, freed from the gilded arts and ambitious schemes through which, unfortunately for the age, most men advance in power and greatness." He was known above all for "his humanity, his benevolence, his strict integrity, and singleness of purpose." General Taylor is a "moral" man, "a friend and observer of temperance." He only drinks "pure cold water." Finally, "like Washington, he is plain, direct, and honest . . . brave and just, and generous and humane."[11]

The exaltation of the Whig candidate did include a number of familiar public policy arguments as well. When Taylor became president, the pamphlet writer suggested, members of Congress would resume their rightful place in the U.S. government and no longer be "the cringing slaves of Executive power." The will of the people would not be "crushed by the veto." Duties would be laid on foreign imports and Americans' labor "adequately protected from ruinous competition with the pauper labor of Europe." Internal improvements "necessary certainly to the success of the commerce [of the nation] . . . will be prominent among the reforms" Taylor pursued. And always, although he was nominated by the Whig Party, he was "the people's candidate," a no-party candidate, not a sectarian politician.[12]

If Taylor lost, Whigs argued, the consequences to the nation would be dire. Given what the American people had seen over the previous four years, his defeat "will justify war at the mere caprice of the President, will degrade the character of Congress, deny to the majority the right to govern, and make the 'one-man Power' supreme and dictatorial against the popular will." Zachary Taylor, in sum, was a person of unusual authority and distinction, holding the best interests of the country at the center of his being, a bulwark against the dangerous follies of the other side—clearly the candidate best suited to lead the nation.[13]

The Whigs' case against the Democratic presidential candidate was equally strong. When anyone compared Lewis Cass to Taylor, there was no contest. First, the former was the embodiment of a narrow-minded politician, having no other distinction than unswerving blind loyalty to his party. What else had he ever been than a mere party hack follow-ing Democratic leaders' dictates at every turn? Cass's vaunted military experience, of which party orators were making so much, was hardly in the same league as Taylor's. Whig publicists delighted in making fun of Cass's record as a soldier (Abraham Lincoln, with his sharp tongue, played a prominent part in this effort). The Democratic candidate had been present at one of the nation's great military debacles, the surrender of Detroit to the British during the War of 1812. Cass's partisans argued that he had attempted to avoid being part of the surrender and claimed that he had personally broken his sword rather that give it up to the enemy. This was hardly the stuff, the Taylorites pointed out in rebut-tal, of being the commander of the victorious U.S. Army at Palo Alto, Monterey, and Buena Vista.[14]

Furthermore, Whigs insisted, Cass lacked integrity. He and his sup-porters were two-faced about the Wilmot Proviso, saying one thing about it in the North to win support there, quite another in the South for the same reason. Moreover, they claimed that Cass had engaged in financial misbehavior to his benefit while governor of the Michigan Territory and had been an incompetent secretary of war. He was, in short, no more than "a time-serving demagogue—a political trickster—who has grown wealthy on extra pay from the public treasury." Which of the two ma-jor candidates could be trusted? Which of them would make the better president?[15]

In following this antipartisan, Taylor-celebrating tactic, the Whig strategists engaged in a delicate balancing act. Despite their wish to fo-cus so much attention on Taylor's military accomplishments, they also had to expand their arguments in his favor into other areas of concern in their world. There was not always a distinct line between all of the is-sues on the campaign agenda. When it came to candidates, for example, their appeal stemmed not only from their personal qualities but because they embodied other matters. Whatever Taylor's heroic, nonpartisan qualities, there were additional questions about him to which potential voters needed to hear answers. As partisans had long understood, in the general's case, it was electorally significant that he was both a south-ern slaveholder and had identified himself as a Whig, committed to the party program, the primacy of Congress, and other welcome govern-ment practices. From the first, Whig strategists picked up on these dif-ferent elements of his political appeal as they interacted with the public to draw even more support to Taylor's candidacy.[16]

Whig leaders had always believed Taylor's apparent appeal to southerners regardless of party was a great plus for them. Party campaigners in the slaveholding states played on sectional sensitivity throughout the campaign, contrasting their southern-born, slaveowning candidate, obviously empathetic to the South's needs, with the northerner the Democrats were putting forward. At a time of increasing assaults on southern interests, values, and way of life, Whig leaders suggested to non-Whigs in the slave states and still-hesitant supporters there who clung to Clay's leadership to consider where their protection lay. Despite Cass's assurances to the South, a northern politician could not be relied upon. He would succumb to the pressures of the antisouthern activists in his home section, Whigs argued. He would have no other choice but to do so. As Whig leaders developed this line of reasoning, their arguments became more compelling (they hoped), when Congress became enmeshed in an effort to organize the Oregon Territory. The bill under debate included the language of the Wilmot Proviso in one of its clauses, which aggravated sectional sensitivity and provoked a harsh reaction against it from some southerners.[17]

The Whig southern campaign strategy was complicated, however. First, Whig leaders had to deal with the accusation that their vice presidential candidate was an abolitionist. Unfriendly voices spread the charge among the party's southern contingent that Millard Fillmore had once referred to slavery as "evil" and had supported the House of Representatives receiving abolitionist petitions when he served there in the 1830s despite fervent southern objections to Congress receiving them. In response to these attacks on him, Fillmore's supporters circulated a pamphlet among southern Whigs that defended him and his record. He had, for instance, they claimed, taken the position that whatever one's beliefs about the institution, power over slavery was "vested" in the states where it existed, not in the federal government. There was nothing in his past behavior, the pamphlet writer concluded, "calculated to lessen our confidence in his integrity, or to excite any alarm for the safety of the South should he be chosen."[18]

This appeal to defenders of slavery was only one aspect of the situation. As Whig leaders in the South made their case, their colleagues in the northern states, desperate to limit defections to the Free Soilers, appealed to sectionally sensitive voters among their usual supporters in quite a different manner. The Whig State Convention in Massachusetts presented Taylor to the state's voters "not only as a Whig, but as a 'free soil' Whig." Other northern Whig meetings articulated similar messages about their candidate along with passing resolutions in favor of the Wilmot Proviso.[19]

Beyond that, the standard Whig appeal in nonslaveholding areas was that the Louisianan, Taylor, was a better bet to achieve antiextension goals than the southern lackey, Cass. Party campaigners such as Lincoln reiterated the argument made after their convention that the Free Soil Party was not necessary. As president, Taylor would not allow slavery to extend any further than its present boundaries. If enough northern Whigs were elected to Congress, that northern-dominated body would pass the Wilmot Proviso, and Taylor, even if he had sympathy for southern interests, which they denied, would not veto it when it reached his desk. Like the true Whig he was, Taylor was committed to congressional authority on such legislative matters. Cass, in contrast, they reminded their hesitant colleagues, would follow the tradition of earlier Democratic presidents, particularly that of the Constitution wrecker Andrew Jackson, and be quick to veto any such bill. Which of the two, Whig publicists summed up, would better serve those who wanted to pass the proviso?[20]

As for Van Buren and the Free Soilers, the Whig argument never wavered. Any support thrown to them by Whigs would be a catastrophe. Van Buren's record was against him. He had been willingly subservient to southern pressure throughout his political life. In one campaign he had written several letters, "all of which are as southern as could have been written by John C. Calhoun." Where in that record Whigs could extract anything positive, and then cast their votes for him, "we cannot imagine." Why should anyone believe that he had really changed—or repented "some of his vile acts"? Voting for him now would be wrongheaded if one was against the extension of slavery. Such a vote would take votes away from Taylor, probably elect Cass, and "perpetuate the southern dynasty which, in foreign measures, brought on the war with Mexico and the annexation of Texas, and which, at home, has destroyed the protective policy, a wise system of internal improvements, and contributed to a large public debt." Voting Free Soil, William Seward wrote to his New York supporters, "is only a negative protest against the Slavery party." It accomplishes nothing useful. Is that what antislavery Whigs wanted? With whom did northern interests lie? "For myself," Seward continued, "I shall cast my suffrage for General Taylor and for Millard Fillmore, freely and conscientiously, on precisely the same grounds on which I have hitherto voted."[21]

As some of these remarks indicate, despite the sectional pressures, party leaders also understood that the continued "potency of party ties" remained in the electoral mix, and was a most powerful weapon when the voters went to the polls regardless of recent developments that might challenge such commitments. Thus the first task of party leaders was to keep their normal supporters—their partisan base, in later terminology—happy, excited, and committed by flexing their partisan muscles and reminding them why they were loyal Whigs. To accomplish this, they had to concentrate on the traditional issues separating the parties, their reasons for resisting the claims of the other candidates and parties, and linking Taylor ever more firmly to Whig issues.[22]

They proceeded to remind their audience that the Democrats, "for all practical purposes, reduce the Constitution to a dead letter" in their policy advocacy. Democratic domestic policies such as opposing federal financing for internal improvements and clinging to a low tariff policy only hurt the national economy, their foreign adventures led to bloodshed, and "the whole odious catalogue of errors, blunders, lies, and meddlesome experiments of the Polk administration" led to further conflict for the country. Finally, echoing an old theme, Democratic leaders and their party were "rotten with corruption," only "held together" by the strong "cohesive power of public plunder."[23]

Cass was the perfect Democratic Party man. He had been a loyal supporter and outspoken advocate of all of Polk's failed policies, including the latter's overaggressive policy toward other countries and his willingness to threaten Congress and even go to war to achieve his policy objectives. A Cass presidency would be nothing but a dangerous rerun of those of his Democratic predecessors. He would expose the country "to all the dangers and difficulties of further annexation and conquest." In contrast, as a southern Whig member of Congress summed up the case, whereas "the Democratic Party is committed to a policy which leads to aggression, war, and conquest . . . the Whigs desire to preserve peace with all the world, to stimulate the industry, and to develop the resources of the country."[24]

In response to Democratic failure in the economic realm, the Whigs reiterated their familiar arguments from earlier times. They continued to favor certain federal legislation, particularly the establishment of sound financial institutions they considered necessary to promote economic development, a higher tariff, and federal financing of internal improvements to state transportation infrastructure, instead of the Democrats' low tariff of 1846, Polk's independent treasury, and the Democratic blind resistance to spending federal money on needed construction projects. The tariff issue, they believed, would be particularly potent in the key large state of Pennsylvania, where the situation in the coal and iron industries was particularly bleak because of foreign competition and the lack of concern about their needs from the Polk administration. Similarly, given the anger of usually loyal Democrats in several of the Great Lakes states about Polk's veto of the much desired Rivers and Harbors Act Congress had passed in 1846 (with some Democratic support), the Whigs made much of the situation in the areas where anger still festered. Critics particularly went after Cass's allegedly lukewarm attitude, at best, toward his home region's needs, and thus his failure to support efforts to obtain federal aid. Such Whig opportunities in states where they had not previously done well at election time further strengthened the party's optimism as the campaign developed.[25]

In a number of places in the North, the electoral influence of anti-immigrant, anti-Catholic nativist groups highlighted another familiar electoral issue (usually argued at the local level) and influenced Whig calculations. Stimulated by the success of Lewis Levin's Native American movement in Pennsylvania and its hostility to proimmigration Democrats, Whig Party leaders reawakened many Whigs' negative attitudes toward outsiders and worked with Levin and his supporters on behalf of Taylor's candidacy. The Pennsylvania nativists did throw their support to Taylor, with Levin running for reelection to Congress on both the Whig and Native American tickets. The relationship was not as overt in other states, but Whig hostility to immigrants was well known from past experience and remained strong.[26]

Synthesizing all the Whigs were arguing, the party's Chicago *Journal* summed up its case against the Democrats in the northern states: "Cass is proslavery, prowar, and anti-[internal] Improvement." A Pennsylvania party newspaper added Taylor's support for the Walker Tariff of 1846 to the list. To the editor, the main themes of the campaign in his state were "Taylor and the [high Whig] tariff of 1842." Other Whig newspapers echoed similar notions throughout the country, adding other items (or subtracting some) where helpful. The message was familiar, repetitious, and clear enough. The country needed new leadership, new directions, and new policies, rejecting the failed party in power over the previous four years. Cass and his Democratic associates were not the answer. They constituted "the Veto party, the advocate of war and carnage," which Cass unhesitatingly supported according to his opponents. Finally, Cass's alleged opposition to the Rivers and Harbors Act continued to be emphasized in the anti-Cass publications distributed in the upper Great Lakes area and wherever else they would do the most good against his and the Democratic Party's bid to retain the presidential office.[27]

This focus on the traditional partisan approach to national politics came to the fore among Whig leaders, especially in the northern states, as party strategy developed during the campaign. As the weeks passed, Whigs found that their candidate-centered appeal was not having the desired effect. Democrats were not coming over to Taylor in sufficient numbers, nor was there a rush of uncommitted voters to the Whig standard. Something had to be done as well to ensure the support of those uncertain Whigs who had held back from supporting Taylor since the Philadelphia convention. He remained at the center of their appeal in all of his guises, as a general, southerner, and committed Whig, but, as Michael Holt points out, party strategists began to shift their focus to rely more heavily than they had originally on the traditional issues that had long divided them from the Democrats, particularly in those geographic areas where the antiparty Taylor was not as popular among Whig loyalists as he was elsewhere. The party leaders certainly did not give up on the candidate-centered issues they had been advocating, but they clearly indicated that partisanship, never absent, was back in favor as a campaign weapon.[28]

"THE GALLANT CASS OF MICHIGAN"

The Democratic campaign was neither innovative nor adventurous. Party publicists followed the usual elements of the argument that had been a recognized pattern of their appeal for two decades. They believed their party's history of accomplishment from Jackson to Polk was their greatest strength, and Cass was a perfect embodiment of the principles for which they stood. To turn their supporters out in force, therefore, and convince potential defectors to stay loyal to their natural political home, Democratic leaders emphasized the party's magnificent record of beneficial policies "that had done so much good for mankind," and that their candidate was a distinguished and committed follower of Andrew Jackson. They saw the party record, carried forward by its presidential candidate, as "THE ARTILLERY OF DEMOCRATIC TRUTH," a force that had proved strong enough to defeat all of their enemies.[29]

"Everything indicates," the editor of the Washington *Union* wrote early in 1848, "that the coming political battle is to be fought upon the old party issues, though the Whigs may attempt to evade them." And, as the campaign developed, the *Union* editor as well as other party leaders tried hard to keep those issues before their supporters. They knew as well as the Whigs did that some of their policy commitments were hurting them among usually loyal Democrats in a number of places. For example, Polk's veto of the Rivers and Harbors Act had already eroded party loyalty in parts of the western states, as had the Walker Tariff in Pennsylvania, where, as one of the Hunker leaders complained, normally staunch party colleagues thought it necessary "to out tariff the Whigs." (And, he sourly continued, to "out promise the abolitionists.")[30]

Nevertheless, most Democratic strategists gladly played up their position on these and other familiar economic and social issues as they had gelled over the past two decades, which distinguished them from the Whigs. They celebrated Polk's many achievements in restoring the country to the right course after the Whig administration of Harrison and Tyler and warned about the dangers that still lurked from "odious Whig doctrines" such as a national bank, high tariffs, oppressive federal power, and other indignities if they returned to power. Remember, Democrats warned, "endeavoring to conceal their purpose of fastening unadulterated federalism upon the government," the Whigs "labor to keep in the background their cherished policy of special privileges" for the few.[31]

Echoes of the differences over the war with Mexico and the future territorial aims of the United States added to the damning Democratic litany against the "federalists." Taylor is the candidate of "the MEXICAN WHIGS . . . the object of which is to defeat and destroy the American patriots whom he led to victory in Mexico. What spectacle can be more disgusting? . . . As well might he attempt to reinstate Benedict Arnold and the Tories of the revolution in the affections of the American people, as the Whig allies of Mexico who are now clinging to his skirts." The Whigs had allegedly laid aside "all patriotic principles" during the war. Of course, according to the Democrats, their behavior was unfortunately nothing new. Their "want of patriotism" had been "manifested" in every war the nation fought "by their reprehensible, not to say treasonable, conduct," reminding everyone of one of their favorite accusations against the "federalists," the party's behavior during the War of 1812. They had protracted that war by their encouragement of the enemy in their public speeches and repeated attacks on Polk's policies. Further, their opposition to acquiring territory "as indemnity for the manifold injuries inflicted upon us by Mexico . . . disgraced the country."[32]

Democrats were also quick to attack Taylor and his colleagues for their links to the nativists, referring to the Whigs as the party of "federal nativism." The party "openly leagues with the proscriptive Native Americans," they warned their immigrant neighbors, in order "to overthrow the democracy who stand for your rights and privileges." They pointed out to Irish American voters, in particular, that "your enemies are the Whigs of the United States. They insult you on all occasions." Taylor was the nativists' "favored candidate," they concluded, because they knew the Whigs would support anti-immigrant demands.[33]

Finally, echoing similar Whig allegations against Cass, Democrats claimed it was Taylor who had proven himself personally dishonest, engaging in financial improprieties at the expense of the American people. Party newspapers charged that during his recent military service in Mexico and immediately thereafter, he had drawn extra pay from the government to which he was not entitled. When challenged, he had not paid it back. They also pointed out that even after he became a candidate for political office, he continued to draw a salary from the federal government. This was, they insisted, hardly appropriate behavior.[34]

Their own presidential candidate, however, was above reproach. They certainly waxed as enthusiastically about him as Whigs did about Taylor. Cass was "a statesman of enlarged experience—of extensive attainments—honest in his principles—pure in his private life—amiable in his manners—faithful to his friends—liberal to his opponents." They celebrated his political history as firmly in the mold of the Jacksonian Democrats. His service as a territorial governor and then in Jackson's cabinet proved his devotion to their cause. His record and votes in the Senate since 1845 fully supported President Polk and the advancement of the party's policies. "He has been one of the most decided and the most faithful advocate of an administration which yields to no other in the glory and benefit which it has shed upon its country." He was a tried and true Democrat, and everyone knew what he believed in and would do as president—unlike the situation with his opponent. He "requires no censor to ask his principles, or to ascertain his qualifications. Besides, he is, like his party, clear and manly in the exposition of his principles."[35]

Cass had some other electorally attractive virtues as well. If voters insisted on military prowess when choosing a president, Democrats reminded their audiences of the service of "the Gallant Cass of Michigan" in the War of 1812. Contrary to Whig lies about his record, he had been recognized as an outstanding militia officer and a brave soldier, making his reputation against the British along the Great Lakes frontier even when others had faltered. He was always "to be found where the shot flew thickest." He had been, Democrats claimed, the first soldier to enter Canada during the U.S. Army's invasion of that British province, and General William Henry Harrison had called him "an officer of the highest merit." Democrats were quick to trumpet such achievements, the plaudits Cass received as a result of them, and his subsequent well-deserved promotions to higher rank.[36]

As with the Whigs' strategy, a large part of the Democrats' argument consisted of attacks on their opponents. They never let up on their denunciations of the Whigs' refusal to tell the voters what they really stood for and would do in office. The Whigs were "that party which either has no principles, or is ashamed to express them," and their candidate follows that unacceptable course with his "storehouse of unknown political principles." Unlike the Whigs, Cass and his colleagues do not "seek to decoy" to their side "the false or the unwary of other parties." They scorn efforts "to corrupt and seduce, or to mislead and entrap, by allurements and rewards, or by device or trickery, the rank and file of . . . [their] enemy." The Whigs, however, by running Taylor, "abandon all principle, and fight only for office." Their campaigners are "deceiving, deluding, humbugging" with their candidate. Taylor was, according to the Democrats, "a mere sham." His "affected independence of party consists altogether in [his] profound ignorance of political questions."[37]

Further, the American people would not be fooled by the no-party tricks played by these "most intolerant, malignant, and persecuting partisans," who had nominated a presidential candidate without "obtaining a solitary pledge" from him about where he stood on the issues of the day. Democrats accused Whigs of behaving like "the conquered Mexicans" by "surrendering to Gen. Taylor" and bowing "before the idol of availability." Whigs were motivated only by their desire to win and in service of such an aim hid any policy commitments they had previously espoused and tried to impose on the nation. Instead, they acted with "complete mendacity and want of principle." As a result, Democrats maintained, the present contest was between an unacceptable "motley gang of factions" and "the party of principle."[38]

Ultimately, Democratic leaders summed up their traditional argument in a direct fashion. First, "we scorn and repudiate the famous maxim that 'all is fair in politics.' We believe that nothing is fair in politics, but that which is founded on great principles, on truth, on justice." Therefore, "if you vote for General Cass, you vote to continue and perpetuate the Democratic policy, which has brought the country to such a high state of prosperity." If you vote Whig, you are supporting the party that "has not the manliness to take any position." But the most critical argument remained that if you vote for "General Mum," then "you vote for a national bank, high protective tariff, an enormous and wasteful system of internal improvements . . . and the whole catalogue of Whig measures." The enactment of such, all Democrats were sure, would be a disaster for the nation.[39]

Like the Whigs, Democrats were sensitive to the sectional impulses present in the political landscape. They could not avoid the issue of slavery extension, as much as many of them wanted to. As with the Whigs, they could only try to gain some advantage from the importance of this issue to some of their supporters. They began by trying to deal with the difficulty in familiar ways. First, when arguing with those northern Democrats attracted to the Free Soil Party, leaders made a case for party unity and the consequences of breaking ranks. Every step northern Democrats took in support of the Free Soilers moved them "away from the democracy and into federalism, abolitionism, and disunion." They had to resist such sectional splintering and the consequences it would have for the future of the nation. Thomas Hart Benton, a longtime colleague and friend of Van Buren, campaigned actively for Cass and on behalf of "harmony, union, and concession among the Democrats." Such was "the only sure guaranty of success" in this election. And success had to be the goal of all Democrats, even those who were unhappy with Polk's behavior and policies. Their position was succinctly summed up by antislavery U.S. Representative John Wentworth from Illinois: "Let us Barnburners strive to lick Taylor first," he wrote. "He must be beaten, and if we have an independent organization in Democratic states, he will beat us."[40]

The Democrats wanted unity, as they pointed out, for a purpose beyond simply winning the election. As much as they despised the renegade Van Buren on a personal level for his apostasy, and presumably thirsted for revenge, there were also critical policy matters involved in the decision as to who would be the next president. The United States was in danger from the sectional turmoil. A Van Buren victory or a substantial vote for him in the North "would strike a deep and fatal blow at the Union." "His present principles . . . are open and undisguised war against a particular section of the union, and his success would at once and forever place the North and the South in an attitude so hostile that peace and brotherly love could never be restored." The issue before them was clear to the Democrats: "If this country is [to be] saved from anarchy and disunion, from sectional strife and civil commotions, it must be by the great National Union of the Democratic Party." That party "is now the only hope of the Union. The fidelity of Northern Democrats to the Compromises of the Constitution . . . will defeat all the base sectional maneuvers of fanatics and knaves."[41]

Democratic leaders celebrated Cass's vision of popular sovereignty as expressed in his letter to Nicholson and codified in the party platform. They reminded everyone Congress did not have the power to interfere with the institution of slavery. The Wilmot Proviso was a "humbug." Congress could not constitutionally "legislate," a Democratic U.S. representative from Ohio argued, "on the question of slavery in the Territories." Furthermore, in addition to Cass's view of constitutional authority in the states, Democrats worked hard to remind their colleagues in the South that even though Cass was not a southerner, he was responsive to their interests both as a Jacksonian and as a longtime friend of the section. Northern Democrats such as Cass "have been reared in a school which has ever taught the principle of noninterference with slavery by the General government." In office, the northern Democrats would leave it to the people in the states and territories to decide what should be done.[42]

Southern Democratic loyalists picked up on this theme and reminded their colleagues in the slave states of their party's stated commitment to upholding their rights as citizens in the territories. They lauded the "small but gallant squad of Democratic senators" from the North for their quickness to support the South when it was under attack. As Senator Jefferson Davis of Mississippi put it in a campaign speech in his state's capital, some say Cass, as a northerner, "cannot be trusted by the South." This was not true. "So long as we have friends in the North, it is not only a moral duty to cherish and sustain them, but it is dictated by policy to do so." They had proven their commitment—they had no intention, unlike the Whigs and Free Soilers, of interfering with southern interests.[43]

Southern Democratic leaders constantly urged their local compatriots to remember, also, that there was a wide gulf separating Whig from Democratic policies in other matters of concern. In speeches in Congress and on the stump from such loyal party members as Howell Cobb of Georgia, there was strong advocacy of party loyalty and the reminder that few consensual elements existed in U.S. politics and there was always much for the parties to fight about. The Democrats' well-established economic policies, including the low tariff, demand for rigorous economy, and resistance to wasteful large government, had served the nation and the southern states well and would continue to do so in the future under a Cass administration. Taylor and the Whigs would not. For any southern Democrat to question his party commitment and its value now was wrongheaded and harmful to his section. Much would be lost if the Democrats did not remain as stalwart as they had always been. They should unite behind Cass without hesitation and with great enthusiasm.[44]

Finally, the Democrats fused several strategies by echoing charges their opponents were making against them: the Whigs were duplicitous on the slavery issue by saying one thing in the South, another in the North, an unacceptable way for a political party to argue, and their use of Taylor as a slaveholder was hypocritical. "We leave it to the intelligent voter to say whether such a man can ever be friendly to free soil, or anything but extreme southern measures," Whigs told southerners, while at the same time to northerners, they portrayed their candidate as willing to let the Wilmot Proviso become law. In selling him there as an antiextension candidate, Whigs were trying to have it both ways. They continued to knowingly "assert a falsehood" for electoral advantage.[45]

The Democrats' campaign strategy began with their traditional perspectives as its core component and added to it, out of necessity, an exposition of the way they would handle the slavery extension matter within their traditional ideological framework. Their leaders clearly believed their most effective appeal, as in previous elections, was to draw a sharp contrast with their Whig opponents and the continuing relevance of that contrast even under current conditions. Because of their devotion to a range of issues critical to their voters, they pointed out the consequent danger if any of their supporters deserted the party for the single-issue Free Soilers or Yancey's group of southern rights advocates. The Democrats remained, as they always had been, the best hope for the country on all matters of concern as it faced the future.

"THERE IS NO MIDDLE COURSE; YOU ARE FOR SLAVERY OR YOU ARE AGAINST IT"

The members of the Free Soil Party would have none of this focus on traditional policy matters the two major parties preferred. Instead, they presented a different story to the voters about their society and its politics. They began with a typical outside challenger's position. There was something very wrong, they claimed, with the system. The dominance of the Whigs and Democrats over the minds of the voters in the late 1840s—the "old and defunct party ties"—prevented the nation from facing the consequential problems in U.S. society. The party leaders were "passion-minded partisans who resolve to see nothing but through the mist of an unreasonable prejudice." Unfortunately, they contended, most voters blindly followed their leaders and thus were politically limited in the same manner. The Whigs, when asked what they stood for, only answer "General Taylor," indicating that "they have no principle left to electioneer with." The Democrats had been reduced to incessantly repeating only the "obsolete" concerns of another age when Andrew Jackson ruled the nation.[46]

Americans' failure to face up to what was now the most critical, indeed the only, issue would not be remedied by either of the old parties. Whatever the Whigs' claims about the attractiveness of General Taylor or the Democrats' about the importance of the old divisions between them, both the inexperienced general and "the exploded issues" of the past were irrelevant to the current situation facing the country. Free Soilers wanted instead a clear focus on the one vital matter before the American people. "The principles of Free Soil," one of their leading newspaper editors wrote, "are the only ones at issue in the contest for President." And members of the new party believed they held the moral high ground on that matter. They were "bound together by the firmest and most sacred ties, in a Cause which engages all their heart."[47]

To accomplish their purpose in the campaign, the Free Soilers had to break down the too-powerful party loyalties of northern voters, their "blind adherence" to "the tyranny of the old parties," by convincing them of the need to think differently. They found it easy and, they believed, politically telling, to unstintingly assail the old parties for being indifferent toward or cowardly about the issue of slavery's further extension. But the growing tensions over that issue made it impossible, Free Soil leaders argued, for Whig and Democratic campaigners to evade the matter despite their desire to do so. Still, the old parties continued to ignore the reality now before them. The Free Soil mantra, in response, challenged

and denigrated the old parties, constantly reminding the voters that neither would do anything about the crisis created by the slaveholders: their
demand for the further extension of slavery. The Free Soilers, in contrast, would.[48]

The advocates of the Wilmot Proviso had sought to contain slavery
within its existing boundaries, and the Free Soil campaign became the
electoral expression of that position in 1848. Party leaders' arguments
against further extension closely followed the debates of the previous
few years, echoing the oratory in which supporters of the proviso had
repeatedly engaged since 1846, and which the Free Soil Party had enshrined in its Buffalo platform: "It was the settled policy of the nation [at
its outset] not to extend, nationalize, or encourage, but to limit, localize,
and discourage slavery; and to this policy, which should never have been
departed from, the Government ought to return." That perspective was
the core of the party's belief system and remained its emphasis throughout the months leading up to the election, supplemented by references
to a number of other challenges and desired reforms advocated by its
supporters.[49]

Most important, as the Free Soilers saw it, was combining their resistance to the further extension of slavery with powerful oratorical condemnation of the reasons for its recent expansion. Those reasons were
clear-cut: they lay in the long-standing maldistribution of power within
the U.S. Congress, that is, the South's control of the federal government,
which slaveowners aggressively used to defend their section and advance
their own interests at the expense of the interests of other Americans
outside the slave states.[50]

Southerners had "hitherto ruled the republic with a rod of iron" from
their base in the Democratic Party. They had dominated that party since
the days of Thomas Jefferson, but never more completely and aggressively than in the previous few years under President Polk. This power
was abused by those of Polk's followers who remained loyal to his policies, such as Lewis Cass, who had earned his nomination "by multiple
acts of the most obsequious and crouching servility to his southern over-
seers." The party "is so openly and recklessly committed to the slave
power," one Free Soil pamphlet writer charged, "that it seems like a
needless work to offer any proofs of its proslavery character." The Whigs
were no better, as clearly indicated by their choice of a presidential candidate, a plantation owner who held 300 slaves. Taylor, "the dealer and
buyer of slaves, does not often care for human life." Both of the old

party candidates, the Whig general and the Democratic political hack, were "the pledged guardians of the Slave Interest" and part of a longtime conspiracy to extend slavery further on the continent. This conspiracy, Free Soil leaders argued, had to be exposed, and southern control of the nation's political process had to be broken.[51]

Furthermore, if the Democrats and Whigs were occasionally pressured by the voters to talk about the issue, their responses were deceitful, both claiming to hold positions they did not out of political expediency. Each party engaged in a "stupendous and monstrous fraud" by saying one thing about their position in the slave states and quite another elsewhere. The Democrats had actually issued two different versions of Cass's biography, "one for the North and the other for the South." Such deceit had to be punished by the electorate—both of the old parties had to be defeated.[52]

Their presidential candidates' expressed, or unexpressed, attitudes about slavery extension were typical examples of the parties' failures on the main issue before them, Cass because of his championship of popular sovereignty, a policy that could lead to more slave territory being added to the Union, and Taylor for ignoring the issue entirely while his party colleagues lied about his position and what he was likely to do as president. In reality, the Free Soilers repeatedly argued, "there is absolutely no difference between Cass and Taylor." One of them "is a Northern man with Southern principles, the other is a Southern man with Southern principles. Both candidates are utterly unworthy [of] the suffrage of a free people."[53]

Given the situation, voters had to choose someone better than either of these two men to lead the country. The old parties, their issues, their evasions, and their candidates, no longer mattered even as they blindly fought on, whatever the consequences. Martin Van Buren stood out as something different, and better, than the other candidates. He was clear about what he believed; his stances on issues were "distinctly known" and decidedly what the country needed at this juncture. Therefore, the choice was obvious: a new political template had to replace the obsolete one. "Forthwith, let the party lines be drawn" on the main issue. "There is no middle course; you are for slavery or you are against it."[54]

Despite their single-issue intensity, the Free Soilers did occasionally reach beyond their primary focus. When they discussed other matters, they followed the traditional party practice of allowing tactical considerations to shape their arguments and presented them in places where they believed that initiative could draw other reform-minded people to them on election day. In Maine, for example, they offered arguments and suggested legislation against allowing individual overindulgence in alcohol along with their Free Soil planks. Temperance was a major issue in parts of New England; the impulse was beginning to grow in political force there with the aim of legislating state regulation of alcohol consumption. In the Great Lakes region, Free Soilers argued in favor of federal aid to internal improvements, an issue that they knew never stopped roiling many westerners of both old parties. Free Soil leaders remained committed to land reform, a "free grant to actual settlers," as they had promised in their Buffalo platform, and appealed for support from leaders of that movement. They attacked the Whigs for bolstering anti-immigrant sentiments in many places: "The alliance of Taylorism with Nativism is complete," they argued, and had to be exposed and defeated. The Free Soil advocacy of these issues certainly was not as widespread or as fervent as their antisouthern, antiextension stance, but it was used as part of the electoral calculus that defined their chances against the old parties.[55]

As for the Free Soil presidential candidate, Van Buren's biography was both like, and quite unlike, that of his two rivals. He had never been a soldier as had Taylor and Cass, although party advocates argued that as a state legislator he had played an important role in building up New York's military capability during the War of 1812. His principal vocation was, like Lewis Cass's, to maintain and exploit the kind of partisan politics many Free Soilers rejected as irrelevant and destructive of the republic. But, the party leaders insisted, what he once had advocated and had been were no longer important in 1848. "The past is laid aside," they said in relation to Van Buren's candidacy, and the crucial thing was for all those who opposed slavery's extension to unite behind him in this "desperate struggle for freedom."[56]

Still, party campaigners had relatively little to say about Van Buren, certainly much less than the other parties offered about their candidates. In his present incarnation he did not have the draw of Taylor and Cass. In the places where the Free Soilers were appealing for the votes of antislavery Whigs, the former Democratic president's name remained anathema to many of the longtime adversaries of all that he had been in his political career. As one Whig leader remarked, "The nomination of any other man than Van Buren would have made a large hole in our ranks, but I think with work we will bring in nearly all the Whigs." And the Whig leaders whipped up that long-standing hostility as much as they could in order to undercut the Free Soilers. As for the Cass Democrats, they were hopeless when it came to Van Buren and what he now stood for because they were, as the charge went, "so openly and recklessly committed to the slave power." There was no hope of ever persuading them of Van Buren's virtues given his present affiliation.[57]

Nevertheless, when the Free Soilers did openly discuss their candidate, they argued that Van Buren had qualities that significantly benefited the movement against slavery's further extension. They believed his long experience in politics and government and the talents that he had displayed there were useful now in advancing a good cause and seeing it through to triumph—leading the country into redefining itself in a particular, better way. Whatever everyone's memories of him may have been, those who supported the cause he had now joined—the reformist, antislavery vanguard—should acknowledge him as he was in 1848. He was "the man for these circumstances and this battle."[58]

As did their opponents, the Free Soilers found their campaign voice in emphasizing the common denominator among the party's different factions that had led them to Buffalo in August. Given their political heterogeneity, their task of forging unity was, of course, harder for them than for the Whigs and Democrats, whatever the latter's current divisions. But, despite the Free Soilers' different backgrounds, their common resistance to antisouthern aggression and their commitment to the containment of slavery kept them united as they argued together relentlessly on behalf of that key issue.

To be sure, their case was about more than their own unity. Like all party campaigns their argument reflected a strong (and, they hoped, compelling) perspective on the state of the nation and what actions should be taken in the face of its current difficulties. As experienced and prudent political activists as well as challengers and reformers, they did not push this campaign into issue areas in which some of their supporters wanted to confront the status quo, such as calling for the abolition of slavery where it already existed or promoting racial and gender equality throughout the nation. Free Soil leaders did not think that any large part of the electorate was ready to support such views. However, their platform could and would, they believed, attract the kind of support that would make a significant statement about where the electorate now stood on that critical issue, and thus lead further along the path they were breaking.[59]

So far as the two major parties were concerned, putting together arguments to arouse the voters and cause them to give their support to one or the other candidate was an important exercise calling for tactical ingenuity and knowledge of the past as well as of the playing field in the current election. But the stories the parties told—their usually harsh, always aggressive, and certainly mostly prosecutorial assault on their opponents as well as the celebration of their own candidate and party—also involved their notions of what was true and desired, their existing commitments, and their attitudes. The old parties argued throughout the campaign largely in the same manner, and with the same rhetorical weapons, as they had in previous races, whatever new factors had been added. They did not offer a random hodgepodge of ideas and hope that some would be electorally effective and stick. Each had several strings to their bow and played them with different emphases as needed. But they did not often stray from the core beliefs that defined them as parties or cross partisan lines into the others' territory when they offered their arguments. The Whigs may not have talked about their favored legislative agenda all of the time, certainly not to the satisfaction of their opponents, but they had not discarded any of the items that comprised it and had no intention of doing so.

Party leaders did not directly deceive the public about what they stood for or shift their commitments so much as when necessary in a specific situation choose to emphasize those aspects of what they believed that would best serve their electoral purposes. They drew campaign resources from their beliefs, traditions, and outlook, particularly those they believed increased their chances of victory. They distinguished themselves from one another on the issues of the day, denounced the other side, and exalted their own candidates and principles. And, over the course of the campaign, they shifted emphases to meet new conditions and changed perceptions of what should be said, but within the boundaries of their belief system.

Sectional combat was, of course, an addition to the normal agenda of Whig and Democratic warfare, and heightened difficulties for the major parties throughout. Both tried to control its impact on their parties, maximize its negative impact on the other side, and crush, if they could, the Free Soil attempt to make the slavery extension issue trump all else and be the centerpiece of the campaign. The third party also began with strong, distinct commitments as the foundation of all that its members argued. Whatever the unfinished business of the past, other issues and previous loyalties had to be put aside in this new era with new forces now in play. In short, they sought to change the subject and thereby crack the fortress of partisan power. In doing so, they were as harsh and prosecutorial as their opponents, an approach dictated by their experience in previous political campaigns under other banners.

Many factors had come into play during the campaign. The center of gravity of this complex of arguments was persistent interweaving of the many matters of concern to somebody somewhere who could vote. The sectional roars were certainly loud enough throughout, and the reality of the tensions manifested by them was palpable. As noted, party leaders had to take them into account whether they wanted to or not. But running through the rhetorical combat of this election was also the continuing relevance of long-held party outlooks, traditional issue commitments, and issues raised by attention focused on the candidates by the Whigs and Democrats—both positive and negative.

By early November all that party leaders could say had been said. Many arguments had been put forward; many had heard them. The word had gone out; the voters had been primed. By now, party organizers and workers were exhausted and each organization's hoarse-voiced speakers were ready to end their efforts, although they did not do so quickly. The antagonists kept up their advocacy, assaults, and celebrations right up to the last moment. But it had now become the voters' moment, not theirs. They had been convinced, party leaders hoped, as had been said earlier more than once, that "there never was an election for a chief magistrate of the United States of greater importance to the interests of the whole country." Beyond that, everyone's calculations, hopes, and arguments would be tested at the polls. Some party leaders retained their optimism. Others were aware that the other side had made hits on them during the campaign. "Like skillful military engineers," their enemies (of whichever party) "have been searching out the vulnerable points in our ramparts, and directing all the energies of their missiles to those points."[60] What would be the result of the efforts made by all sides? Everyone was about to find out. The campaign was over. Election day had arrived. The polls were, at last, about to open.

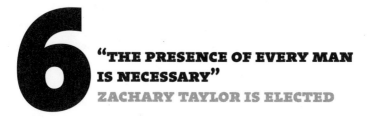

6

"THE PRESENCE OF EVERY MAN IS NECESSARY"

ZACHARY TAYLOR IS ELECTED

On Tuesday, November 7, 1848, the polls opened early throughout the United States. Local officials appointed by the relevant government authority of an area, for example, a village or town clerk, a constable, or a sheriff's deputy, oversaw the proceedings and prepared for the arrival of the voters. Others joined them, some acting as clerks to receive the votes, a number serving as election judges who would decide on any challenges, usually against someone claiming to be eligible to vote who allegedly was not, and also deal with other problems as they arose. Political agents from each of the parties were on hand as well, energized for this one final, decisive moment of their long struggle. Election day was another critical working opportunity for them. They came out holding the lists they had compiled containing the names of party supporters in their locality to make sure that all of their known supporters turned up, checking off each. They watched carefully that everything went off without too many problems or any misdeeds from the other side—the parties were always alert for evidence of fraud, intimidation, or corruption by their opponents.[1]

The activists were not the only ones out and about on election day. The parties had exhorted their loyal supporters to come early to the polling venues, obviously first and foremost to vote but also to stay around and help observe the proceedings, keep an eye out for the tricks their opponents would surely try and, always, encourage others to vote their way. "Shut up your shops and stores of every description, Whigs! And go to the polls," one of the latter's newspapers pleaded. "The presence of every man is necessary." Democrats agreed. Under the heading "STAY ALL DAY AT THE POLLS," the editor of the *Albany Atlas* reminded his readers; "it encourages our friends, it animates their exertions, it sustain[s] the week [*sic*] and encourages the hesitating." Although election day was not an official holiday, many campaigners appealed to their employers to treat it as one and followed through as they were asked by their parties. Clearly the partisan armies were geared up from top to bottom and ready for the payoff of their intense exertions over the previous months.[2]

The polling sites varied in different localities. In county seats they were often in the courthouse or another official building; in urban wards, smaller towns, and rural areas, they were in a local building, a saloon perhaps, or a general store, occasionally someone's home, or even set up outside depending on the weather. The actual place for casting ballots, such as a table, counter in a store, window of a building, or some similar accessible surface, was roped off or otherwise separated from the crowds. The voters came forward, identified themselves to the designated clerk, and handed over their ballot to him. The clerk then entered the voter's name in a poll book and deposited the paper in the official ballot box.[3]

Under the U.S. Constitution the question of who was eligible to vote was left to the individual states. The specific requirements varied throughout the Union, but in general in 1848, voters had to be white adult males, residents of the state, county, town, or school district for some period (usually six months or one year for the first two; thirty days or less for the smallest entity), and not be a convicted felon. Previous requirements that a voter had to be a property owner to be eligible had all but disappeared by 1848. The few states that held out soon gave way. Nor in many places did the voter have to prove that he was literate, and being a U.S. citizen was not universally required. In some states simply declaring an intention to become one was accepted in permitting a resident noncitizen to vote. African American men could vote in a few, but only a few, northern states, mostly in New England, under the same terms as their white counterparts. In New York State they could cast ballots as well but had to meet a property requirement that was not imposed on anyone else in the state.[4]

Whatever the legal requirements were, they were not always rigorously enforced. Many of the voters were known to the election officials and that was enough. If they were challenged—and some always were— for not being a resident long enough or for not yet being an adult— the voter could swear that he met the requirement and election judges decided the issue, usually on the spot. Not many challenges were accepted. When there were claims of fraudulent voters, there were often partisan reasons to ignore or override complaints as well as some sense that the right to vote should be allowed for those who fell within the main categories of eligibility without too much fuss—unless, of course, a party's control in some area was threatened by too many allegedly questionable voters showing up.

As voters approached the place where their ballots were to be received, moving through the assembled crowd of noisy spectators, the latter made their partisan feeling well known. (Whatever their enhanced role during the campaign may have been, women were discouraged from being near the polls on election day itself because of the raucousness of the crowd's behavior and the vulgarity of the verbal exchanges near the polling site.) Some of those about to cast ballots had come a short distance; others had traveled relatively far as individuals or with their families or as part of a group transported by the party organizations.

After marking and handing to the clerk the ballots they had brought with them or picked up from a party agent, many of the voters did stay around, as suggested, to join the ongoing verbal exchanges and wait to hear the election results. Because the ballots were supplied by the parties, they contained only the names of a party's candidates: either a single one for the presidency or a list of those running for the various lesser offices. A voter could scratch out the names listed and replace them by writing in others if he wished to. Throughout the day, the party agents constantly exhorted everyone to vote a straight party ticket. Most complied; some did not.

The whole process from start to finish was remarkably open as was commonly accepted as appropriate. Often the ballots were differently colored according to party and easily seen by those present. Even if they were not, the party managers present knew who their supporters (and opponents) were and watched them as they marked their ballots and handed them over to the clerk. In a number of places *viva voce* voting was still the rule although much less common than in its heyday. When a voter's name was called, he announced his choice aloud to the clerk within the hearing of those assembled.

Liquor was plentiful near the polls and well disposed of during the day. Some participants brought food with them, and party agents made some available as well. A reasonable level of order was usually maintained, although fights—even riots—broke out in particularly tense moments, especially when allegedly ineligible aliens appeared in urban areas and sought to vote or tempers became too hot for the faithful to control as the excitement grew. A U.S. election day in the late 1840s was recognized as a civic event as well as a social occasion to be enjoyed by everyone but it was rarely as peaceful as it might have been given the contentious atmosphere of the campaign and the stakes of its final day.[5]

Still, the main business of the moment was accomplished. By the time the balloting was over, everyone on hand had worked a long day. The polls were open from dawn to dusk in many places or for some similarly extensive period, and they were often kept open after the official closing time to allow those still in line to cast their votes. The whole process, for all the partisan tumult, alleged trickery attempted by the other side, shoving, and other threatening actions, was about serious matters. The campaign had aroused the electorate and, party leaders hoped, intensified their determination to vote and their commitment to follow through and do the right thing at the polls. As the crowds came out, ballots in hand, the strenuous efforts by party activists over the previous few months seemed about to be rewarded. The presence of the large number of enthusiastic partisans and the mass of voters who came forward to advance their particular cause indicated that the parties had done their work effectively. Given all of that effort, their leaders hoped or believed their side would now prevail.

THE CONSENT OF THE GOVERNED

At the end of the day, the officials declared the polls closed, gathered and opened the ballot boxes, and commenced the count, always under the watchful eyes of the party workers on the scene. By then, almost 2.9 million people had voted for president across the United States on that November day compared to the 2.7 million who had gone to the polls in 1844. Of course, these were not the first votes cast in 1848. There was a great deal of election activity throughout the nation in addition to the race for president. Earlier, state and congressional elections had been held on different dates in many places, with anxious observers looking to them for clues as to the electorate's mood. But the results had been ambiguous. The Whigs, behind their popular veteran leader John Crittenden, won Kentucky's governorship in August as expected. But they barely won the same office in North Carolina, a state considered strongly leaning to the Whigs that year—the closeness of the vote was not a good omen for them. They narrowly won usually Democratic Pennsylvania in October, a better sign for the party. But the congressional and legislative races in Illinois and Indiana had not turned out well for the Whigs, whatever their perhaps inflated hopes had been before the polls opened.[6]

The Democrats, in contrast, won more than expected of the state races in Ohio. In another surprise, in the only state where the electors were still chosen by that institution rather than by popular vote, the South Carolina legislature seemed likely, according to the state's main newspaper, to pick Lewis Cass for president by a large majority over the southerner Taylor. No one could be sure how all of this pre-November evidence added up so far as the final outcome was concerned as November 7 dawned—although there were plenty of optimistic statements from the party camps despite their uncertainty.[7]

There was little ambiguity about the November returns for president. Both of the main parties received substantial support from the voters. But when the returns had been counted, first at the local level and then officially tallied in state capitals, a process that took some days, Zachary Taylor won the battle for a majority of the 290 electoral votes in play. He won 163 from 15 states to Cass's 127, also from 15 states. Taylor received just more than 1,360,000 popular votes, 47.4 percent of the national total, to Cass's 1,220,000-plus and 42.7 percent of the whole number cast (see Table 6.1). Martin Van Buren received just more than 290,000 votes, 10.1 percent of the national tally (and 14.2 percent when only returns from the northern states were computed). The Free Soil candidate received votes in 17 states including the border slave states of Maryland and Delaware. He came in second in several, including New York, Vermont, and Massachusetts, where in each he pushed Cass into third place. Although he received votes throughout the North, in many places they totaled only a very few. Finally, there was a scattering of ballots in different areas for other candidates, including Gerrit Smith and the Liberty League, who won just more than 2,500 votes in the North, many of them in New York State, with several hundred other votes cast for other names, a few of them familiar but many not.[8]

The electoral map in general was similar to the one for the contest four years before. By 1848, four new states had entered the Union since Polk's victory: Iowa, Wisconsin, and Texas, all of which went to Cass, and Florida, which was won by Taylor. For the rest, Whig states largely remained Whig and most Democratic states were loyal to their partisan heritage as well. (There was a substantial +.90 statistical correlation

Table 6.1. Popular and Electoral Votes (Entire Nation)

Candidate	Popular Vote	Percentage	Electoral Vote
Taylor	1,361,393	47.3	163
Cass	1,223,460	42.5	127
Van Buren	291,501	10.1	0

Source: *Congressional Quarterly's Guide to U.S. Elections* (Washington, D.C.: Congressional Quarterly, Inc., 1975).

between the popular vote in 1844 and that in 1848.) The big difference between the two contests was the switch of five of the twenty-six states that had cast votes in 1844 from one party to the other. Unlike four years before, this time the Whigs won New York, Pennsylvania, Georgia, and Taylor's home state of Louisiana, and the Democrats took Ohio.[9]

A number of states overwhelmingly favored one or the other candidate. Taylor's largest margins were in Rhode Island, Kentucky, and North Carolina, traditional Whig strongholds. Cass's biggest leads were in Texas and usually Democratic New Hampshire, Arkansas, and Missouri. In addition, each of the major candidates benefited—or did not—from a number of almost-but-not-quite results in which the popular vote margins between the two parties were close. In Georgia, for example, with its 10 electoral votes, Taylor won by fewer than 3,000 popular votes of the 90,000 cast. He took Connecticut, with its 6 electoral votes, by just more than 3,000 popular votes of the 62,000 counted. On the other side, there was his close-run defeat in Virginia: Cass took its 16 electors by fewer than 1,500 votes of the 90,000-plus cast. Also in Mississippi, the Democratic candidate held on to win its 6 electors by fewer than 600 votes of the more than 52,000 recorded. The combination of traditional supporters for each party, defections from one to another, and failure to turn out combined in each of these states to produce the close calls (see Table 6.2).

But these narrow outcomes meant little in the final reckoning of the election—such small-margin opportunities existed in every presidential contest, depending often on unpredictable events, but they could not be changed after the votes were in or affect anything—except, perhaps, causing frustrated party leaders to think to themselves, if only we had done more of this or tried that, the outcome could have been different, and, of course, their realization that different results were not far from being attainable the next time the parties faced each other.

Both the Whigs and Democrats drew significant support throughout the country. In sectional terms, Cass won his electors in seven of

Table 6.2. Popular Vote for President by State (Percentage of Votes in Parentheses)

State	Taylor (W)	Cass (D)	Van Buren (FS)
Alabama	30,482 (49.4)	31,173 (50.6)	
Arkansas	7,587 (44.9)	9,301 (55.1)	
Connecticut	30,318 (48.6)	27,051 (43.4)	5,005 (8.0)
Delaware	6,440 (51.6)	5,910 (47.5)	82 (0.7)
Florida	4,120 (57.2)	3,083 (42.8)	
Georgia	47,532 (51.5)	44,785 (48.5)	
Illinois	52,585 (42.4)	55,952 (44.9)	15,702 (12.6)
Indiana	69,668 (45.7)	74,695 (49.0)	8,031 (5.3)
Iowa	9,930 (44.6)	11,238 (50.5)	1,103 (5.0)
Kentucky	67,145 (57.5)	49,720 (42.5)	
Louisiana	18,487 (54.6)	15,379 (45.4)	
Maine	35,273 (40.3)	40,195 (45.9)	12,157 (13.9)
Maryland	37,702 (52.1)	34,528 (47.7)	129 (0.2)
Massachusetts	61,072 (45.3)	35,281 (26.2)	38,833 (28.5)
Michigan	23,947 (36.8)	30,742 (47.2)	10,393 (16.0)
Mississippi	25,911 (49.4)	26,545 (50.6)	
Missouri	32,671 (44.9)	40,077 (55.1)	
New Hampshire	14,781 (29.5)	27,763 (55.4)	7,560 (15.1)
New Jersey	40,015 (51.5)	36,901 (47.5)	829 (1.1)
New York	218,583 (47.9)	114,319 (25.1)	120,497 (26.4)
North Carolina	44,054 (55.2)	35,772 (44.8)	
Ohio	138,656 (42.2)	154,782 (47.1)	35,523 (10.8)
Pennsylvania	185,730 (50.3)	172,186 (46.7)	11,176 (3.0)
Rhode Island	6,705 (60.7)	3,613 (32.7)	726 (6.6)
Tennessee	64,321 (52.5)	58,142 (47.5)	
Texas	5,281 (31.1)	11,644 (68.5)	
Vermont	23,117 (48.3)	10,493 (22.9)	13,837 (28.9)
Virginia	45,265 (49.2)	46,739 (50.8)	
Wisconsin	13,747 (35.1)	15,001 (38.3)	10,418 (26.6)

Source: *Congressional Quarterly's Guide to U.S. Elections* (Washington, D.C.: Congressional Quarterly, Inc., 1975).

the fifteen slave states, Taylor in the other eight (see Table 6.3). In the North, the split was just the reverse, eight states went to Cass, and Taylor won seven—neither party had a slave- or non-slave-state advantage (see Map 6.1). The five top states in terms of percentage for Taylor included four from the South and one from the North. The five top states supporting Cass included four from the South and one from the North. The Democrats remained strong in the five states of the Old Northwest as expected as well as neighboring Iowa voting in its first presidential race. The Whigs took the three middle Atlantic states (two of them the

Table 6.3. State Electoral Vote Distribution by Number of Electors

Taylor	Electoral Votes	Cass	Electoral Votes
New York	33	Ohio	23
Pennsylvania	26	Virginia	17
Tennessee	13	Indiana	12
Kentucky	12	Alabama	9
Massachusetts	12	Illinois	9
North Carolina	11	Maine	9
Georgia	10	South Carolina	9
Maryland	8	Missouri	7
New Jersey	7	Mississippi	6
Connecticut	6	New Hampshire	6
Louisiana	6	Michigan	5
Vermont	6	Iowa	4
Rhode Island	4	Texas	4
Delaware	3	Wisconsin	4
Florida	3	Arkansas	3

Source: *Congressional Quarterly's Guide to U.S. Elections* (Washington, D.C.: Congressional Quarterly, Inc., 1975).

largest—and most important—in the Union in terms of their number of electoral votes), four of the five states in the border region, and four of the six New England states.

In contrast to his rivals, Van Buren won no states or any electoral votes. He received his largest bloc of support in New York State, winning 120,497 of his 291,501 national total there. In percentage of votes cast, his strongest state was tiny Vermont, where the Free Soil ticket won 38.9 percent, followed by the two large states of Massachusetts and New York, where he received 28.5 percent and 26.4 percent, respectively. In Ohio, where there had been much expression of Free Soil sentiment and much activity promoting that cause, he received about 11 percent of the state's vote, which placed Ohio ninth on the list of the seventeen states in which Van Buren gained any support. Free Soil did particularly poorly in New Jersey, receiving only 1.1 percent of the ballots cast there, and in Pennsylvania, where the Van Buren ticket picked up only 3.0 percent of the votes—most of it in the counties in David Wilmot's congressional district in the northern part of the state bordering New York.

The Whigs would control the presidency for the second time in the past three elections. Their jubilation was tempered, however, by the realization that the outcome was not a complete triumph for them. Most members of Congress who ran for reelection held on to their seats. But

Map 6.1. States Won by Each Candidate

there had been enough changes in the results that the Democrats would control not one but both houses of the new Congress. The outgoing House of Representatives was made up of 109 Democrats, 116 Whigs, and a few others listed as independents or Native American (the nativist Lewis Levin of Philadelphia). The Senate consisted of 36 Democrats and 21 Whigs. In the elections for the 31st Congress, just over than 140 House seats were contested in 1848 (most of the rest had been elected in 1847 before the organization of the Free Soil Party; some others would be chosen in 1849). When the results were all finally in from all of the contests, there would be 113 Democrats, 108 Whigs, one native American (Levin again), and 10 members who had been elected either as Free Soilers or as coalition candidates identifying themselves as Free Soil Whigs or Free Soil Democrats (the last including David Wilmot).[10]

The new Senate would remain in Democratic hands. It would be made up of thirty-three Democrats, twenty-five Whigs, and two Free Soilers (both of them former Democrats), Chase of Ohio and John P. Hale of New Hampshire, elected two years before by a free soil coalition that came together before there was a Free Soil Party. (The Free Soil bloc in the Ohio legislature joined with the Democrats there to form a majority sufficient to elect Chase.) The Democrats would add two more senators to their totals in this Congress with the admission of California in 1850.[11]

In sectional terms, sixteen of the Democrats elected in 1848 to the House of Representatives of the 31st Congress came from the slave states (including one from South Carolina who labeled himself a Taylor Democrat), and thirty-seven were from the North. For the Whigs, seven of those who won seats in the presidential election year came from the slaveholding South (one more than they had elected there two years earlier), and seventy-two were from the rest of the country. Although their percentage of the vote in these races picked up slightly over their 1846 totals, the Whigs' southern results were hardly impressive given the earlier hopes of many of their leaders that a southerner at the head of their ticket would strengthen them in other races in the section. As for the Free Soilers, Ohio voters elected three of the party's congressional hopefuls to the House. Massachusetts and Pennsylvania sent two each. New York chose one (the radical Barnburner Preston King), and the voters in the western states of Michigan and Wisconsin elected one each. (Later runoff elections for seats that had not been decided in the first round of balloting would add two more Free Soilers from Massachusetts, one from New Hampshire, and one from Indiana—the last the hardworking campaigner George Julian.)[12]

"THE FORCE OF OLD PARTY ORGANIZATIONS"

The Whigs had been successful at the presidential level behind their singular candidate. What produced Taylor's victory? Was it the appeal Whigs had made in their campaign to southerners that he was one of them and could be counted on to be sympathetic to their outlook and demands? Was it strong support for him by the members of the Whig Party because he was its nominee, and he would, therefore, be loyal to the party's traditional policies and do what they hoped with the federal government? Was it the attraction of his exalted military reputation for so many voters and the qualities of character and leadership he had displayed on the battlefields of Mexico? The parties had organized and run the campaigns, as was their responsibility, with these possibilities in mind. First, the outcome reflected the reality that since their inception, they had presented contrasting programs, emphasized different issues, and traditionally attracted distinct voter blocs, each party's particular attraction based on diverse economic interests, cultural values, regional origins, members' attitudes toward government power, or some combination of all or some of them—matters that had developed during the political battles of the Jacksonian years over the national bank, tariff policy, and the social and economic direction of the nation.[13]

Second, party strategists never forgot that these different blocs had been remarkably steadfast in their voting behavior. Their partisan constancy in successive elections, federal and state, was a hallmark of U.S. politics in this era and could be expected to repeat history, with each party receiving the repeated support of a substantial number of people when they came to the polls because they voted in a predictable way in election after election. The bulk of voters rarely, if ever, did not do their duty to the party of Andrew Jackson and his successors, or to the Whigs of Henry Clay, Daniel Webster, and the rest who had followed in the footsteps of the party founders.[14]

Strategists also knew, however, that an individual voter's commitment to his party had never been total. At every election, there had been some window of opportunity provided by defectors from both the Whigs and Democrats to the other side as well as by the failure of others to show up at the polls at all despite their previous loyalty and participation. Now, obviously, the Free Soil intervention in the election added to that threat to the normal pattern of partisan divisions because of the intense commitment and energy of the numbers of activists involved in the antislavery extension movement along with its leaders' determination to draw major party members to vote for Van Buren. These potential variations and shifts again raised the central question: What determined how people voted in 1848? What was the relative importance of traditional loyalties and issues as against new and different concerns or the kind of campaign strategies implemented in shaping the final outcome?

The key to answering these questions, of course, starts with the consideration as to whether, as some observers suggested at the time and others have echoed since, political matters in the United States were indeed different in 1848 from previous presidential elections. It was a new political day—a moment when, as one pamphlet writer declared, "the ordinary themes of the tariff, Finance, Commerce, etc. that have usually been the rallying cries of party warfare are not heard at this time. Minor topics like these have sunk out of sight," so that, he concluded, "for both northern and southern voters the only issue of major significance was that of slavery in the territories."[15]

That challenging assertion, the centerpiece of Free Soil rhetoric, proved not to be the case. Despite much political instability throughout the year and the reality of partisan fragmentation as well as the new issue in the election, the most compelling aspect of the voting returns in 1848 was familiar and not surprising, the persistence of traditional party loyalties among most of the electorate, "the force of old party organizations," in David Wilmot's words. The Free Soilers did draw much of their support from voters usually committed to one or the other of the major parties. But overall, partisan commitment, not defection, remained a powerful influence on November 7 and was central to the outcome. And that was quickly recognized: "The great body of the democracy could not be seduced from their [*sic*] party attachments," the editor of the Albany *Argus* wrote some weeks after the votes had been counted.[16]

The same was true of the Whigs. They, too, stayed loyal to their political home. The fact that so many of their leaders, men such as the veteran William Seward and the newcomer Abraham Lincoln, both of whom (among many others) opposed the further extension of slavery, refused to join the Free Soil bandwagon and remained loyal instead to their traditional commitments, undercut the arguments the Free Soilers directed toward northern antislavery Whigs. It was a telling indicator of the mood that year. The basic rock on which both major parties rested in 1848 was, as before, this all but automatic support they received from most members of their normal constituencies. As before, Democrats continued to vote Democratic and Whigs continued their Whiggery. Only a relatively few party members crossed over to the other side or chose to join the new antislavery coalition. Although there were, as always, interesting deviations from the norm, as one historian has recently summed up, "party identities born of the political clashes of the 1830s remained stubborn, as did fears of letting the other side prevail."[17]

Van Buren had many sympathizers among his former Democratic associates throughout the northern states. But outside of New York, not many of his erstwhile party colleagues were willing to break ranks and vote for him as the Free Soil candidate. It has been estimated that the Democrats retained roughly 89 percent of their 1844 vote in the North and 91 percent in the South; the Whigs held 97 percent of their 1844 vote generally. Little had changed among voters in elections since 1844 either. The constancy figures are as impressive when 1848 is compared with the most recent state elections in 1846 and 1847. Such behavioral persistence continued to give each party a firm basis on which to build its support on behalf of hoped-for victory.[18]

But there were cracks in the partisan structure. In the South, despite holding on to so much support there overall, the Democrats lost ground in the region. Cass was not as popular among his party colleagues south of the Mason-Dixon Line as Polk had been four years before. Cass received 17,000 fewer votes in the slave states than his Democratic predecessor, and Taylor gained 39,000 more votes in the region than Clay's 1844 total. Taylor drew defecting Democrats throughout the slave states and held most of the Whigs there who came to the polls. An estimate of the results in three of the deep South states concludes that about 10 percent of Polk voters in 1844 supported Taylor four years later. Stung Democratic leaders were nonplussed by what happened. "Hundreds of Democrats have come to the polls," one Georgia politician wrote to U.S. Representative Howell Cobb, "only to vote against us. . . . This wholesale defection is entirely unexpected and inexplicable."[19]

But there was another matter to consider: not voter defections but abstentions. "A full vote is a Democratic vote," one southern party editor argued before the election. But Cass and his party had not received a full vote in the slaveholding states or anywhere else in the country. A most compelling aspect of the election of 1848 in the South and elsewhere was that national voter turnout was the lowest it had been since 1836, that is, before the two parties had fully matured their messages and developed their organizations. The 80.2 percent of those eligible who had come to the polls in 1840 and the 78.9 percent that did so in 1844 had established new participation records for national elections. In 1848, there was a startling drop of 7.2 percent from the previous contest as total turnout fell to 72.7 percent of those eligible. Something had clearly happened within the electorate to cause turnout to be depressed to this degree.[20]

Although some southern Democrats defected to Taylor because of the slavery issue, others who refused to vote for Cass did not. They stayed home on election day instead. (One estimate suggests, for example, that 25 percent of 1844 Polk voters in Alabama, Mississippi, and Louisiana abstained in 1848.)[21] Some were undoubtedly repelled by the harshness of the political din during the campaign or the candidate choices offered. But many of them probably chose not to vote because they were cross-pressured between party loyalty and the sectional push under way in the South because of the alleged dangers it faced. They would not vote for Taylor. He may have been a southerner but he was also the candidate of the Whig Party with all that meant to them in negative terms.

In the North, there was a similar pattern of sagging turnout because of significant abstention as well as defection among the antislavery Whigs and among many Democrats in general. In New York State, for example, the turnout of 80 percent in the presidential race fell below what it had been in the previous two contests and would prove the lowest in any presidential election in that state in the half century after 1840 except for 1872. Equally important, there was not an even degree of abstention between members of the two parties, that is, one that affected both about the same. One-fifth of those who had voted for Polk four years before failed to vote at all in 1848, but 90 percent of Clay's supporters came out in support of Zachary Taylor despite the resistance to the Whig candidate expressed by many party activists in the state—clearly a difference in behavior that was a serious blow to the divided Democrats. Elsewhere the results were similar. As one historian has suggested as one example that had widespread resonance elsewhere, some major party loyalties weakened in New Hampshire in 1848, "but the result was abstention, not desertion to the Free Soil Party."[22]

FREE SOIL

Finally, of course, the Free Soilers made some inroads into the major parties' dominant position, if not as much as the leaders of the movement had hoped. Their 290,000 votes came from both the Democrats and the Whigs as well as from Liberty Party voters who had supported James Birney in 1844 and from others who had not come to the polls four years before. The sources of the defections to Van Buren from the major parties varied significantly across the political spectrum. Although both Whigs and Democrats were part of the Free Soil totals, they were so in different proportions in different states—the Free Soil support from them depended on what was happening in the diverse polling places. In contrast, Liberty supporters did not split their votes; they, unsurprisingly, went overwhelmingly for Van Buren.[23]

In New York, their banner popular vote state, Free Soil support came largely from Democratic ranks with fewer Whigs crossing party lines to vote for Van Buren. The former president also received most of the state's Liberty Party vote of 1844 and strong support in areas where there was substantial land reform sentiment. Beyond the presidency, the Free Soilers also helped wreck the Democrats' congressional vote in the state. The Whigs won thirty-one of thirty-four House seats there compared to only twenty-three two years before. They also swept New York's legislative seats up for election that autumn and won the governorship. The Free Soil gubernatorial candidate, John A. Dix, finished second.[24]

The same Democratic bias as in New York was true of the small number of Van Buren votes in Pennsylvania. But these two states were not predictive models of the source of Free Soil support elsewhere. In Indiana and Ohio, the portion of the Van Buren vote that came from defectors largely consisted of former Whig voters. In some other states in the region there was, in contrast, marked defection from both parties. Throughout the Old Northwest, many who had not voted at all in 1844 now came out and marked their ballots for Free Soil. In some New England states as well, the Free Soilers drew support from the Democrats, but in others their support came predominantly from Whigs. In the largest New England commonwealth, Massachusetts, almost half of the Free Soil voters had voted Whig four years before, about 30 percent had supported Polk, and the rest came from the Liberty Party. The variation from state to state in Free Soil voters' previous behavior at the polls was a notable aspect of an election characterized by new pressures and different notions than in previous contests.[25]

Not everyone who supported the Free Soil ticket did so because of the party's anti–slavery extension commitment. Whatever its clear aura of hostility to the South's peculiar institution, the coalition drew support for several reasons in 1848. The first of these was, to be sure, the strong antislavery attitudes among Liberty supporters and in important blocs in both of the major parties who were willing to abandon their usual electoral moorings. At the same time, other Free Soil supporters came over to Van Buren for more parochial reasons. Many of his most devoted allies in the Free Soil camp, whatever their views about slavery, were seeking to regain their place in the Democratic Party through applying electoral force against their old party and its leaders to punish them for their treatment of the ex-president and his colleagues.[26]

Finally, as historian Thomas Alexander suggests, some Free Soil voters were less than independent when they made their decision, apparently following the opinion of a local or state leader when they went to the polls. The latter had, according to Alexander, "a profound effect" on the decisions some people made when they voted. This was not surprising. Political leaders had often set the tone for the rank and file in election season, recognized as the font of party ideology and appeal they were—and apparently did so among many voters in the 1848 election.[27]

Still, whatever the Free Soil voters' reasons for their choice—antislavery commitment, hostility to the old parties and their ways, or subservience to those seen as their leaders—the final results were clear. When they came out to vote they added strength to a party whose anti–slavery extension perspective defined it and gave it public meaning against a different political framework.

All of this analysis leads to another critical question. How much did the Free Soil vote influence the outcome of the presidential election? The mixture of defection and abstention affected both parties and caused each of them problems at least to some degree. But in separate analyses, two historians who have made close studies of state-by-state voting patterns in 1848 suggest that, as Michael Holt sums up, the Free Soil vote "had only minimum impact on the outcome." Thomas P. Alexander agrees. The argument that Van Buren's vote determined the winner in 1848, he suggests, "cannot bear close scrutiny." Although the Free Soil vote reduced the major party totals and their margins in several states, they point out, the evidence is not conclusive that it determined the overall outcome of the national balloting.[28]

Nor was the election determined by the voter abstentions that were such a feature of the contest. Although often dramatically reducing a party's vote totals in places, such noninvolvement did not necessarily change the outcome in a particular state. It was not large enough to do so. In Alabama, for example, the Democrats' total fell from 37,401 votes for president in 1844 to 31,173 four years later, much of that because of abstentions by previous supporters. But they still won the state, even though the Whigs increased their vote there between the two presidential contests. Other states in other parts of the country where Free Soil was on the ballot, such as Maine and Illinois, demonstrated a similar pattern.[29]

However, in New York, Ohio, and Indiana, the significant disruption of the Free Soil presence apparently did affect the final outcome. At first glance, Taylor's victory in the nation's largest state with its thirty-six electoral votes seems the key to his victory. New York went narrowly for Polk in 1844, but in 1848 its people voted for Taylor and put him over the top in the Electoral College. His victory in the Empire State was because of the extraordinary fragmenting of the Democrats, the heavy defections from them to Van Buren and the Free Soilers, and the abstention from voting of others. Nevertheless, this is not the complete story. At the same time, both Ohio and Indiana, with almost as many electoral votes as New York, a total of thirty-five between them, went to Cass largely because of Whig, not Democratic, defections to Free Soil as well as the abstentions of other unhappy potential voters. If these three are considered together as the critical states, they successfully cancelled out each other's determinative influence in the final results.[30]

"THE BONE AND SINEW IN PENNSYLVANIA"

In summary, Americans made their choices at the polls in 1848 for many reasons. Their decisions on election day were evidence of the different elements in the campaign that year: traditional partisan behavior, sectional reactions to events, the embracing and rejecting of candidates, and the occasional other issue specific to a particular group in a particular place. All played a role in the contest. But what put Taylor over the top in the Electoral College? Given the way various states acted, the result of the contest hinged, finally, on Pennsylvania. There, with its twenty-six electoral votes, lay the key to Taylor's victory. It was normally a Democratic state. Polk had won it in 1844 with 167,535 votes to Clay's 161,203. In 1848 that changed: the Whigs won with more than 185,000 votes to Lewis Cass's just over 171,000. But the Free Soil tumult had not roiled the political waters deeply there. The party's vote was small in the state— Van Buren received just under 11,200 of its votes. There was nativist support for Taylor in the Philadelphia area that helped his candidacy, but the key to what happened, a number of observers suggested at the time, and historians have agreed, were the hard economic times in parts of a state that usually went Democratic and the blame its voters placed for their distressed conditions on the Polk administration's economic and financial program, particularly its low-tariff policy.[31]

Democrats in the state's coal-producing region refused to support the party with their usual dedication. They deserted the Cass-Butler ticket in droves in reaction against the traditional Democratic policy initiatives most party members elsewhere had celebrated when they were originally proposed, and then enacted, by the Polk administration. Now, however, the Democrats in the coal and iron region "could not be controlled," a state party leader wrote to James Buchanan. "They said it was bread and they would not stand to principle," that is, their usual party commitment. If they had behaved in their normal loyal ways toward the party of Andrew Jackson, would the result have been different? Probably. But no one can be certain of that, given Pennsylvania's often close-run results in previous elections. As Zachary Taylor accurately put it, "I have no doubt that many democrats, particularly the bone and sinew in Pennsylvania, voted for me. Otherwise I could not have been elected."[32]

The way people voted in 1848 had many familiar and some distinctive qualities, the latter stemming from the amount of excitement engendered by activists of different persuasions over the slavery issue and the appearance of the Free Soilers. The argument that makes the Free Soilers the centerpiece of the 1848 election, that it had the force to trump everything else in play along with what their presence and strength forecast about the future, has obviously caught the attention of historians and affected the way they perceive that election.[33]

The Free Soilers made inroads and their efforts frightened the other parties' leaders throughout the contest. But the issue pushed so hard by the Van Buren coalition did not dominate the scene when the voters cast their ballots. It did contribute to defections and abstentions. So did other matters. Voters had much else on their minds—the presidential campaign had been about many issues. When it came down to the reactions of the voters and their final decisions made at their polling places, despite some crumbling in the two major parties' usual support, the dominant perspective was partisan even amid the real upsurge of sectional feeling.

To be sure, partisans integrated sectional matters into their appeals in some instances if they felt it necessary to do so. But all of the sectional excitement was not strong enough at this stage to alter matters to any significant degree, whatever the fears of some party leaders and the omens others perceived in the situation. Coming back to the original point, "the force of a seemingly regular nomination" outshone all other considerations in the contest between Cass and Taylor.[34] As the latter prepared to enter the White House, he did so at the head of a victorious coalition that had apparently overcome internal turmoil to take advantage of its opponents' major difficulties. The issue now was what would follow. Would the partisan emphasis be sustained or would the sectional upsurge not only remain but be able to grow beyond its dimensions in 1848?

7

"A CONSPICUOUS MILESTONE IN THE ANTISLAVERY JOURNEY"—OR NOT

In the aftermath of the results on November 7, 1848, party leaders were quick to take stock of how the experience had affected the nation's political landscape and what Taylor's victory portended for the future. Whigs basked in their success even as some of the antislavery advocates among their members remained in the schismatic stance they had adopted during the election. Most members of the party leadership saw their defeat of Cass as a great moment in Whig history both for the achievement of their policy agenda and for its meaning for the Union. First, the electorate had rejected "the whole odious catalogue of errors, blunders, lies, and meddlesome experiments" of the Polk administration. Second, the Whig's triumph, as Millard Fillmore wrote, "raises up a national party, occupying a middle ground, and leaves the fanatics and disunionists, North and South, without the hope of destroying the fair fabric of our Constitution." Further, under President Taylor, "the will of the people, as expressed through their representatives in Congress, is to control" and will not "be defeated by the arbitrary imposition of the veto power." With Whiggery now in command all would be well for the United States and undoubtedly become even better as time passed.[1]

Democrats were obviously less enthralled by the outcome. Taylor's triumph, as Martin Van Buren later wrote in his study of the origin and history of the nation's political parties, resulted in "the elevation of an old-school Federalist to the Presidency, and an administration of the Federal Government upon the long-exploded principles of Federalism." Party leaders looked inward at what had happened to them and reached the obvious conclusion that all of the warring groups would "have to come together" to be successful. There was no hope for victory "when we are divided." How this was to happen, given all that had occurred and the still evident deep antipathies among them, was less clear as the year ended.[2]

Leaders of the Free Soilers wanted to believe that it was too late for the old parties to have such optimistic hopes despite the Whig triumph and the expected push for Democratic reunion. They had argued as the contest began that "the bulwarks of the old parties [were] crumbling beneath the weight and force of the deluge" of anti–slavery extension sentiment. Whatever their popular vote totals in the contest, they continued to say (not only in public) after the election that they had begun to force a sea change in the shape and substance of U.S. politics. Because of their efforts "the public mind has been stirred on the subject of slavery to depths never before reached," Charles Sumner wrote to Salmon P. Chase a few days after Taylor's triumph. "Much information in regard to the Slave Power has been diffused in quarters heretofore ignorant of this enormous tyranny."[3]

It is easy to understand the importance many of the participants placed on this moment in history as well as the uncertainty some felt. Although the old parties had managed to maintain their position despite the tumult and drama of the rise of the Free Soil Party, the latter certainly caused a political stir in 1848 and put extra strains on traditional political leaders as they scrambled to keep their ranks intact against the antislavery threat. Although both Democrats and Whigs hoped the disarray had now ended and they could return to their normal concerns, contrary to their hopes, the disruption continued for a time.

All began well enough. The president-elect arrived in Washington from Louisiana in late February. He met briefly with the outgoing president at the White House and conferred with Whig congressional leaders, finding time to also meet Lewis Cass. He spent much of each day putting the final touches on his cabinet and preparing for his inauguration, which would take place on March 5 because the normal date, March 4, fell on a Sunday in 1849. On the designated day he was driven from his hotel to the Capitol, accompanied by Vice President Fillmore and the departing President Polk. After a brief welcome inside, Taylor moved out onto the eastern portico of the building to present his inaugural address.[4]

In his speech Taylor promised to govern constitutionally alongside the coordinate branches of the federal government. As president he would recommend to Congress "such constitutional measures . . . as may be necessary and proper." These would include measures to protect U.S. agriculture and manufacturing and to improve the nation's rivers and harbors. But it was up to Congress, "in which all legislative powers are vested . . . to regulate these and other matters"—to move forward on his suggestions (or not as that body determined). He looked forward to its action. He made a few other brief remarks including his hope "to assuage the bitterness which too often marks unavoidable differences of opinion."[5]

One of Taylor's biographers has remarked that his address was one of the shortest in history and "cannot be ranked among the most eloquent presidential papers." And, he continued, it was quite vague about policies, although Taylor's conception of Whiggery certainly came through. Finally, the message contained no direct mention of recent controversies about slavery in the territories or references to any lingering difficulties from recent confrontations over the issue. (Congress, which had just adjourned, had between the November election and the inauguration continued to wrestle with issues of territorial organization and whether slavery would be allowed in them—so far unsuccessfully. What would follow remained unclear.)[6]

Zachary Taylor's presidency was brief. He died suddenly in July 1850 after just sixteen months in office. During his time as chief executive he had not turned out to be quite what many of his supporters hoped for or expected when they had voted for him or heard him speak on the steps of the Capitol on inauguration day. Like many newly installed presidents before him, in office he disappointed some of his early supporters— Abraham Lincoln among them. (That avid campaigner for Taylor was not offered the government position he desired: commissioner of the General Land Office. It went to another deserving Whig instead.) Other loyal Whigs who were also left off the new president's list of appointments complained as well. At the same time, there continued to be those, including the president, who wanted to broaden their coalition beyond the party's usual supporters and build a so-called Taylor republican coalition. But this was never a full-throttle initiative and did not advance very far. Taylor may not have been an "ultra" Whig, but his commitment to his particular notion of the Whig Party was evident whether he wanted to be nonpartisan or not. The members of his cabinet and those close to him on Capitol Hill were well-known Whigs as well. Taylor led a Whig administration, whatever some wanted to believe and others wanted to change.[7]

More critically, President Taylor proved a more determined, forceful leader than many of his supporters had foreseen, often independent in his behavior. He was willing to challenge the leaders of his own party, for instance, and—shades of Andrew Jackson—to confront Congress as well when he disagreed with the latter's initiatives on the territorial issue. Legislators had taken up the question of slavery in the new territories once more when the new Congress convened in late 1849 as angry sectional tensions continued to boil up on Capitol Hill with the Mexican cession still unorganized and the status of slavery there not yet determined. During the time Congress was away, however, Taylor had pursued his own initiative without waiting for Congress to act. The state of Texas was also fomenting trouble, claiming that its boundary extended into New Mexico. The California area was in turmoil because of the discovery of gold there and the resulting rush of people to the Sierra Nevada. The president sent a personal emissary to push the Californians into organizing a state government and petitioned Congress to admit it to the Union. He made it clear that he would resist the Texas territorial claims as well. There were many party members, however, with different ideas and demands, especially about the status of slavery. But Taylor insisted on the acceptance of his California statehood plan, resisting the compromise legislation fashioned by Henry Clay and Stephen A. Douglas working its difficult way through Congress.[8]

As a result of his intransigence and what they saw as actions that were prejudicial against them, Taylor proved no friend of their section in the eyes of many southerners, nor a protector of its rights. Some were convinced the southern-born president had come under the malignant influence of their bete noir, the antislavery Whig leader William H. Seward of New York. Throughout the debates in Congress things remained heated as southerners made their unhappiness known and antislavery northerners harshly responded. Despite their small numbers, the Free Soilers contributed to these legislative debates and occasionally with their votes helped shape some of the action in an all but evenly divided House of Representatives, to the annoyance of the members of the major parties.[9]

Sectional tensions also remained high among many people outside of Congress. Notions of the importance of North-South confrontation remained prominent as political activists, editors, and pamphleteers continued to whip them up as much as they could throughout what some labeled "the crisis of 1850." Ironically, it was only with Taylor's death and the ascension of Millard Fillmore to the presidency in his stead that Congress was at last able to shape a series of compromise bills on the territories. In large part they were based on popular sovereignty principles, but not the Wilmot Proviso, and included a number of related matters. The bills passed both houses and were signed by the new president, finally settling the terms of the Mexican cession.[10]

After Fillmore approved the legislation, the sectional uproar began to moderate both inside and outside Congress, although it never totally disappeared from public discourse. Many on both sides of the sectional divide remained angry; North-South hostility always simmered just below the surface and would break through several more times during the Fillmore administration, particularly over the recently passed fugitive slave law, which allowed slaveowners to call upon the federal and state governments to aid them in capturing and returning slaves who had escaped. The leaders of the Free Soil Party were heartened when tensions did erupt and remained determined to continue their fight. But, despite the optimism some of them articulated, the coalition found itself increasingly on the defensive and proved to be more fragile and have less staying power than its leaders wanted to believe. As sectional tensions eased somewhat, many Free Soilers drifted back to their previous political homes or dropped out of the electoral arena entirely. Echoes of the old parties' internal divisions remained disturbingly present. But those who returned to them tried to focus their attention once more on familiar policy matters and on the reunion with their recent party adversaries. They had much in common, after all, and a long history together. Martin Van Buren and his closest associates along with many, but not all, of their Barnburner supporters once more became members in good standing in the Democratic camp.[11]

In 1852 the leaders of the Free Soil Party again organized a run for the presidency. Their ticket was headed this time by New Hampshire's John P. Hale. Although they still faced troublesome internal disagreements and continuing apathy in some quarters that caused voter turnout to drop again, the two major parties were in better shape than they had been four years before and, when the campaign was over, the results were familiar. The reunited Democrats returned to power, electing New Hampshire party stalwart and former militia general in Mexico Franklin Pierce as president. The Whigs, behind the candidacy of Winfield Scott, did poorly in the Electoral College and slipped some in their percentage of popular votes from what they had received four years before. They still could claim substantial popular support. But the Democrats claimed

more as they had in four of the six elections since 1828. The Free Soilers did worse than in their first run. This time they won just more than
156,000 votes nationwide, 4.5 percent of the national total, a little fewer
than half of what they had garnered in 1848. (To be sure, their support
added up to much more than the Liberty Party had received in 1844 but
was still indicative of the Free Soilers' failure to expand their support
base as much as they hoped in order to influence the nation's territorial
and related policies.)[12]

"NOT YET READY FOR A PURELY SECTIONAL PARTY"

What, then, was the significance of the presidential election of 1848?
It capped a decade of extraordinary political turmoil that had raised the
issue of slavery to a prominence it had not previously had in national
politics, caused important splits in the two major political parties, and
led to the organization of a new party dedicated to preventing any further extension of the institution on U.S. soil. Such a transition of the
antislavery impulse into an organized political coalition was an important moment in U.S. history. Free Soil U.S. Representative George Julian of Indiana long afterward referred to the Buffalo convention in his
memoirs as "a conspicuous milestone in the antislavery journey." More
contemporaneously, Salmon P. Chase saw it as "the beginning of the
end" of slavery.[13]

Many historians, although acknowledging the strong ongoing influence of partisan loyalties, have accepted Julian and Chase's formulation
of the Free Soil Party's enduring impact on the conventional politics of
the time. The election, one scholar has written, "determined the fate of
the Jacksonian party system." Others agree with him that it was a most
significant moment in shaping and forecasting the sectional future,
even given the potency of party loyalties. "The events of 1848 mark a
turning point in the political status of slavery," William Brock suggests.
In its aftermath, the nation's "political center was fragile." The Free Soil
challenge "helped to break 'the thralldom of party'" and "point toward
the likelihood of a more successful challenger in the future."[14]

However relevant these claims seem in retrospect, given the momentous events that occurred a decade later as the result of another presidential election and the subsequent secession of the South, in my judgment,
they claim too much. Such notions about the election of 1848 suggest
the interpretive influence of "the Civil War synthesis," a perspective that

has usually dominated historical analysis. This approach links most of the era's political battles primarily to the growing centrality of sectional confrontation in the period after 1815. In this retrospective view, despite the politically familiar impulses in the Taylor-Cass contest, the swelling sectional power was one of a series of foundation stones of a broader, ultimately successful, challenge to the nation's political system that led to breakdown and civil war at the outset of the 1860s.[15]

Such an approach raises the question of whether, looking back, we understand such events as the people at the time did. The situation in 1848 was a nuanced one. A sectional crisis had certainly erupted, but the reigning political world, if shaken, had not unraveled. Despite some threats of secession by angry southerners, the Union had prevailed. The Free Soil disruption of the normal course of U.S. politics, given the nation's long-standing complacency about such unacceptable things as the practice of slavery, had not accomplished a great deal of what its supporters desired. As in Europe in 1848, in the end, the dominant forces proved not to be the challengers but the more traditional players in the political arena who were able to retain control of the process and the outcome.

The election of 1848 had demonstrated that the Free Soilers were premature in their advocacy and demands, the results revealing "bluntly," in the words of Richard Sewell, "how slight was the Free Soil impact upon the North." Although hostility to the further expansion of slavery had sharpened, had become more focused and better organized, and had grown into a larger political movement than such an impulse had ever before attained, the energetic Free Soil effort in 1848 had not quite established the elements for a subsequent confrontation between the sections over the issue of slavery's further expansion. A political change of the magnitude sought by the Free Soilers came slowly. Although many northerners did hold antislavery opinions, the election showed that most of them had no intention of voting against it at the polls on election day. And although many southerners resented and feared the attacks on their social and economic system based on slavery, they, too, were not prepared to focus on it to the exclusion of everything else in their political world. Both northerners and southerners still had other things on their minds when they engaged in political warfare. The "crisis" had not as yet come. The outlook in parts of political leadership circles was certainly more sectionalized than it had been. But that condition had not extended far beyond the elite cadre. Neither the Free Soilers or their southern sectionalist counterparts were able to mobilize the rank-and-file U.S. voters to embrace the cause and either confront slavery head on or defend it all out regardless of other interests.[16]

Voters had reacted to the issue in many different ways, not in a united or a preponderant rush to let it determine the future of U.S. politics. Despite the importance of the issue to some, most politically engaged Americans remained disinterested or preferred to avoid the matter. "We cannot shut our eyes to the fact," a Whig member of Congress said in the House in early 1849, "that there is very often to be found a vast difference between the Representative and those who send him here." Some political activists may have been more than ready, but as Frederick Blue has written, most voters "were not yet ready for a purely sectional party." Differences over slavery were part of the nation's issue complex. But they paled before the importance still imparted to traditional political loyalties and the still relevant issues of the Jacksonian party system. "The partisan imperative" remained, as suggested throughout this book, most compelling to most politically active Americans in the late 1840s.[17]

The 1848 electoral experience reveals much about U.S. politics and the elements that underpin it and suggests how much Julian's "antislavery journey" was, unsurprisingly, not along a straight highway running from the first dramatic sectional encounter over slavery in the Missouri debates of 1819–1821 through a number of other signposts to its denouement in the secession of South Carolina and its sister states in 1860–1861 and, finally, on to emancipation. There were barriers, delays, diversions, alternate routes, and many twists and turns along the way, as interest in and confrontation about the slavery issue rose and fell. There were, in the words of William H. Seward, "action and reaction," occasionally the "temporary triumph" of antislavery advocates, and then sinking "into inactivity again," all of which constituted the national experience.[18]

The election of 1848 was one of the moments demonstrating this ebb and flow. Sectional perspectives and tensions had arisen, had a great deal of resonance in certain quarters, and had dramatically shaped important aspects of the election. But ultimately the traditional quality of U.S. politics was in evidence as the people came to a specific moment of decision. To repeat, the particular context in which the Free Soilers emerged was not attuned to their outlook and purpose. The partisan dynamic had been forcefully challenged but not overthrown. As a result, the sectional issue, although sometimes loudly and forcefully pressed, remained more under control than it seemed to many, in retrospect, looking back at a later time from a different vantage point.

However, does this mean the Free Soil coalition had no political impact? Not at all. Whatever its normal qualities, that is, the continuing
dominance of traditional party-determined voting behavior, the contest
in 1848 was not an ordinary election. The fact was that the political situation in the late 1840s had lost some of its partisan stability and was
more fluid, however briefly and shallowly, even as national party leaders
fought hard to maintain it. I have previously argued that the furor in the
North in reaction to the annexation of Texas, the way Polk handled the
matter, and the southern reaction to northern outrage had unhinged, for
a time, the nation's normal political processes. The sectional forces unleashed were more intense than expected and, most critically, although
they subsequently fell back, strengthened a collective memory that, filled
as it was with suspicion and hostility about the motives of the other side,
in retrospect, when stimulated, more readily provoked sectional confrontation than had ever happened before.[19] The question was whether the
impulses released would penetrate deeply beyond the political elite and
become the norm of U.S. politics rather than reverting to the intermittent quality of the usual aftermath of other less coherent or organized
sectional uprisings. The election of 1848 was the first test of that.

In that contest, the Free Soilers had made an impression. Although
aware of the obvious limitations of their impact, they could be upbeat
about what they had accomplished in organizing their campaign for the
presidential election. In many ways, the experience had been a water-
shed event. The challengers had established a beachhead of sectionally
driven politics, if not yet a breakthrough, that clung to life in the early
1850s, if more shallowly than they desired. Their efforts gave the idea
of Free Soil some political traction in both the North and South even as
many turned away from them. That was something for the optimists
among them to celebrate.

Still, whatever the positive qualities of the election of 1848 for antislavery activists, they remained far from being the force they hoped to
be. Nor was anything further in favor of achieving their goals ordained
or inevitable. There were no guarantees on the horizon, or even many
promising omens in its aftermath through 1852, that could be cited
with confidence that the movement against slavery's extension would
continue to grow and ultimately become something more wide-ranging
in its appeal and powerful in its influence. In the late 1840s and early
1850s, the ebb and flow of the challenges to slavery indicated that more

work was still needed to enlarge and sustain the challengers' presence—or at minimum, a significant, explosive event that would stimulate the memories that lay below the surface into political play before it would expand and develop into a major force—a force more extensive and, it would prove, more durable than anything before it.

When the explosion did occur between 1854 and 1856 because of several converging factors, beginning with an anti-Catholic, anti-immigrant uproar against the two major parties but ultimately dominated by an even more angry confrontation over slavery's expansion—this time into the area long denied to slavery by the Missouri Compromise—the previous experience of intermittent sectional uproars and behavior now hardened into something more durable. Both of the old parties were seriously weakened by the powerful voter upsurge against them in the mid-1850s, one that did not retreat from its initial surge but led to an electoral realignment of wide reach and major consequence—something that had not occurred in 1848. Voters abandoned their long-standing party moorings in search of a more compatible political home. As a result, political conditions in the United States changed significantly. The Whigs collapsed as a significant force on the national scene and the Republican Party established itself as the voice of those opposed to the further extension of slavery. As such, it drew its voters primarily from areas of Free Soil support in the previous decade—Democrats, Whigs, and members of the Liberty Party—in much larger numbers than heretofore.[20]

As a result of this voter relocation and resettlement, the Free Soil Party of 1848 could now be seen as the "harbinger" of its successor coalition. Most critically, given the new conditions present, the coalition that became the Republican Party was able to sustain its role in U.S. politics as it grew strong enough to win the presidency in 1860 behind non–Free Soiler Abraham Lincoln, on what was essentially the Free Soil platform, against a badly divided—along sectional lines—Democratic Party. At that moment in 1860, in the words of the Ohio party address in 1848, the "crisis" had indeed "come."[21]

DEMOCRATIC NATIONAL PLATFORM, 1848

Resolved, That the American Democracy place their trust in the intelligence, the patriotism, and the discriminating justice of the American people.

Resolved, That we regard this as a distinctive feature of our political creed, which we are proud to maintain before the world as the great moral element in a form of government springing from and upheld by the popular will; and we contrast it with the creed and practice of Federalism, under whatever name or form, which seeks to palsy the will of the constituent, and which conceives no imposture too monstrous for the popular credulity.

Resolved, therefore, That, entertaining these views, the Democratic party of this Union, through their Delegates assembled in general convention of the States, coming together in a spirit of concord, of devotion to the doctrines and faith of a free representative government, and appealing to their fellow-citizens for the rectitude of their intentions, renew and reassert before the American people the declaration of principles avowed by them when, on a former occasion, in general convention, they presented their candidates for the popular suffrage.

1. That the Federal Government is one of limited powers, derived solely from the Constitution; and the grants of power shown therein ought to be strictly construed by all the departments and agents of the Government; and that it is inexpedient and dangerous to exercise doubtful constitutional powers.

2. That the Constitution does not confer upon the General Government the power to commence and carry on a general system of internal improvements.

3. That the Constitution does not confer authority upon the Federal Government, directly or indirectly, to assume the debts of the several States, contracted for local internal improvements, or other State purposes; nor would such assumption be just and expedient.

4. That justice and sound policy forbid the Federal Government to foster one branch of industry to the detriment of another, or to cherish the interests of one portion to the injury of another portion of our

common country; that every citizen, and every section of the country, has a right to demand and insist upon an equality of rights and privileges, and to complete and ample protection of persons and property from domestic violence or foreign aggression.

5. That it is the duty of every branch of the Government to enforce and practice the most rigid economy in conducting our public affairs, and that no more revenue ought to be raised than is required to defray the necessary expenses of the Government, and for the gradual but certain extinction of the debt created by the prosecution of a just and necessary war, after peaceful relations, shall have been restored.

6. That Congress has no power to charter a national bank; that we believe such an institution one of deadly hostility to the best interests of the country, dangerous to our republican institutions and the liberties of the people, and calculated to place the business of the country within the control of a concentrated money power, and above the laws and the will of the people; and that the results of Democratic legislation, in this and all other financial measures upon which issues have been made between the two political parties of the country, have demonstrated to candid and practical men of all parties, their soundness, safety, and utility in all business pursuits.

7. That Congress has no power under the Constitution to interfere with or control the domestic institutions of the several States, and that such States are the sole and proper judges of everything appertaining to their own affairs, not prohibited by the Constitution; that all efforts of the Abolitionists or others made to induce Congress to interfere with questions of slavery, or to take incipient steps in relation thereto, are calculated to lead to the most alarming and dangerous consequences; and that all such efforts have an inevitable tendency to diminish the happiness of the people, and endanger the stability and permanence of the Union, and ought not to be countenanced by any friend to our political institutions.

8. That the separation of the moneys of the Government from banking institutions is indispensable for the safety of the funds of the Government and the rights of the people.

9. That the liberal principles embodied by Jefferson in the Declaration of Independence, and sanctioned in the Constitution, which makes ours the land of liberty, and the asylum of the oppressed of every nation, have ever been cardinal principles in the Democratic faith, and every attempt to abridge the present privilege of becoming citizens and the

owners of soil among us, ought to be resisted with the same spirit which swept the alien and sedition laws from our statute book.

Resolved, That the proceeds of the public lands ought to be sacredly applied to the national object specified in the Constitution; and that we are opposed to any law for the distribution of such proceeds among the States, as alike inexpedient in policy and repugnant to the Constitution.

Resolved, That we are decidedly opposed to taking from the President the qualified veto power, by which he is enabled, under restrictions and responsibilities amply sufficient to guard the public interests, to suspend the passage of a bill whose merits cannot secure the approval of two-thirds of the Senate and House of Representatives, until the judgment of the people can be obtained thereon, and which has saved the American people from the corrupt and tyrannical domination of the Bank of the United States, and from a corrupting system of general internal improvements.

Resolved, That the war with Mexico, provoked on her part by years of insult and injury, was commenced by her army crossing the Rio Grande, attacking the American troops, and invading our sister State of Texas; and that, upon all the principles of patriotism and laws of nations, it is a just and necessary war on our part, in which every American citizen should have shown himself on the side of his country, and neither morally nor physically, by word or by deed, have given "aid and comfort to the enemy."

Resolved, That we would be rejoiced at the assurance of peace with Mexico founded on the just principles of indemnity for the past and security for the future; but that, while the ratification of the liberal treaty offered to Mexico remains in doubt, it is the duty of the country to sustain the administration in every measure necessary to provide for the vigorous prosecution of the war, should that treaty be rejected.

Resolved, That the officers and soldiers who have carried the arms of their country into Mexico, have crowned it with imperishable glory. Their unconquerable courage, their daring enterprise, their unfaltering perseverance and fortitude when assailed on all sides by innumerable foes, and that more formidable enemy, the diseases of the climate, exalt their devoted patriotism into the highest heroism, and give them a right to the profound gratitude of their country, and the admiration of the world.

Resolved, That the Democratic National Convention of the thirty States composing the American Republic, tender their fraternal congratulations to the National Convention of the Republic of France, now assembled as the free-suffrage representatives of the sovereignty of thirty-five millions of republicans, to establish government on those eternal principles of equal rights for which *their* Lafayette and *our* Washington fought side by side in the struggle for our own national independence; and we would especially convey to them, and to the whole people of France, our earnest wishes for the consolidation of their liberties, through the wisdom that shall guide their counsels, on the basis of a democratic constitution, not derived from grants or concessions of kings or parliaments, but originating from the only true source of political power recognized in the States of this Union—the inherent and inalienable right of the people, in their sovereign capacity, to make and to amend their forms of government in such manner as the welfare of the community may require.

Resolved, That in view of the recent development of the grand political truth, of the sovereignty of the people, and their capacity and power for self-government, which is prostrating thrones and erecting republics on the ruins of despotism in the Old World, we feel that a high and sacred duty is devolved, with increased responsibility, upon the Democratic party of this country, as the party of the *people,* to sustain and advance among us constitutional "liberty, equality, and fraternity," by continuing to resist all monopolies and exclusive legislation for the benefit of the few at the expense of the many, and by a vigilant and constant adherence to those principles and compromises of the Constitution which are broad enough and strong enough to embrace and uphold the Union as it was, the Union as it is, and the Union as it shall be, in the full expansion of the energies and capacity of this great and progressive people.

Voted, That a copy of these resolutions be forwarded, through the American Minister at Paris, to the National Convention of the Republic of France.

Resolved, That the fruits of the great political triumph of 1844, which elected James K. Polk and George M. Dallas President and Vice-President of the United States, have fulfilled the hopes of the Democracy of the Union—in defeating the declared purposes of their opponents to create a national bank; in preventing the corrupt and unconstitutional distribution of the land proceeds, from the common treasury of the Union, for local purposes; in protecting the currency and the labor of the country from ruinous fluctuations, and guarding the money of the people for the use of the people, by the establishment of the constitutional treasury; in the noble impulse given to the cause of free trade, by the repeal of the tariff in 1842 and the creation of the more equal, honest, and productive tariff of 1846; and that, in our opinion, it would be a fatal error to weaken the bands of political organization by which these great reforms have been achieved, and risk them in the hands of their known adversaries, with whatever delusive appeals they may solicit our surrender of that vigilance, which is the only safeguard of liberty.

Resolved, That the confidence of the Democracy of the Union in the principles, capacity, firmness, and integrity of James K. Polk, manifested by his nomination and election in 1844, has been signally justified by the strictness of his adherence to sound Democratic doctrines, by the purity of purpose, the energy and ability which have characterized his administration in all our affairs at home and abroad; that we tender to him our cordial congratulations upon the brilliant success which has hitherto crowned his patriotic efforts, and assure him, that at the expiration of his Presidential term, he will carry with him to his retirement the esteem, respect, and admiration of a grateful country.

Resolved, That this Convention hereby present to the people of the United States, Lewis Cass, of Michigan, as the candidate of the Democratic party for the office of President, and William O. Butler, of Kentucky, as the candidate of the Democratic party for the office of Vice-President of the United States.

Source: Donald Bruce Johson and Kirk H. Porter, *National Party Platforms, 1840–1964* (Urbana: University of Illinois Press, 1966), 10–12.

WHIG PARTY STATEMENT OF PRINCIPLES PASSED AT A MASS MEETING AFTER THE NATIONAL CONVENTION (IN LIEU OF A FORMAL PLATFORM)

1. *Resolved,* That the Whigs of the United States, here assembled by their Representatives, heartily ratify the nominations of General Zachary Taylor as President and Millard Fillmore as Vice President of the United States, and pledge themselves to their support.

2. *Resolved,* That the choice of General Taylor as the Whig candidate for President we are glad to discover [in] sympathy with a great popular sentiment throughout the nation—a sentiment which, having its origin in admiration of great military success, has been strengthened by the development, in every action and every word, of sound conservative opinions, and of true fidelity to the great example of former days, and to the principles of the Constitution as administered by its founders.

3. *Resolved,* That General Taylor, in saying that, had he voted in 1844, he would have voted the Whig ticket, gives us the assurance—and no better is needed from a consistent and truth-speaking man—that his heart was with us at the crisis of our political destiny, when Henry Clay was our candidate and when not only Whig principles were well-defined and clearly asserted, but Whig measures depended on success. The heart that was with us then is with us now, and we have a soldier's word of honor, and a life of public and private virtue, as the security.

4. *Resolved,* That we look on General Taylor's administration of the Government as one conducive of Peace, Prosperity, and Union. Of Peace—because no one better knows, or has greater reason to deplore, what he has seen sadly on the field of victory, the horrors of war, and especially of a foreign and aggressive war. Of Prosperity—now more than ever needed to relieve the nation from a burden of debt, and restore industry—agricultural, manufacturing, and commercial—to its accustomed and peaceful functions and influences. Of Union—because we have a candidate whose very position as a Southwestern man, reared on the banks of the great stream whose tributaries, natural and artificial, embrace the whole Union, renders the protection of the interests of the whole country his first trust, and whose various duties in past life have

been rendered, not on the soil or under the flag of any State or section, but over the wide frontier, and under the broad banner of the Nation.

5. *Resolved,* That standing, as the Whig Party does, on the broad and firm platform of the Constitution, braced up by all its inviolable and sacred guarantees and compromises, and cherished in the affections because protective of the interests of the people, we are proud to have, as the exponent of our opinions, one who is pledged to construe it by the wise and generous rules which Washington applied to it, and who has said (and no Whig desires any other assurance), that he will make Washington's Administration the model of his own.

6. *Resolved,* That as Whigs and Americans, we are proud to acknowledge our gratitude for the great military services which, beginning at Palo Alto, and ending at Buena Vista, first awakened the American people to a just estimate of him who is now our Whig Candidate. In the discharge of a painful duty—for his march into the enemy's country was a reluctant one; in the command of regulars at one time and volunteers at another, and of both combined; in the decisive though punctual discipline of his camp, where all respected and beloved him; in the negotiations of terms for a dejected and desperate enemy; in the exigency of actual conflict, when the balance was perilously doubtful—we have found him the same—brave, distinguished, and considerate, no heartless spectator of bloodshed, no trifler with human life or human happiness, and we do not know which to admire most, his heroism in withstanding the assaults of the enemy in the most hopeless fields of Buena Vista—mourning in generous sorrow over the graves of Ringgold, of Clay, or of Hardin—or in giving in the heat of battle, terms of merciful capitulation to a vanquished foe at Monterey, and not being ashamed to avow that he did it to spare women and children, helpless infancy, and more helpless age, against whom no American soldier ever wars. Such a military man, whose triumphs are neither remote nor doubtful, whose virtues these trials have tested, we are proud to make our Candidate.

7. *Resolved,* That in support of this nomination we ask our Whig friends throughout the nation to unite, to co-operate zealously, resolutely, with earnestness in behalf of our candidate, whom calumny cannot reach, and with respectful demeanor to our adversaries, whose Candidates have yet to prove their claims on the gratitude of the nation.

Source: Donald Bruce Johson and Kirk H. Porter, *National Party Platforms, 1840–1964* (Urbana: University of Illinois Press, 1966), 14–15.

FREE SOIL NATIONAL PLATFORM, 1848

Whereas, We have assembled in Convention as a union of *Freemen,* for the sake of Freedom, forgetting all past political differences in a common resolve to maintain the rights of Free Labor against the aggressions of the Slave Power, and to secure Free Soil for a Free People:

And whereas, The political Conventions recently assembled at Baltimore and Philadelphia, the one stifling the voice of a great constituency entitled to be heard in its deliberations, and the other abandoning its distinctive principles for mere availability, have dissolved the national party organizations heretofore existing, by nominating for the Chief Magistracy of the United States, under Slaveholding dictation, candidates, *neither of whom* can be supported by the opponents of Slavery-extension, without a *sacrifice of consistency, duty,* and *self-respect.*

And whereas, These nominations so made finish the occasion and demonstrate the necessity of the union of the People under the banners of Free Democracy, in a solemn and formal *declaration* of their *independence* of the *Slave Power,* and of their fixed determination to rescue the Federal Government from its control:

Resolved, therefore, that we, the people here assembled, remembering the example of our fathers in the days of the first Declaration of Independence, putting our trust in God for the triumph of our cause, and invoking his guidance in our endeavors to advance it, do now plant ourselves upon the *National Platform of Freedom,* in opposition to the Sectional Platform of Slavery.

Resolved, That Slavery in the several States of this Union which recognize its existence, depends upon the State laws alone, which cannot be repealed or modified by the Federal Government and for which laws that Government is not responsible. We therefore propose no interference by Congress with Slavery within the limits of any State.

Resolved, That the *Proviso* of Jefferson, to prohibit the existence of Slavery, after 1800 in all the Territories of the United States, Southern and Northern; the votes of six States, and sixteen delegates, in the Congress of 1784, for the Proviso, to three States and seven delegates against it; the actual exclusion of Slavery from the Northwestern Territory by the

Ordinance of 1787, unanimously adopted by the States in Congress, and the entire history of that period, clearly show that it was the settled policy of the nation, *not to extend, nationalize,* or *encourage,* but to limit, localize, and discourage, Slavery; and to *this policy* which should never have been departed from, the Government ought to *return.*

Resolved, That our fathers ordained the Constitution of the United States, in order, among other great national objects, to establish justice, promote the general welfare, and secure the blessings of Liberty; but expressly *denied* to the Federal Government, which they created, all constitutional power to *deprive any person* of life, *liberty,* or property, without due legal process.

Resolved, That in the judgment of this Convention, Congress has no more power to make a *slave* than to make a *king;* no more power to institute or establish *Slavery,* than to institute or establish a *Monarchy.* No such power can be found among those specifically conferred by the Constitution, or derived by just implication from them.

Resolved, That it is the duty of the Federal Government to relieve itself from all responsibility for the existence or continuance of Slavery wherever that Government possess constitutional power to legislate on that subject, and is thus responsible for its existence.

Resolved, That the true, and, in the judgment of this Convention, the *only* safe means of preventing the extension of Slavery into territory now free, is to prohibit its existence in all such territory by *an act of Congress.*

Resolved, That we accept the issue which the Slave Power has forced upon us, and to their demand for more Slave States and more Slave Territory, our calm but final answer is: No more Slave States and no more Slave Territory. Let the soil of our extensive domains be kept free, for the hardy pioneers of our own land, and the oppressed and banished of other lands seeking homes of comfort and fields of enterprise in the New World.

Resolved, That the bill lately reported by the Committee of Eight in the Senate of the United States, was no compromise, but an absolute surrender of the rights of the non-slaveholders of the States; and while we rejoice to know that a measure which, while opening the door for the introduction of Slavery into Territories now free, would also have opened the door to litigation and strife among the future inhabitants thereof, to the ruin of their peace and prosperity, was defeated in the House of Representatives,—its passage, in hot haste, by a majority, embracing several Senators who voted in open violation of the known will of their constituents, should warn the People to see to it, that their representatives be not suffered to betray them. There must be no more compromises with Slavery: if made, they must be repealed.

Resolved, That we demand Freedom and established institutions for our brethren in Oregon, now exposed to hardships, peril, and massacre, by the reckless hostility of the Slave Power to the establishment of Free Government for Free Territories—and not only for them, but for our new brethren in California and New Mexico.

And whereas, It is due not only to this occasion, but to the whole people of the United States, that we should also declare ourselves on certain other questions of national policy, therefore,

Resolved, That we demand *cheap postage* for the people; a retrenchment of the expenses and patronage of the Federal Government; the *abolition* of all *unnecessary* offices and salaries; and the election by the People of all civil officers in the service of the Government, so far as the same may be practicable.

Resolved, That *river* and *harbor improvements,* when demanded by the safety and convenience of commerce with foreign nations, or among the several States, are objects of *national concern;* and that it is the duty of Congress, in the exercise of its constitutional powers, to provide therefore.

Resolved, That the FREE GRANT TO ACTUAL SETTLERS, in consideration of the expenses they incur in making settlements in the wilderness, which are usually fully equal to their actual cost, and of the public benefits resulting therefrom, of reasonable portions of the public lands, under suitable limitations, is a wise and just measure of public policy, which will promote, in various ways, the interest of all the States of this Union; and we therefore recommend it to the favorable consideration of the American People.

Resolved, That the obligations of honor and patriotism require the earliest practical payment of the national debt, and we are therefore in favor of such a tariff of duties as will raise revenue adequate to defray the necessary expenses of the Federal Government, and to pay annual installments of our debt and the interest thereon.

Resolved, That we inscribe on our banner, "FREE SOIL, FREE SPEECH, FREE LABOR, AND FREE MEN," and under it we will fight on, and fight ever, until a triumphant victory shall reward our exertions.

Source: Donald Bruce Johson and Kirk H. Porter, *National Party Platforms, 1840–1964* (Urbana: University of Illinois Press, 1966), 13–14.

ZACHARY TAYLOR'S INAUGURAL ADDRESS, MARCH 5, 1849

Elected by the American people to the highest office known to our laws, I appear here to take the oath prescribed by the Constitution, and, in compliance with a time-honored custom, to address those who are now assembled.

@tx:The confidence and respect shown by my countrymen in calling me to be the Chief Magistrate of a Republic holding a high rank among the nations of the earth have inspired me with feelings of the most profound gratitude; but when I reflect that the acceptance of the office which their partiality has bestowed imposes the discharge of the most arduous duties and involves the weightiest obligations, I am conscious that the position which I have been called to fill, though sufficient to satisfy the loftiest ambition, is surrounded by fearful responsibilities. Happily, however, in the performance of my new duties I shall not be without able cooperation. The legislative and judicial branches of the Government present prominent examples of distinguished civil attainments and matured experience, and it shall be my endeavor to call to my assistance in the Executive Departments individuals whose talents, integrity, and purity of character will furnish ample guaranties for the faithful and honorable performance of the trusts to be committed to their charge. With such aids and an honest purpose to do whatever is right, I hope to execute diligently, impartially, and for the best interests of the country the manifold duties devolved upon me.

In the discharge of these duties my guide will be the Constitution, which I this day swear to "preserve, protect, and defend." For the interpretation of that instrument I shall look to the decisions of the judicial tribunals established by its authority and to the practice of the Government under the earlier Presidents, who had so large a share in its formation. To the example of those illustrious patriots I shall always defer with reverence, and especially to his example who was by so many titles "the Father of his Country." To command the Army and Navy of the United States; with the advice and consent of the Senate, to make treaties and to appoint ambassadors and other officers; to give to Congress information of the state of the Union and recommend such measures as he shall judge to be necessary; and to take care that the laws shall be faithfully executed—these are the most important functions intrusted to the President by the Constitution, and it may be expected that I shall briefly indicate the principles which will control me in their execution. Chosen by the body of the people under the assurance that my Administration would be devoted to the welfare of the whole country, and not to the support of any particular section or merely local interest, I this day renew the declarations I have heretofore made and proclaim my fixed determination to maintain to the extent of my ability the Government in its original purity and to adopt as the basis of my public policy those great republican doctrines which constitute the strength of our national existence.

In reference to the Army and Navy, lately employed with so much distinction on active service, care shall be taken to insure the highest condition of efficiency, and in furtherance of that object the military and naval schools, sustained by the liberality of Congress, shall receive the special attention of the Executive.

As American freemen we cannot but sympathize in all efforts to extend the blessings of civil and political liberty, but at the same time we are warned by the admonitions of history and the voice of our own beloved Washington to abstain from entangling alliances with foreign nations. In all disputes between conflicting governments it is our interest not less than our duty to remain strictly neutral, while our geographical position, the genius of our institutions and our people, the advancing spirit of civilization, and, above all, the dictates of religion direct us to the cultivation of peaceful and friendly relations with all other powers. It is to be hoped that no international question can now arise which a government confident in its own strength and resolved to protect its own just rights may not settle by wise negotiation; and it eminently becomes a government like our own, founded on the morality and intelligence of its citizens and upheld by their affections, to exhaust every resort of honorable diplomacy before appealing to arms. In the conduct of our foreign relations I shall conform to these views, as I believe them essential to the best interests and the true honor of the country.

The appointing power vested in the President imposes delicate and onerous duties. So far as it is possible to be informed, I shall make honesty, capacity, and fidelity indispensable prerequisites to the bestowal of office, and the absence of either of these qualities shall be deemed sufficient cause for removal.

It shall be my study to recommend such constitutional measures to Congress as may be necessary and proper to secure encouragement and protection to the great interests of agriculture, commerce, and manufactures, to improve our rivers and harbors, to provide for the speedy extinguishment of the public debt, to enforce a strict accountability on the part of all officers of the Government and the utmost economy in all public expenditures; but it is for the wisdom of Congress itself, in which all legislative powers are vested by the Constitution, to regulate these and other matters of domestic policy. I shall look with confidence to the enlightened patriotism of that body to adopt such measures of conciliation as may harmonize conflicting interests and tend to perpetuate that Union which should be the paramount object of our hopes and affections. In any action calculated to promote an object so near the heart of everyone who truly loves his country I will zealously unite with the coordinate branches of the Government.

In conclusion I congratulate you, my fellow-citizens, upon the high state of prosperity to which the goodness of Divine Providence has conducted our common country. Let us invoke a continuance of the same protecting care which has led us from small beginnings to the eminence we this day occupy, and let us seek to deserve that continuance by prudence and moderation in our councils, by well-directed attempts to assuage the bitterness which too often marks unavoidable differences of opinion, by the promulgation and practice of just and liberal principles, and by an enlarged patriotism, which shall acknowledge no limits but those of our own widespread Republic.

Source: James D. Richardson, comp., *A Compilation of the Messages and Papers of the Presidents, 1789–1902* (Washington, D.C.: Bureau of National Literature and Art, 1905), 5:4–6.

NOTES

AUTHOR'S PREFACE

1 Oliver C. Gardiner, *The Great Issue, or the Three Presidential Candidates* (New York: William C. Bryant, 1848), 72.
2 "To the People of Ohio, Proceedings and Address of the Democratic State Convention Held at Columbus, May 10, 1848" (Columbus, Ohio, 1848), 15.
3 This comment was made in a speech by U.S. Representative John G. Palfrey of New Hampshire, *Congressional Globe*, 30th Cong., 1st Sess., Appendix, 133.

CHAPTER 1 TROUBLED POLITICAL TIMES

1 Douglas C. North, *Economic Growth of the United States, 1790–1860* (Englewood Cliffs, N.J.: Prentice Hall, 1961); Paul Wallace Gates, *The Farmer's Age: Agriculture, 1815–1860* (New York: Holt, Rinehart, and Winston, 1960); George Rogers Taylor, *The Transportation Revolution, 1815–1860* (New York: Rinehart, 1951); Walter Licht, *Industrializing America: The Nineteenth Century* (Baltimore, Md.: Johns Hopkins University Press, 1995); Bruce Laurie, *Artisans into Workers: Labor in the Nineteenth Century* (New York: Hill and Wang, 1989).
2 There is a great deal of literature on the political developments under way, well integrated in Charles G. Sellers Jr., *The Market Revolution: Jacksonian America, 1815–1846* (New York: Oxford University Press, 1991). See also "The Road to 1838," in Joel H. Silbey, *The American Political Nation, 1838–1893* (Stanford, Calif.: Stanford University Press, 1991), 5–32. On the Missouri controversy, see, most recently, Robert P. Forbes, *The Missouri Compromise and Its Aftermath: Slavery and the Meaning of America* (Chapel Hill: University of North Carolina Press, 2007).
3 On the election of 1840, see William N. Chambers, "Election of 1840," in Arthur M. Schlesinger, ed., *History of American Presidential Elections, 1789–1968*, vol. 1 (New York: Chelsea House, 1971), 643–744; and the analysis by Michael F. Holt in his *Political Parties and American Political Development from the Age of Jackson to the Age of Lincoln* (Baton Rouge: Louisiana State University Press, 1992), 151–191. On the expansion of the electorate, see Alexander Keyssar, *The Right to Vote: The Contested History of Democracy in the United States* (New York: Basic Books, 2000); and Chilton Williamson, *American Suffrage from Property to Democracy* (Princeton, N.J.: Princeton University Press, 1960).
4 Robert Gunderson, *The Log Cabin Campaign* (Lexington: University Press of Kentucky, 1957). The Whigs issued Ogle's speech as a widely circulated campaign pamphlet, "Speech of Mr. Ogle of Pennsylvania on the Regal Splendor of the Presidential Palace" (Boston: Weeks Jordan, 1840).

5 Chambers, "Election of 1840"; Holt, *Political Parties.*

6 Chambers, "Election of 1840"; Gunderson, *Log Cabin Campaign.*

7 On the 1844 contest, see Charles G. Sellers, "Election of 1844," in Schle-singer, *History of Presidential Elections,* vol. 1, 747–860; Sellers, *James K. Polk, Continentalist, 1843–1846* (Princeton, N.J.: Princeton University Press, 1957); and Michael Holt, *The Rise and Fall of the American Whig Party: Jacksonian Politics and the Onset of Civil War* (New York: Oxford University Press, 1999). Silbey, *American Political Nation,* describes the political scene during the campaign and on election day.

8 On the election of 1828, see Robert Remini, *The Election of 1828* (Philadel-phia, Pa.: Lippincott, 1963). On Van Buren's role, see John Niven, *Martin Van Buren: The Romantic Age of American Politics* (New York: Oxford University Press, 1983); and Donald Cole, *Martin Van Buren and the American Political System* (Princeton, N.J.: Princeton University Press, 1984).

9 Donald Cole, *The Presidency of Andrew Jackson* (Lawrence: University Press of Kansas, 1993); Harry L. Watson, *Liberty and Power: The Politics of Jackso-nian America,* rev. ed. (New York: Hill and Wang, 2006).

10 There is an enormous body of excellent scholarship on the evolution of the U.S. political system, in which the election of 1848 was embedded, begin-ning with Richard P. McCormick, *The Second American Party System: Party Formation in the Jacksonian Era* (Chapel Hill: University of North Carolina Press, 1967). Since its publication, three other studies have been particularly helpful in adding to our understanding: Holt, *Rise and Fall of the American Whig Party;* Sean Wilentz, *The Rise of American Democracy, Jefferson to Lin-coln* (New York: Norton, 2005); and Daniel Walker Howe, *What Hath God Wrought: The Transformation of America, 1815–1848* (New York: Oxford University Press, 2007).

11 Holt, *Rise and Fall of the American Whig Party;* and Daniel Walker Howe, *The Political Culture of the American Whigs* (Chicago, Ill.: University of Chicago Press, 1979).

12 Lawrence F. Kohl, *The Politics of Individualism: Parties and the American Character in the Jacksonian Era* (New York: Oxford University Press, 1989); David J. Russo, *Major Political Issues of the Jacksonian Period and the Devel-opment of Party Loyalty in Congress, 1830–1840* (Philadelphia, Pa.: American Philosophical Society, 1972); Bruce Collins, "The Ideology of the Ante-Bellum Northern Democrats," *Journal of American Studies* 11 (April 1977): 103–121.

13 Lee Benson, *The Concept of Jacksonian Democracy: New York as a Test Case* (Princeton, N.J.: Princeton University Press, 1961); and John Ashworth, *"Agrarians and Aristocrats": Party Political Ideology in the United States, 1837–1846* (London: Royal Historical Society, 1983) are excellent studies of party ideology.

14 Silbey, *American Political Nation,* discusses the development of partisan or-ganization and leadership in the 1830s and 1840s. See also Roy F. Nichols, *The Invention of the American Political Parties: A Study of Political Improvisa-tion* (New York: Macmillan, 1967).

15 "The Grounds of Difference between the Contending Parties," *Whig Almanac, 1843* (New York: n.p., 1843), 16; Elizabeth Varon, *"We Mean to Be Counted": White Women and Politics in Antebellum Virginia* (Chapel Hill: University of North Carolina Press, 1998).

16 The intensity of voter commitment to the parties is a constant theme of many studies of the politics of this period. See also Silbey, "The Shrine of Party," in *American Political Nation*, 125–140.

17 For a discussion suggesting the existence of important limits to party commitment in this era, see Glenn C. Altschuler and Stuart Blumin, *The Rude Republic: Americans and Their Politics in the Nineteenth Century* (Princeton, N.J.: Princeton University Press, 2000).

18 The voting returns in this and the following paragraph are taken from *Congressional Quarterly's Guide to U.S. Elections* (Washington, D.C.: Congressional Quarterly Press, 1975).

19 Ronald G. Walters, *American Reformers, 1815–1860* (New York: Hill and Wang, 1978), is a good introduction to the reform impulse. See also Robert H. Abzug, *Cosmos Crumbling: American Reform and the Religious Imagination* (New York: Oxford University Press, 1994); Ray Billington, *The Protestant Crusade, 1815–1860: A Study of the Origins of American Nativism* (New York: Macmillan, 1938); Walters, *The Antislavery Appeal: American Abolitionism after 1830* (Baltimore, Md.: Johns Hopkins University Press, 1976); Jonathan Earle, *Jacksonian Antislavery and the Politics of Free Soil, 1824–1854* (Chapel Hill: University of North Carolina Press, 2004); Yonatan Eyal, *The Young America Movement and the Transformation of the Democratic Party, 1828–1861* (New York: Cambridge University Press, 2007).

20 Jonathan Messerli, *Horace Mann: A Biography* (New York: Knopf, 1972); Ian Tyrell, *Sobering Up: From Temperance to Prohibition in Antebellum America, 1800–1860* (Westport, Conn.: Greenwood, 1979); Ellen C. Dubois, *Feminism and Suffrage: The Emergence of an Independent Women's Movement in the United States* (Ithaca, N.Y.: Cornell University Press, 1980); Reeve Huston, *Land and Freedom: Rural Society, Popular Protest, and Party Politics in Antebellum New York* (New York: Oxford University Press, 2000).

21 James Brewer Stewart, *Holy Warriors: The Abolitionists and American Slavery,* 2d ed. (New York: Hill and Wang, 1997). The best examination of southerners' reactions to attacks on their institution and the gag rule controversy is William Freehling, *The Road to Disunion*, Vol. 1: *Secessionists at Bay, 1776–1854* (New York: Oxford University Press, 1990). See also William J. Cooper, *The South and the Politics of Slavery, 1828–1856* (Baton Rouge: Louisiana State University Press, 1978).

22 Aileen Kraditor, "The Liberty and Free Soil Parties," in Arthur M. Schlesinger, *History of U.S. Political Parties*, vol. 1 (New York: Chelsea House, 1973), 741–882; Richard Sewell, *Ballots for Freedom: Antislavery Politics in the United States, 1837–1860* (New York: Oxford University Press, 1976).

23 The most recent of the many biographies of Calhoun is Irving Bartlett, *John C. Calhoun: A Biography* (New York: Norton, 1993). See also Manisha Sinha,

The Counterrevolution of Slavery: Politics and Ideology in Antebellum South Carolina (Chapel Hill: University of North Carolina Press, 2000).

24 Jonathan Nathan to Hamilton Fish, January 3, 1844, Hamilton Fish Papers, New York Historical Society.

25 *Congressional Quarterly's Guide to U.S. Elections*, 267.

26 (Washington, D.C.) *Daily Union*, June 17, 1847; Athens (Ga.) *Southern Banner*, February 2, 1847.

27 There is a useful, brief discussion of South Carolina's Whigs in Lacy K. Ford, *Origins of Southern Radicalism: The South Carolina Upcountry, 1800–1860* (New York: Oxford University Press, 1988).

28 William E. Gienapp, "The Crisis of American Democracy: The Political System and the Coming of the Civil War," in Gabor Boritt, ed., *Why the Civil War Came* (New York: Oxford University Press, 1996), 83.

29 In addition to Holt, *Rise and Fall of the American Whig Party*, see the older but still helpful George R. Poage, *Henry Clay and the Whig Party* (Chapel Hill: University of North Carolina Press, 1936).

30 Holt, *Rise and Fall of the American Whig Party*; and Poage, *Henry Clay and the Whig Party*. See also Norma Lois Peterson, *The Presidencies of William Henry Harrison and John Tyler* (Lawrence: University Press of Kansas, 1989).

31 Holt, *Rise and Fall of the American Whig Party*, 331.

32 *Congressional Quarterly's Guide to U.S. Elections*, 267. The turnout figure is from U.S. Bureau of the Census, *Historical Statistics of the United States: Colonial Times to 1970* (Washington, D.C.: Government Printing Office, 1975).

33 Sellers, *Polk, Continentalist*; and Holt, *Rise and Fall of the American Whig Party*, are the relevant sources. See also Paul H. Bergeron, *The Presidency of James K. Polk* (Lawrence: University Press of Kansas, 1987).

34 The citations in Note 33 discuss these matters.

35 Edward L. Widmer, *Young America: The Flowering of Democracy in New York City* (New York: Oxford University Press, 1999); David M. Pletcher, *The Diplomacy of Annexation, Texas, Oregon, and the Mexican War* (Columbia: University of Missouri Press, 1973); and Thomas Hietala, *Manifest Design: American Exceptionalism and Empire*, rev. ed. (Ithaca, N.Y.: Cornell University Press, 2003); Eyal, *Young America Movement*.

36 See Holt, *Rise and Fall of the American Whig Party*; Michael A. Morrison, *Slavery and the American West: The Eclipse of Manifest Destiny and the Coming of the Civil War* (Chapel Hill: University of North Carolina Press, 1997).

37 Holt, *Rise and Fall of the American Whig Party*, 211.

38 Sellers, "Election of 1844"; Bergeron, *Presidency of Polk*.

39 Morgan Dix, comp., *The Memoirs of John Adams Dix* (New York: Harper, 1883), 205. The split in the New York Democratic Party is the subject of Walter Ferree, "The New York Democracy: Division and Reunion, 1847–1852," unpublished Ph.D. diss., University of Pennsylvania, 1953.

40 John Adams Dix to Silas Wright, April 16, 1846, in Martin Lichterman, *John Adams Dix*, unpublished Ph.D. diss., Columbia University, 1952, 173. On Van Buren and his associates' anger see the biographies of Van Buren and

Joel H. Silbey, *Storm over Texas: The Annexation Controversy and the Road to Civil War* (New York: Oxford University Press, 2005).

41 James D. Richardson, comp., *A Compilation of the Messages and Papers of the Presidents, 1789–1902* (Washington, D.C.: Bureau of National Literature and Art, 1905), 381.

42 Jackson's comment is in Andrew Jackson to Lewis Cass, July 8, 1843, Lewis Cass Papers, William E. Clements Library, University of Michigan. On the Oregon compromise, see Pletcher, *Diplomacy of Annexation*.

43 As a student of this group has recently written, "Moving away from the agrarian roots of Andrew Jackson's original coalition, Young America Democrats accepted the market revolution, loosened their interpretation of the Constitution, and adopted various reform causes." Eyal, *Young American Movement*, 2.

44 Silbey, *Storm over Texas*, 91–121.

45 John C. Calhoun to Richard Pakenham (the British minister in Washington), April 18, 1844, in Clyde N. Wilson, ed., *The Papers of John C. Calhoun*, vol. 18 (Columbia: University of South Carolina Press, 1988), 273–281. On the perception that Polk was following southern interests regarding Texas and subsequently, see Leonard L. Richards, *The Slave Power: The Free North and Southern Domination, 1780–1960* (Baton Rouge: Louisiana State University Press, 2000), 134–161; William Dusinberre, *Slavemaster President: The Double Career of James Polk* (New York: Oxford University Press, 2003).

46 Silas Wright to John L. Russell, May 15, 1844, in Ransom H. Gillet, *The Life and Times of Silas Wright*, vol. 2 (Albany, N.Y.: Argus, 1874), 1518.

47 One can follow the Democratic Party disarray in Ferree, "The New York Democracy" and in the biographies of Van Buren listed above.

48 See the record of congressional voting behavior during the Polk administration in Joel H. Silbey, *The Shrine of Party: Congressional Voting Behavior, 1841–1852* (Pittsburgh, Pa.: University of Pittsburgh Press, 1967), 83–97.

49 On the Whigs, see Holt, *Rise and Fall of the American Whig Party*, 208–258.

50 On general opposition to the war with Mexico, see John H. Schroeder, *Mr. Polk's War: American Opposition and Dissent, 1846–1848* (Madison: University of Wisconsin Press, 1973).

51 "The 29th Congress: Its Men and Measures; Its Professions and Its Principles; What It Has Done for Itself, What for the Country, and What against the Country—Being a Review of the First Session of the 29th Congress" (Washington, D.C.: n.p., 1846), 10; *Congressional Globe*, 30th Cong., 1st Sess., Appendix, 213; Henry Clay to O. W. Laver, November 6, 1846, in James F. Hopkins et al., eds., *The Papers of Henry Clay*, vol. 10 (Lexington: University Press of Kentucky, 1959–1992), 285.

52 Clay's speech is in the *Whig Almanac, 1848*, 7–16. On Lincoln's assault on Polk regarding the war, see, among many others, David H. Donald, *Lincoln* (New York: Simon and Schuster, 1995). Lincoln's career in Congress is the subject of Donald Riddle, *Congressman Abraham Lincoln* (Urbana: University of Illinois Press, 1957). On Stephens, see Thomas E. Schott, *Alexander H. Stephens*

of Georgia: A Biography (Baton Rouge: Louisiana State University Press, 1988).

53 Mark Neely, "War and Partisanship: What Lincoln Learned from James K. Polk," *Journal of the Illinois State Historical Society* 74 (Autumn 1981): 205; *Congressional Globe*, 30th Cong., 2nd Sess., Appendix, 957.

54 Schroeder, *Mr. Polk's War;* Holt, *Rise and Fall of the American Whigs;* and Ferree, "The New York Democracy" all offer evidence of the intense political anger against Polk.

55 Holt, *Rise and Fall of the American Whig Party* is excellent on the Whigs' opposition to Polk after 1845.

CHAPTER 2 "A NORTHERN NO!"

1 *A Northern No! Addressed to the Delegates from the Free States to the Whig National Convention at Philadelphia, 1848* (n.p., 1848).

2 Michael A. Morrison, *Slavery and the American West: The Eclipse of Manifest Destiny and the Coming of the Civil War* (Chapel Hill: University of North Carolina Press, 1997); David Pletcher, *The Diplomacy of Annexation: Texas, Oregon, and the Mexican War* (Columbia: University of Missouri Press, 1973).

3 On the Whigs "no territory" policy, see Morrison, *Slavery and the American West,* 19–26.

4 On the origins and introduction of the Wilmot Proviso, see Charles G. Sellers, Jr., *James K. Polk: Continentalist* (Princeton, N.J.: Princeton University Press, 1966), 476ff; Jonathan H. Earle, *Jacksonian Antislavery and the Politics of Free Soil* (Chapel Hill: University of North Carolina Press, 2004), 123–143; Chaplain W. Morrison, *Democratic Politics and Sectionalism: The Wilmot Proviso Controversy* (Chapel Hill: University of North Carolina Press, 1967); Charles Going, *David Wilmot, Free Soiler: A Biography* (New York: Appleton, 1924).

5 The wording is in all of the books cited in Note 4. Polk's complaint is in Milo M. Quaife, ed., *The Diaries of James K. Polk during His Presidency, 1845–1849,* vol. 2 (Chicago, Ill.: Jansen, McClurg, 1910), 75.

6 See Earle, *Jacksonian Antislavery;* Eric Foner, "The Wilmot Proviso Revisited," *Journal of American History* 46 (September 1969): 262–279; and Richard Sewell, *Ballots for Freedom: Antislavery Politics in the United States, 1837–1860* (New York: Oxford University Press, 1976), 131 and passim.

7 On John P. Hale in New Hampshire, see Richard H. Sewell, *John Parker Hale and the Politics of Abolition* (Cambridge, Mass.: Harvard University Press, 1965).

8 Morrison, *Slavery and the American West,* is particularly good on this.

9 Holt, *Rise and Fall of the American Whig Party* effectively discusses Whig strategy during the Polk administration.

10 *Congressional Globe*, 30th Cong., 1st Sess., 89; Philadelphia *Pennsylvanian*, February 5, 1847.

11 John A. Garraty, *Silas Wright* (New York: Columbia University Press, 1949).

12 There were now 116 Whigs and 108 Democrats in the House compared with 76 Whigs and more than 135 Democrats in the 29th Congress.

13 Ernest Muller, "Preston King: A Political Biography," unpublished Ph.D. diss., Columbia University, 1949; Earle, *Jacksonian Antislavery*, 67–68.

14 Walter Ferree, "The New York Democracy: Division and Reunion, 1847–1852," unpublished Ph.D. diss., University of Pennsylvania, 1953. The standard work on the Barnburners for many years has been Herbert D. A. Donovan, *The Barnburners* (New York: New York University Press, 1925). A history of them written at the time, including pertinent documents, is Oliver C. Gardiner, *The Great Issue, or the Three Presidential Candidates* (New York: William C. Bryant, 1848). The quotation is from the "Address" to the Utica Convention in *The Great Issue*, 83.

15 In addition to Ferree, "New York Democracy," see Sewell, *Ballots for Freedom*, 148ff; and Earle, *Jacksonian Antislavery*, 132ff.

16 Joseph Rayback, *Free Soil: The Election of 1848* (Lexington: University Press of Kentucky, 1970), 171–185 and elsewhere, has a good discussion of the selection of delegates. Frederick J. Blue, *The Free Soilers: Third-Party Politics, 1848–1854* (Urbana: University of Illinois Press, 1973), details the fragmentation of parties under way and the move toward a separate Free Soil Party.

17 Kinley J. Brauer, *Cotton versus Conscience: Massachusetts Whig Politics and Southwestern Expansion* (Lexington: University Press of Kentucky, 1967), discusses developments in Massachusetts; Stephen Maizlish, *The Triumph of Sectionalism: The Transformation of Ohio Politics, 1844–1856* (Kent, Ohio: Kent State University Press, 1983), those in Ohio.

18 In addition to the books cited above, see the biographies by David H. Donald, *Charles Sumner and the Coming of the Civil War* (New York: Knopf, 1960); James Brewer Stewart, *Joshua R. Giddings and the Tactics of Radical Politics* (Cleveland, Ohio: Case Western Reserve University Press, 1970). Sewell, *Ballots for Freedom;* and Blue, *The Free Soilers*, follow these moves and reactions very well.

19 John Niven, *Salmon P. Chase: A Biography* (New York: Oxford University Press, 1995), 87–113, describes these efforts, as do Sewell, *Ballots for Freedom;* Maizlish, *Triumph of Sectionalism;* Blue, *The Free Soilers.*

20 Niven, *Chase.*

21 See ibid. On the Liberty Party generally, see Bruce Laurie, *Beyond Garrison: Antislavery and Social Reform* (New York: Cambridge University Press, 2005).

22 On the Liberty League and the Smith nomination, see Blue, *Free Soilers*, 9–14; Sewell, *Ballots for Freedom*, 117–120.

23 On the southern reaction to the rise of political antislavery, see William J. Cooper, *The South and the Politics of Slavery* (Baton Rouge: Louisiana State University Press, 1978); William Freehling, *The Road to Disunion: Secessionists at Bay*, vol. 1: *1776–1854* (New York: Oxford University Press, 1990).

24 On Calhoun and his resolutions, see Irving H. Bartlett, *John C. Calhoun: A Biography* (New York: Norton, 1993), 342ff.

25 Milledgeville (Ga.) *Federal Union*, September 7, 1847; Columbus (Ga.) *Times* quoted in *Nashville Union*, September 24, 1847.

26 On the Alabama Platform and its author, see Eric Walther, *William Lowndes Yancey and the Coming of the Civil War* (Chapel Hill: University of North Carolina Press, 2006).

27 Charleston *Mercury,* December 4, 1847.

28 Wilson Lumpkin to John C. Calhoun, August 27, 1847, *Correspondence Addressed to John C. Calhoun, Annual Report of the American Historical Association, 1929* (Washington, D.C.: American Historical Association, 1930), 396; Athens (Ga.) *Southern Banner,* April 6, 1847.

29 Albany *Argus,* December 17, 1847; *New York Globe,* October 14, 1847; see also Springfield *Illinois State Register,* March 26, 1847.

CHAPTER 3 "THE SORE-HEADED LEADERS IN THE STATE OF NEW YORK"—AND SOME OTHERS—NOMINATE A PRESIDENT

1 David Pletcher, *The Politics of Annexation: Texas, Oregon, and the Mexican War* (Columbia: University of Missouri Press, 1973), 549–550, 567ff.

2 In addition to the discussion of party turmoil in Chapters 1 and 2 of this volume, see Frederick Merk, "Presidential Fevers," *Mississippi Valley Historical Review* 47 (June 1960): 3–33.

3 Ibid., 32 and passim; Paul Bergeron, *The Presidency of James K. Polk* (Lawrence: University Press of Kansas, 1987), 247 and chap. 9.

4 The Democrats' preconvention lineup and maneuvering is described in Joseph Rayback, *Free Soil: The Election of 1848* (Lexington: University Press of Kentucky, 1970). Biographies of the potential candidates are particularly helpful. See, for example, Willard Klunder, *Lewis Cass and the Politics of Moderation* (Kent, Ohio: Kent State University Press, 1996); Philip S. Klein, *President James Buchanan: A Biography* (University Park: Pennsylvania State University Press, 1962); Judith K. Schafer, "Levi P. Woodbury," in John A. Garraty and Mark C. Carnes, eds., *American National Biography,* vol. 23 (New York: Oxford University Press, 1999), 792–794.

5 James P. Shenton, *Robert John Walker: A Politician from Jackson to Lincoln* (New York: Columbia University Press, 1961); John M. Behohlavek, *George Mifflin Dallas: Jacksonian Patrician* (University Park: Pennsylvania State University Press, 1977); Donald P. Cole, *Martin Van Buren and the American Political System* (Princeton, N.J.: Princeton University Press, 1984); among others.

6 Stephen A. Douglas to Samuel Treat, April 26, 1848, in Robert Johannsen, ed., *The Letters of Stephen A. Douglas* (Urbana: University of Illinois Press, 1961), 159.

7 In addition to Rayback, *Free Soil,* and the biographies listed above, see Michael F. Holt, *The Rise and Fall of the American Whig Party: Jacksonian Politics and the Onset of Civil War* (New York: Oxford University Press, 1999), chaps. 9–10.

8 Much of this is covered in Holman Hamilton, "The Election of 1848," in Arthur M. Schlesinger, Jr., and Fred L. Israel, eds., *History of U.S. Presidential Elections,* vol. 2 (New York: Chelsea House, 1971), 865–918. See also Rayback, *Free Soil,* passim.

9 In addition to Walter Ferree, "The New York Democracy: Division and Re-union, 1847–1852," unpublished Ph.D. diss., University of Pennsylvania, 1953, see Frederick J. Blue, *The Free Soilers: Third-Party Politics, 1848–1854* (Urbana: University of Illinois Press, 1973), 16–43.

10 Blue, *Free Soilers*, 31–32.

11 Ibid.; Jonathan Earle, *Jacksonian Antislavery and the Politics of Free Soil, 1824–1854* (Chapel Hill: University of North Carolina Press, 2004), 72, 138–139. Wilmot's speech at the Utica convention is reprinted in Oliver C. Gardiner, *The Great Issue, or the Three Presidential Candidates* (New York: William C. Bryant, 1848), 57–62.

12 *New York Globe*, October 28, 1847; Albany *Argus*, January 12, 1848.

13 Springfield *Illinois State Register*, April 24, 1847; John L. O'Sullivan to Samuel J. Tilden, April 30, 1848, Samuel J. Tilden Papers, New York Public Library.

14 Klein, *Buchanan*; Michael A. Morrison, *Slavery and the American West, The Elipse of Manifest Destiny and the Coming of the Civil War* (Chapel Hill: University of North Carolina Press, 1997), 62ff.

15 Morrison, *Slavery and American West*, 58–59. The speech of A. G. Brown is in *Congressional Globe*, 30th Cong., 1st Sess., Appendix, 648.

16 Joseph Rayback, "The Presidential Ambitions of John C. Calhoun, 1844–1848," *Journal of Southern History* 14 (August 1848): 331–356; Camden (S.C.) *Journal* quoted in Charleston *Mercury*, May 11, 1848.

17 Morrison, *Slavery and American West*, 58–59.

18 "Great Speech of the Hon. George Mifflin Dallas, upon the Leading Topic of the Day" (Philadelphia, 1847), 15. See Dickinson's speech in *Congressional Globe*, 30th Cong., 1st Sess., Appendix, 89; Klunder, *Cass*, 84–86; Athens (Ga.) *Southern Banner*, January 13, 1848.

19 *New York Globe*, October 14, 1847; Detroit *Free Press*, December 31, 1847. A local editor in Pennsylvania warned Dallas that "the Wilmot Proviso—a humbug certainly—is doing some mischief." John Congsin to George M. Dallas, George M. Dallas Papers, Historical Society of Pennsylvania. Chaplain W. Morrison, *Democratic Politics and Sectionalism: The Wilmot Proviso Controversy* (Chapel Hill: University of North Carolina Press, 1967), covers the battle over the issue and the tensions it engendered.

20 Philadelphia *Pennsylvanian*, January 14, 1848.

21 Holt, *Rise and Fall of Whig Party*, 259–330, thoroughly explores the available candidates and the thinking about them.

22 Holman Hamilton, *Zachary Taylor: Soldier in the White House* (Indianapolis, Ind.: Bobbs-Merrill, 1951), 38–65, follows the rise of Taylor's candidacy. On Crittenden, see Albert D. Kirwan, *John J. Crittenden: The Struggle for the Union* (Lexington: University Press of Kentucky, 1962); on Corwin, see Norman Graebner, "Thomas A. Corwin and the Election of 1848," *Journal of Southern History* 17 (February 1951): 162–179. The quotation is from *Life of General Zachary Taylor, the Whig Candidate for the Presidency* (Boston: n.p., 1848), 16.

23 Robert C. Winthrop, *Memoir of Robert C. Winthrop, Prepared for the Massachusetts Historical Society* (Boston: Little, Brown, 1897), 24; John C. Critten-

den to Albert T. Burnley, January 8, 1848, cited in Kirwan, *Crittenden*, 226.

24 On the Young Indians, see Holt, *Rise and Fall of Whig Party*, 285–290; on Scott's liabilities, see Holt, *Rise and Fall of Whig Party*, 318.

25 Abraham Lincoln to Thomas Flournoy, February 17, 1848, in Roy P. Basler, ed., *Collected Works of Abraham Lincoln* (New Brunswick, N.J.: Rutgers University Press, 1953–1956), 1:452.

26 Holt, *Rise and Fall of Whig Party*, 285–290. On Webster's encounter with Taylor enthusiasts, see Robert Dalzell, *Daniel Webster and the Trial of American Nationalism, 1843–1852* (Boston: Houghton Mifflin, 1973), 137.

27 Holt, *Rise and Fall of Whig Party*, 315ff; Thomas Stevenson to John J. Crittenden, May 1, 1847, John J. Crittenden Papers, Library of Congress.

28 Columbus *Ohio State Journal*, April 21, 1848; Horace Greeley, *Recollections of a Busy Life* (New York: J. B. Ford, 1868), 215.

29 The sources cited in Notes 21 and 22 for this chapter cover the continuing maneuvers on behalf of the different candidates.

30 James F. Hopkins et al., eds., *The Papers of Henry Clay*, vol. 10 (Lexington: University Press of Kentucky, 1991), 361–377.

31 Henry Clay to Daniel Ullman, May 12, 1847, in ibid., 328–330; *A Northern No! Addressed to the Delegates from the Free States to the Whig National Convention* (n.p., 1848), 8.

32 On Taylor's letter-writing missteps, Hamilton, *Taylor*, and Holt, *Rise and Fall of the Whig Party*, cover the ground. See also Seth Hawley to Thurlow Weed, September 7, 1847, quoted in K. Jack Bauer, *Zachary Taylor: Soldier, Planter, Statesman of the Old Southwest* (Baton Rouge: Louisiana State University Press, 1985), 227.

33 As Henry Clay wrote before the party's convention, Taylor was "a sort of non-descript Whig, a Whig in name, without the principles of the Whigs." Clay to Horace Greeley, June 15, 1848, Hopkins, et al., *The Papers of Henry Clay*, vol. 10, 490.

34 M. J. Heale, *The Presidential Quest: Candidates and Images in American Political Culture, 1787–1852* (London: Longman, 1982), 127. The Allison letter is printed in Hamilton, "The Election of 1848," 913–914.

35 Louisville *Daily Journal*, May 3, 1848. U.S. Representative Robert Toombs of Georgia wrote in anger that Henry Clay "has behaved very badly this winter. His ambition is as fierce as at any time of his life, and he is determined to rule or ruin the party." Toombs to James Thomas, April 16, 1848, in Ulrich B. Phillips, ed., *The Correspondence of Robert Toombs, Alexander H. Stephens, and Howell Cobb: Annual Report of the American Historical Association, 1911* (Washington, D.C.: American Historical Association, 1913), 103.

36 *The Proceedings of the Democratic National Convention, Held at Baltimore, 1848* (Washington, D.C.: Democratic National Committee, 1848), passim. On Commander, see Rayback, *Free Soil*, 187; and Charleston *Mercury*, May 20, 1848.

37 On the Barnburners at Utica, see Gardiner, *Great Issue*, chap. 4; on "The

Barnburner Manifesto," that is, "Address of the Democratic Members of the Legislature of the State of New York, April 12, 1848," see John Bigelow, ed., *The Writings and Speeches of Samuel J. Tilden*, vol. 2 (New York: Harper, 1885), 537–574.

38 All of this is detailed in *Proceedings of Democratic Convention;* Gardiner, *Great Issue*, 96–137.

39 Raleigh (N.C.) *Standard*, May 24, 1848.

40 In addition to the material in *Proceedings of Democratic Convention*, 8, see the summary of the vote in *Congressional Quarterly's Guide to U.S. Elections* (Washington, D.C.: Congressional Quarterly Press, 1975), 124.

41 The balloting for president is listed in ibid., 124.

42 The Barnburner reaction and walkout is reported in several places. See, for example, Blue, *Free Soilers*, 47–48.

43 Alfred Balch to James K. Polk, October 25, 1847, James K. Polk Papers, Library of Congress. There has been little interest in King by historians, including those who have written about the election.

44 Kirk H. Porter and Donald Bruce Johnson, eds., *National Party Platforms, 1840–1964* (Urbana: University of Illinois Press, 1966), 10–12.

45 Ibid., 11.

46 Eric H. Walther, *William Lowndes Yancey and the Coming of the Civil War* (Chapel Hill: University of North Carolina Press, 2006), 102–103.

47 Thomas W. Thomas to Howell Cobb, June 5, 1848, in Phillips, *Correspondence of Toombs, Stephens, and Cobb*, 107; Milledgeville (Ga.) *Federal Union*, June 27, 1848; James Seddon to Robert M. T. Hunter, June 16, 1848, *Correspondence of Robert M. T. Hunter: Annual Report of the American Historical Association, 1916* (Washington, D.C.: American Historical Association, 1918), 91.

48 In addition to Walther, *Yancey*, see J. Mills Thornton III, *Politics and Power in a Slave Society: Alabama, 1800–1860* (Baton Rouge: Louisiana State University Press, 1978), 173–177.

49 Among many discussions of the Van Buren group's reaction, see John Niven, *Martin Van Buren: The Romantic Age of American Politics* (New York: Oxford University Press, 1983), 180–181. Their own perspective on what happened in Baltimore is "Report of the New York Delegates to the National Democratic Convention of 1848," in *Writings and Speeches of Tilden*, 232–247.

50 *Barnburner* 5, July 29, 1848.

51 Both Holt, *Rise and Fall of the Whig Party*, 320–330, and Hamilton, *Taylor*, 86–97, cover the events in Philadelphia.

52 Holt, *Rise and Fall of the Whig Party*, describes the backstage maneuvering.

53 In addition to Holt and Hamilton, Rayback, *Free Soil*, 196–198, describes the roll-call voting for the presidential nomination.

54 Hamilton, *Taylor*, 94–95.

55 The quotation is in Holt, *Rise and Fall of the Whig Party*, 327. See also Henry Clay to James Brooks, September 8, 1848, in Hopkins et al., *Papers of Henry Clay*, vol. 10, 534.

56 Hamilton, *Taylor*, 95–97; Rayback, *Free Soil*, 198–200, among others.

57 The resolutions adopted at the meeting are included in Porter and Johnson, *National Party Platforms*, 14–15.

58 *Young Guard* 4 (August 5, 1848); Henry Clay to Daniel Ullman, September 16, 1848, Daniel Ullman Papers, New York Historical Society.

59 Horace Greeley to Schuyler Colfax, September 15, 1848, Greeley-Colfax Correspondence, New York Public Library.

60 See Henry Wilson, *History of the Rise and Fall of the Slave Power in America*, vol. 2 (Boston: Houghton Mifflin, 1872–1877), 142–144.

61 See Note 49 to this chapter.

62 "'A Great Crisis Has Arrived': Address of the Free Territory Convention of the State of Ohio," Columbus, 1848.

63 Gardiner, *Great Issue*, 96–137.

64 Blue, *Free Soilers*, 58–59. Blue suggests that this meeting "proved to be the successful climax to the entire Conscience Whig movement" (59).

65 This was the tenor of statements by party leaders and comments by editors, perhaps with their fingers crossed. See, as one example, *Young Guard* 1 (July 4, 1848).

66 The various works cited on the development of the Free Soil Party all deal with the efforts under way. The quotation is from a speech by John Gorham Palfrey reported in the *Congressional Globe*, 30th Cong., 1st Sess., Appendix, 133.

67 See, among other sources, Sewell, *Ballots for Freedom*, 188–206.

68 Oliver Dyer, *Phonographic Reports of the Proceedings of the National Free Soil Convention* (Buffalo, 1848), 12; George W. Julian, *Political Recollections, 1840–1872* (Chicago, Ill.: Jansen, McClurg, 1884), 59.

69 On the Seneca Falls meeting, see Judith Wellman, *The Road to Seneca Falls: Elizabeth Cady Stanton and the First Woman's Rights Convention* (Urbana: University of Illinois Press, 2004).

70 See Dyer, *Phonographic Reports*, generally; and Gardiner, *Great Issue*, 151–176.

71 In addition to Dyer, Gardiner, and the other sources referred to, see also Henry B. Stanton, *Random Recollections* (New York: Macgowan and Slipper, 1887), 81.

72 Porter and Johnson, *National Party Platforms*, 13–14.

73 Ibid., 14.

74 Salmon P. Chase to John Parker Hale, June 5, 1848, in John Niven, ed., *The Salmon P. Chase Papers*, vol. 2 (Kent, Ohio: Kent State University Press, 1993–1998), 174.

75 See, among other sources, Blue, *Free Soilers*, 71. The crucial element was, as the non-Democrats among the Free Soilers kept repeating when contemplating Van Buren as their candidate, "it was part of the work of earnest antislavery men to forget party memories and prejudices for the sake of the cause." Julian, *Political Recollections*, 59.

76 Rayback, *Free Soil*, 229.

77 On Adams, see Martin Duberman, *Charles Francis Adams, 1807–1886* (Boston: Houghton Mifflin, 1960).

78 Sewell, *Ballots for Freedom*, 161–162; Porter and Johnson, *National Party Platforms*, 14.

79 Richard Carwardine, *Evangelicals and Politics in Antebellum America* (New Haven, Conn.: Yale University Press, 1993), 151.

80 Holt, *Rise and Fall of Whig Party*, 347–348.

81 Henry Clay to James Brooks, September 8, 1848, in Hopkins, et al., *Papers of Henry Clay*, vol. 10, 534.

82 See, for example, the Philadelphia *Pennsylvanian*, June 3, 1848, in an editorial titled "The New York Disorganizers," and September 5, 1848, in which the writer referred to "the heart-eating Revenge which is poisoning the sunset of his life."

83 Joseph Baldwin to George B. Saunders, June 12, 1848, in Malcolm C. McMillan, ed., "Joseph Baldwin Reports on the Whig National Convention of 1848," *Journal of Southern History* 25 (August 1959): 378; Columbus *Ohio State Journal*, June 16, 1848.

84 Horace Greeley to Schuyler Colfax, September 15, 1848, Greeley-Colfax Papers; Holt, *Rise and Fall of Whig Party*, 344ff.

85 L. E. Crittenden, *Personal Reminiscences, 1840–1890* (New York: Richmond, Croscup, 1893), 5. For the reaction of Van Buren's former associates, see, among others, Thomas Hart Benton, *Thirty Years' View*, vol. 2 (New York: Appleton, 1854–1856), 723; and John Wentworth to E. S. Kimberly, June 27, 1848, E. S. Kimberly Papers, Chicago Historical Society.

86 Morgan Dix, comp., *Memoirs of John Adams Dix*, vol. 1 (New York: Harper, 1883), 239.

87 *Campaign* 1, May 31, 1848.

88 Benjamin F. Wade to Elisha Whittlesy, July 3, 1848, quoted in Hans Trefousse, *Benjamin Franklin Wade: Radical Republican from Ohio* (New York: Twayne, 1963), 58. See also Stephen E. Maizlish, *The Triumph of Sectionalism: The Transformation of Ohio Politics, 1854–1856* (Kent, Ohio: Kent State University Press, 1983), 99–120.

89 *Charleston Mercury*, September 5, 1848; Isaac Stevenson to John J. Crittenden, September 24, 1848, John J. Crittenden Papers, Library of Congress; Manisha Sinha, *The Counterrevolution of Slavery: Politics and Ideology in Antebellum South Carolina* (Chapel Hill: University of North Carolina Press, 2000), 75–76.

90 Stephen A. Douglas to Lewis Cass, June 13, 1848, Lewis Cass Papers, William E. Clements Library, University of Michigan; William L. Yancey to John C. Calhoun, June 14, 1848, in Clyde N. Wilson, ed., *The Papers of John C. Calhoun*, vol. 25 (Columbia: University of South Carolina Press, 1999), 482.

91 Athens (Ga.) *Southern Banner*, June 1, 1848; James T. McIntosh, ed., *The Papers of Jefferson Davis*, vol. 3 (Baton Rouge: Louisiana State University Press, 1981), 375.

92 Howard H. Bell, "The National Negro Convention, 1848," *Ohio Historical Quarterly* 47 (October 1958): 364–365. On Douglass, see Frederick Douglass, *The Life and Times of Frederick Douglass* (Hartford, Conn.: Park, 1881), 721ff.

93 Dyer, *Phonographic Reports*, 13.

94 Edward L. Widmer, *Young America: The Flowering of Democracy in New York City* (New York: Oxford University Press, 1999).

95 The acceptance letters were reprinted in the main newspapers of the parties: the Democrats' *Union;* the Whigs' *National Intelligencer;* and the Free Soilers' *Barnburner.*

CHAPTER 4 "THE WORK TO BE DONE": THE PARTIES ORGANIZE

1 Springfield *Illinois State Register,* October 6, 1848.

2 Edwin Croswell to Horatio Seymour, July 29, 1848, Fairchild Collection, New York Historical Society.

3 Michael Holt, *The Rise and Fall of the American Whig Party: Jacksonian Politics and the Onset of Civil War* (New York: Oxford University Press, 1999), 331–382 and elsewhere, has a good discussion of the Whigs' outlook. See also Charles Sumner to Joshua R. Giddings, September 3, 1848, discussing the Free Soilers, in Francis P. Weisenburger, *Life of John McLean* (Columbus: Ohio State University Press, 1937), 138.

4 *Albany Atlas* quoted in *New York Globe,* October 6, 1848; Albany *Evening Journal,* August 1, 1848; *Battery,* August 3, 1848.

5 *Nashville Union,* October 19, 1848; *Barnburner* 5 (July 29, 1848).

6 *Congressional Quarterly's Guide to U.S. Elections* (Washington, D.C.: Congressional Quarterly Press, 1975), 268, 369ff, 587–588.

7 Holt, *Rise and Fall of the Whig Party,* 354ff.

8 Joel H. Silbey, *The American Political Nation, 1838–1893* (Stanford, Calif.: Stanford University Press, 1991), 47–61; Roy F. Nichols, *The Invention of the American Political Parties* (New York: Macmillan, 1967), 328–377.

9 Nichols, *Invention;* Richard Sewell, *Ballots for Freedom: Anti-Slavery Politics in the United States, 1837–1860* (New York: Oxford University Press, 1973), 166.

10 Groton, Mass. *Spirit of the Times,* September 6, 1848; Milledgeville (Ga.) *Federal Union,* May 23, 1848.

11 Holman Hamilton, *Zachary Taylor: Soldier in the White House* (Indianapolis, Ind.: Bobbs-Merrill, 1951), 113.

12 *New York Daily Globe,* October 6, 1848; Albany *Evening Journal,* October 21, 1848.

13 Columbus *Ohio State Journal,* September 28, 1848; *Sketch of the Life and Public Services of General Zachary Taylor, the People's Candidate for the Presidency* (Washington, 1848), 32.

14 *Recruit,* October 3, 1848; Richard John, *Spreading the News: The American Postal System from Franklin to Morse* (Cambridge, Mass.: Harvard University Press, 1995).

15 Silbey, *American Political Nation,* 54–55.

16 George H. Hickman, comp., *The Democratic Textbook, Being a Compendium of Principles of the Democratic Party* (Boston, 1848).

17 The quotation is from George Hickman, *The Life of General Lewis Cass with His Letters and Speeches on Various Subjects* (Baltimore, 1848), 72. There is no author listed for *People's Life of General Zachary Taylor* (Philadelphia, 1848).

18 *Spirit of the Times,* October 25, 1848.

19 There are discussions of these matters in Holt, *Rise and Fall of the Whig Party;* Hamilton, *Taylor;* and, in one state, William H. Adams, *The Whig Party of Louisiana* (Lafayette: University of Southwestern Louisiana Press, 1973), 178.

20 Rallies are reported in all of the campaign newspapers. William Gienapp, "'Politics Seems to Enter into Everything': Political Culture in the North, 1840–1860," in Stephen E. Maizlish and John J. Kushma, eds., *Essays on American Antebellum Politics, 1840–1860* (College Station: Texas A&M University Press, 1982), 32ff, and passim, places these events in context.

21 See the description of Abraham Lincoln's speaking tour of Massachusetts after the Whig convention in William F. Hanna, *Abraham among the Yankees: Abraham Lincoln's 1848 Visit to Massachusetts* (Taunton, Mass.: Old Colony Historical Society, 1983).

22 See Edwin Croswell to Horatio Seymour, February 22, 1848, Fairchild Collection, in which Croswell is lining up Seymour for speaking engagements. The quotation is in Gienapp, "'Politics Seems to Enter into Everything,'" 34. On Seward, see Glyndon G. Van Deusen, *William Henry Seward* (New York: Oxford University Press, 1967), 109–110.

23 Hanna, *Abraham among the Yankees,* 79 and passim.

24 Oliver Dyer, *Phonographic Reports of the Proceedings of the National Free Soil Convention* (Buffalo, 1848), 27–28.

25 See William J. Parrish, *David Rice Atchison of Missouri: Border Politician* (Columbia: University of Missouri Press, 1961), 70–71; Robert Johannsen, *Stephen A. Douglas* (New York: Oxford University Press, 1973), 231–233.

26 Elizabeth Varon, *We Mean to Be Counted: White Women and Politics in Antebellum Virginia* (Chapel Hill: University of North Carolina Press, 1998), 94–95; Richard H. Sewell, *Ballots for Freedom: Antislavery Politics in the United States, 1837–1860* (New York: Oxford University Press, 1976), 160ff.

27 Robert J. Dinkin, *Campaigning in America: A History of Election Practices* (Westport, Conn.: Greenwood, 1989), 37.

28 George W. Julian, *Political Recollections, 1840–1872* (Chicago, Ill.: Jansen, McClurg, 1884), 66–67.

29 There is a general discussion of these efforts in the mid-nineteenth century in Dinkin, *Campaigning in America,* 40; and in Silbey, *American Political Nation,* 55–56. The quotation is from Dinkin, 40.

30 Willard Klunder, *Lewis Cass and the Politics of Moderation* (Kent, Ohio: Kent State University Press, 1996), 176; Oliver Dyer, *Great Senators of the United States Forty Years Ago* (New York: R. Bonner's Sons, 1889), 45; Hamilton, *Taylor,* 21. Van Buren is described by his various biographers.

31 Hamilton, *Taylor,* 127.

32 *Illinois State Register,* August 11, 1848.

33 Adams, *Whig Party of Louisiana,* 178.

34 Hickman, *Democratic Textbook,* 4.

35 On election days in this era see Silbey, *American Political Nation,* 141–158.

CHAPTER 5 "THERE NEVER WAS AN ELECTION ... OF GREATER
IMPORTANCE": THE PARTIES DEFINE WHAT IS AT STAKE

1 The second Allison letter is reprinted in Holman Hamilton, "The Election of
  1848," in Arthur M. Schlesinger, Jr., and Fred L. Israel, eds., *History of American Presidential Elections*, vol. 2 (New York: Chelsea House, 1971), 917.
2 *The Windings and Turnings of Martin Van Buren* (n.p., 1848), 6.
3 Holman Hamilton, *Zachary Taylor: Soldier in the White House* (Indianapolis,
  Ind.: Bobbs-Merrill, 1951), 125.
4 In 1844, in states such as Ohio, Pennsylvania, New York, Georgia, and Indiana, the popular vote difference between the parties was less than 3 percent
  of the total. Michael Holt, *The Rise and Fall of the American Whig Party: Jacksonian Politics and the Onset of the Civil War* (New York: Oxford University Press,
  1999) and Joel H. Silbey, *The American Political Nation, 1838–1893* (Stanford,
  Calif.: Stanford University Press, 1991) have much material on the calculations of party leaders that stemmed from the reality of narrow vote totals.
5 *Sketch of the Life and Public Service of General Zachary Taylor, the People's Candidate for the Presidency* (Washington, D.C.: J. T. Towers, 1848), 32.
6 As was clear in the Democratic platform and in many of the speeches offered during the campaign.
7 See Chapters 1 and 2 of this volume.
8 Much of this is covered in Joseph Rayback, *Free Soil: The Election of 1848*
  (Lexington: University Press of Kentucky, 1970); and Hamilton, *Taylor*,
  among others.
9 *Grape Shot* 10 (September 1, 1948).
10 *American Whig Review* 8 (August 1848): 199; *Congressional Globe*, 30th
  Cong., 1st Sess., Appendix, 783.
11 *Sketch of Life and Public Service of General Taylor*, 1, 15, 23, 25, 29.
12 Ibid., 26, 30.
13 Ibid., 32.
14 Willard Klunder, *Lewis Cass and the Politics of Moderation* (Kent, Ohio: Kent
  State University Press, 1997), 205–206; *Congressional Globe*, 30th Cong., 1st
  Sess., Appendix., 1042.
15 *Facts for Those Who Will Understand Them: General Cass's Position on the
  Slavery Question Defined by Himself and His Friends* (n.p., 1848), passim;
  "The Cass Platform" (Washington, 1848), passim; *Congressional Globe*, 30th
  Cong., 1st Sess., Appendix, 812.
16 Holt, *Rise and Fall of the Whig Party*, and William J. Cooper, *The South and the
  Politics of Slavery, 1828–1856* (Baton Rouge: Louisiana State University Press,
  1978), discuss these matters effectively.
17 Cooper, *South and Politics*, 265; Rayback, *Free Soil*, 242.
18 Millard Fillmore to John Gayle, July 31, 1848, in Frank H. Severance, ed.,
  Millard Fillmore Papers, vol. 9 (Buffalo, N.Y.: Buffalo Historical Society,
  1907), 280; *Facts for Those Who Will Understand Them*, 8.
19 *Address Adopted by the Whig State Convention . . . Worcester, September 13, 1848*
  (n.p., 1848), 12.

20 Lincoln argued several times that Cass would be subservient to southern demands and only Taylor would prevent the further extension of slavery. See his speech in Worcester, Massachusetts, in William F. Hanna, *Abraham among the Yankees: Abraham Lincoln's 1848 Visit to Massachusetts* (Taunton, Mass.: Old Colony Historical Society, 1983), 30ff. See also Caleb Smith's speech to his constituents in *National Intelligencer*, July 20, 1848.

21 *The Windings and Turnings of Van Buren*, 1–2; *The Van Buren Platform, or Facts for the Present Supporters of Martin Van Buren* (n.p., 1848), 8; William Seward to Orleans County Whigs, no date, quoted in Frederick W. Seward, *Seward at Washington, as Senator and Secretary of State: A Memoir of His Life with Selections from His Letters, 1846–1872*, vol. 1 (New York: Derby and Miller, 1891), 77.

22 *New York Globe*, November 2, 1848; Holt, *Rise and Fall of the Whig Party*, chap. 11.

23 *American Whig Review* 7 (May 1848): 532; *American Whig Review* 8 (December 1848): 560; *Grape Shot* 14 (September 30, 1848).

24 Washington *National Intelligencer*, July 20, 1848; *Congressional Globe*, 30th Cong., 1st Sess., Appendix, 942.

25 *Chicago Journal*, September 12 and November 1, 1848; *National Intelligencer*, September 7, 1848; *Sketch of Life and Public Service of General Taylor*, 30.

26 Rayback, *Free Soil*, 266–267.

27 *Chicago Journal*, September 12 and November 11, 1848; Philadelphia *Inquirer*, September 12, 1848, quoted in Henry R. Mueller, *The Whig Party of Pennsylvania* (New York: Columbia University Press, 1922), 153; *National Intelligencer*, September 7, 1848.

28 Holt, *Rise and Fall of the Whig Party*, 354, 365ff.

29 *New York Globe*, November 3, 1848; *Recruit*, August 1, 1848.

30 Washington *Union*, April 11, 1848; Daniel S. Dickinson to S. Brewster, October 23, 1848, Fairchild Collection, New York Historical Society.

31 *Campaign* 5 (June 28, 1848); *Recruit*, June 8, 1848.

32 *Taylor Whiggery Exposed* (Washington, 1848), 3; George H. Hickman, comp., *The Democratic Textbook: A Compendium of the Principles of the Democratic Party* (Boston: n.p., 1848), 3; *Congressional Globe*, 30th Cong., 1st sess., Appendix, 856; Columbus *Ohio Statesman*, September 6, 1848.

33 *Young Guard* 1 (July 4, 1848); *Nashville Union*, October 28, 1848; Silbey, *American Political Nation*, 84.

34 This charge was repeated in various issues of the *Campaign* throughout the fall. See also Klunder, *Cass*, 208.

35 George H. Hickman, *The Life of General Lewis Cass with His Letters and Speeches on Various Subjects* (Baltimore, 1848), introductory page, and 72; *Campaign* 14 (August 30, 1848).

36 Hickman, *Life of Cass*, 13.

37 *Congressional Globe*, 30th Cong., 1st Sess., 799; *Campaign* 1 (May 31, 1848); *Campaign* 19 (October 2, 1848); *Taylor Whiggery Exposed*, 3; Daniel S. Dickinson, "Speech at Tammany Hall, August 19, 1848," in *Speeches, Correspondence, etc. of the Late Daniel S. Dickinson of New York*, vol. 1 (New York:

Putnam, 1867), 272; *United States Magazine and Democratic Review* 23 (October 1848): 208.

38 Benjamin F. Hallet, *Facts for Candid Men and True Democrats* (Albany, 1848), 4; Springfield *Illinois State Register*, June 23, 1848; Dickinson, "Speech at Tammany Hall," in *Speeches, Correspondence*, vol. 1, 272; *Recruit*, October 17, 1848; Silbey, *American Political Nation*, 91.

39 *Campaign* 13 (August 23, 1848), *Campaign* 20 (October 11, 1848); Washington *Union*, June 22, 1848; *Taylor Whiggery Exposed*, 8.

40 Hallet, *Facts for Candid Men*, 14; *Recruit*, August 15, 1848; Benton is quoted in Elbert Smith, *Magnificent Missourian: The Life of Thomas Hart Benton* (Philadelphia, Pa.: Lippincott, 1957), 177, 241; John Wentworth to E. S. Kimberly, E. S. Kimberly Papers, Chicago Historical Society.

41 *Ohio Statesman*, July 1 and September 14, 1848; James Y. Mason to Lewis Cass, September 25, 1848, Lewis Cass Papers, William E. Clements Library, University of Michigan.

42 *Recruit*, August 1, 1848; *Congressional Globe*, 30th Cong., 1st Sess., 1021, Appendix, 796.

43 *Congressional Globe*, 30th Cong., 1st Sess., Appendix, 963; *The Papers of Jefferson Davis*, vol. 1 (Baton Rouge: Louisiana State University Press, 1971), 385.

44 Cobb's speech is in the *Congressional Globe*, 30th Cong., 1st Sess., Appendix, 775. See also ibid., 966.

45 *To the Intelligent and Humane Voters of Pennsylvania* (n.p., 1848), 1; *Young Guard* 13 (October 7, 1848); *Cass and Taylor on the Slavery Question* (Boston, 1848), 4; *Free Soil Almanac, 1849* (Rochester, 1848), 17.

46 New York *Evening Post*, October 1, 1848; New York *Evening Post*, October 6, 1848; *Barnburner* 9 (August 26, 1848); *Cass and Taylor on the Slavery Question*, 4.

47 *Albany Atlas*, September 5 1848; *Albany Atlas*, September 9, 1848; *Evening Post*, October 14, 1848; *Free Soil Almanac*, 17.

48 *Barnburner* 7 (August 11, 1848); *New York Globe*, November 6, 1848.

49 Kirk H. Porter and Donald B. Johnson, *National Party Platforms, 1840–1964* (Urbana: University of Illinois Press, 1967), 13–14.

50 This was a long-standing and growing perspective among northerners, now greatly aggravated by the battle over Texas annexation and the Mexican cession. See Leonard I. Richards, *The Slave Power: The Free North and Southern Domination, 1780–1860* (Baton Rouge: Louisiana State University Press, 2000).

51 George W. Julian, *Political Recollections, 1840–1872* (Chicago, Ill.: Jansen, McClurg, 1884), 51; *Cass and Taylor, Is Either Worthy of a Freeman's Suffrage?* (n.p., 1848), 1; *To the Intelligent and Humane Voters of Pennsylvania*, 4; Washington *National Era*, October 24, 1848, quoted in Frederick Blue, *The Free Soilers: Third-Party Politics, 1848–1854* (Urbana: University of Illinois Press, 1973), 125.

52 *Barnburner* 10 (September 24, 1848); *The Cass Platform*, 8.

53 *Free Soil Almanac*, 19, 23.

54 *New York Globe*, September 26, 1848; *Barnburner* 7 (August 11, 1848).

55 Edward O. Schriver, "Antislavery: The Free Soil and Free Democratic Parties in Maine, 1848–1855," *New England Quarterly* 42 (March 1969): 84; *Albany Atlas*, October 10, 1849.

56 *Barnburner* 7 (August 11, 1848).

57 George W. Patterson to Thurlow Weed, August 24, 1848, in Hamilton, *Taylor*, 114; *Cass and Taylor, Is Either Worthy of a Freeman's Suffrage*, 1, 23.

58 *Free Soil Almanac*, 19.

59 *Democratic Review* 23 (November 1848): 381; Columbus *Ohio State Journal*, October 13, 1848.

60 *Democratic Review* 23 (November 1848): 381; Columbus *Ohio State Journal*, October 13, 1848.

CHAPTER 6 "THE PRESENCE OF EVERY MAN IS NECESSARY": ZACHARY TAYLOR IS ELECTED

1 I have relied on newspaper reports and the descriptions by several historians to recreate election day 1848. See, for example, the *Battery* 5 (October 12, 1848); Kenneth J. Winkle, *The Politics of Community: Migration and Politics in Antebellum Ohio* (New York: Cambridge University Press, 1988); Richard Bensel, *The American Ballot Box in the Mid-Nineteenth Century* (New York: Cambridge University Press, 2004); Joel H. Silbey, *The American Political Nation, 1838–1891* (Stanford, Calif.: Stanford University Press, 1991).

2 Richmond *Whig*, November 7, 1848; *Albany Atlas*, November 6, 1848.

3 Winkle, *Politics of Community*, and Bensel, *American Ballot Box*, describe the process of voting.

4 On who is eligible to vote, see Alexander Keyssar, *The Right to Vote: The Contested History of Democracy in the United States* (New York: Basic Books, 2000), 26–76.

5 See Winkle, *Politics of Community*; Bensel, *American Ballot Box*; Glenn C. Altschuler and Stuart M. Blumin, *Rude Republic: Americans and Their Politics in the Nineteenth Century* (Princeton, N.J.: Princeton University Press, 2000), 69ff.

6 Michael F. Holt, *The Rise and Fall of the American Whig Party: Jacksonian Politics and the Onset of the Civil War* (New York: Oxford University Press, 1999). For other returns, see *Congressional Quarterly's Guide to U.S. Elections* (Washington, D.C.: Congressional Quarterly Press, 1975); Michael J. Dubin, *United States Congressional Elections, 1789–1997: The Official Results* (Jefferson, N.C.: McFarland, 1998).

7 Charleston *Mercury*, October 21, 1848.

8 Thomas P. Alexander, "Harbinger of the Collapse of the Second Two-Party System: The Free Soil Party of 1848," in Lloyd E. Ambrosius, ed., *A Crisis of Republicanism: American Politics during the Civil War Era* (Lincoln: University of Nebraska Press, 1990), 24ff. The voting numbers vary depending on the source. I have relied primarily on *Congressional Quarterly's Guide*.

9 +.90 signifies a very strong statistical relationship.

10 Dubin, *U.S. Congressional Elections*, 150, 159.

11 The final results are listed in the *Biographical Directory of the United States Congress, 1774–1989* (Washington, D.C.: Government Printing Office, 1989), 147–150. On the Ohio coalition, see Stephen E. Maizlish, *The Triumph of Sectionalism: The Transformation of Ohio Politics, 1844–1856* (Kent, Ohio: Kent State University Press, 1983), 124ff.

12 Dubin, *U.S. Congressional Elections*, 151–157.

13 See Chapter 1 of this volume.

14 Silbey, *American Political Nation*, chap. 8; Thomas P. Alexander, "The Dimensions of Voter Partisan Constancy in Presidential Elections from 1840–1860," in Stephen E. Maizlish and John J. Kushma, eds., *Essays on American Antebellum Politics, 1840–1860* (College Station: Texas A&M University Press, 1982), 70–121.

15 *A Northern No! Address to the Delegates from the Free States to the Whig National Convention at Philadelphia, 1848* (n.p., 1848), 5; Frederick J. Blue, *The Free Soilers: Third-Party Politics, 1848–1854* (Urbana: University of Illinois Press, 1973), 130.

16 David Wilmot to Salmon P. Chase, May 29, 1848, in Charles B. Going, *David Wilmot, Free Soiler: A Biography* (New York: Appleton, 1924), 321; Albany *Argus*, November 28, 1848.

17 Sean Wilentz, *The Rise of American Democracy: Jefferson to Lincoln* (New York: Norton, 2005), 630.

18 Holt, *Rise and Fall of the Whig Party*, 370.

19 Peyton McCrary et al., "Class and Party in the Secession Crisis: Voting Behavior in the Deep South, 1856–1861," *Journal of Interdisciplinary History* 8 (Winter 1978), reported in Holt, *Rise and Fall of the Whig Party*, 370; Joseph F. Cooper to Howell Cobb, November 11, 1848, in Ulrich B. Phillips, ed., *The Correspondence of Robert Toombs, Alexander H. Stephens, and Howell Cobb: Annual Report of the American Historical Association, 1911* (Washington, D.C.: American Historical Association, 1913), 157.

20 *Nashville Union*, October 23, 1848.

21 Holt, *Rise and Fall of the Whig Party*, 370.

22 John F. Kirn, "Voters, Parties, and Legislative Politics in New York State, 1846–1876," unpublished Ph.D. diss., University of Virginia, 2003), 381; Lex Renda, *Running on the Record: Civil War Era Politics in New Hampshire* (Charlottesville: University of Virginia Press, 1997), 31.

23 See Holt, *Rise and Fall of the Whig Party*; Alexander, "Voter Partisan Constancy," in Maizlish and Kushma, *Essays*.

24 Kirn, "Voters, Parties, and Legislative Politics," 355–475.

25 On the Midwest, see Ray Shortridge, "Voting for Minor Parties in the Antebellum Midwest," *Indiana Magazine of History* 74 (June 1978): 130–131; on Massachusetts, see Kevin Sweeney, "Rum, Romanism, Representation, and Reform: Coalition Politics in Massachusetts, 1847–1853," *Civil War History* 22 (June 1976): 116–137; Alexander, "Voter Partisan Constancy," in Maizlish and Kushma, *Essays*, 96; Alexander, "Harbinger of the Collapse of the Second Party System," in Ambrosius, *Crisis of Republicanism*, 25.

26 See Joel H. Silbey, *Storm over Texas: The Annexation Controversy and the Road to Civil War* (New York: Oxford University Press, 2005).

27 Alexander, "Harbinger of the Collapse of the Second Party System," in Ambrosius, *Crisis of Republicanism*, 25.

28 Holt, *Rise and Fall of the Whig Party*, 374; Alexander, "Voter Partisan Constancy," in Maizlish and Kushma, *Essays*, 117.

29 See Table 6.2.

30 Holt, *Rise and Fall of the Whig Party*, 331–382; Kirn, "Voters, Parties, and Legislative Politics," 355–475; Alexander, "Harbinger of the Collapse of the Second Party System," in Ambrosius, *Crisis of Republicanism*, passim.

31 For an overview of the state's politics, see Charles M. Snyder, *The Jacksonian Heritage: Pennsylvania Politics, 1833–1848* (Harrisburg: Pennsylvania Historical and Museum Commission, 1958).

32 Holt, *Rise and Fall of the Whig Party*, 331–382, has the fullest discussion of this. Hendrick Wright to James Buchanan, November 13, 1848, in Snyder, *Jacksonian Heritage*, 218. See also James Buchanan to George Bancroft, December 11, 1848, in Mark A. DeWolfe Howe, ed., *Life and Letters of George Bancroft*, vol. 2 (New York: Charles Scribner's Sons, 1908), 40; Zachary Taylor to R. C. Wood, December 10, 1848, in *Letters of Zachary Taylor from the Battlefields of the Mexican War* (Rochester, N.Y.: n.p. [Genesee Press], 1908), 168.

33 See the discussions in Rayback, *Free Soil;* Blue, *The Free Soilers;* and Alexander, "Harbinger of the Collapse of the Second Party System," in Ambrosius, *Crisis of Republicanism*, 24ff.

34 *Albany Atlas*, November 8, 1848.

CHAPTER 7 "A CONSPICUOUS MILESTONE IN THE ANTISLAVERY JOURNEY"—OR NOT

1 *American Whig Review* 8 (December 1848): 560; Millard Fillmore to "a Friend," n.d., in Frank Severance, ed., *Millard Fillmore Papers*, vol. 2 (Buffalo, N.Y.: Buffalo Historical Society, 1907), 285–286. Another leading Whig was less sure. Horace Greeley saw the results of a victory that had been fought on personalities, not principles, as disastrous for the Whigs. "They were at once triumphant and undone." Horace Greeley, *Recollections of a Busy Life* (New York: J. B. Ford, 1868), 214–215.

2 Martin Van Buren, *An Inquiry into the Origin and Course of Political Parties in the United States* (New York: Hurd and Houghton, 1867), 354; *New York Globe*, November 8, 1848; *Barnburner* 9 (August 6, 1848).

3 Charles Sumner to Salmon P. Chase, November 16, 1848, quoted in David Donald, *Charles Sumner and the Coming of the Civil War* (New York: Knopf, 1960), 168–169.

4 Holman Hamilton, *Zachary Taylor: Soldier in the White House* (Indianapolis, Ind.: Bobbs-Merrill, 1951), 149–155.

5 James D. Richardson, comp., *A Compilation of the Messages and Papers of the Presidents, 1789–1902*, vol. 5 (Washington, D.C.: Bureau of National Literature and Art, 1905), 4–6.

6 Hamilton, *Taylor*, 158.

7 Michael F. Holt, *The Rise and Fall of the American Whig Party: Jacksonian Politics and the Onset of the Civil War* (New York: Oxford University Press, 1999), 383–458. Lincoln's patronage failure is mentioned on p. 420.

8 Holman Hamilton, *Prologue to Conflict: The Crisis and Compromise of 1850* (Lexington: University Press of Kentucky, 1964).

9 Ibid. See also Frederick J. Blue, *The Free Soilers: Third Party Politics, 1848–1854* (Urbana: University of Illinois Press, 1973), 188–206.

10 Hamilton, *Prologue to Conflict*; Thelma Jennings, *The Nashville Convention: Southern Movements for Unity, 1848–1851* (Memphis, Tenn.: Memphis State University Press, 1980).

11 Richard H. Sewell, *Ballots for Freedom: Antislavery Politics in the United States, 1837–1860* (New York: Oxford University Press, 1976), 202–230.

12 Roy and Jeanette Nichols, "The Election of 1852," in Arthur M. Schlesinger, Jr., and Fred L. Israel, eds., *History of American Presidential Elections, 1789–1968*, vol. 2 (New York: Chelsea House, 1971), 921–1003.

13 George W. Julian, *Political Recollections, 1840–1872* (Chicago, Ill.: Jansen, McClurg, 1884), 56; Salmon P. Chase to Charles Sumner, November 27, 1848, in John Niven, ed., *The Salmon P. Chase Papers*, vol. 2 (Kent, Ohio: Kent State University Press, 1993–1998), 195.

14 Steven Maizlish, *The Triumph of Sectionalism: The Transformation of Ohio Politics, 1844–1856* (Kent, Ohio: Kent State University Press, 1983), 120; William Brock, *Parties and Political Conscience: American Dilemmas, 1840–1850* (Millwood, N.Y.: K.T.O. Press, 1979), 231; Sean Wilentz, *The Rise of American Democracy: Jefferson to Lincoln* (New York: Norton, 2005), 632; Sewell, *Ballots for Freedom*, 169.

15 Joel H. Silbey, "The Civil War Synthesis in American Political History," *Civil War History* 10 (June 1964): 130–140; Robert Swierenga, *Beyond the Civil War Synthesis: Political Essays of the Civil War Era* (Westport, Conn.: Greenwood, 1975).

16 Sewell, *Ballots for Freedom*, 202.

17 *Congressional Globe*, 30th Cong., 1st Sess., Appendix, 189; Blue, *Free Soilers*, 150.

18 William H. Seward to Salmon P. Chase, March 24, 1847, in Niven, ed., *The Correspondence of Chase*, vol. 2, 146.

19 See Joel H. Silbey, *The Partisan Imperative: The Dynamics of American Politics before the Civil War* (New York: Oxford University Press, 1985).

20 On the importance of 1854 to 1856, see, among many others, Paul Kleppner, *The Third Electoral System, 1853–1892: Parties, Voters, and Political Cultures* (Chapel Hill: University of North Carolina Press, 1979); and especially William E. Gienapp, *Origins of the Republican Party, 1852–1856* (New York: Oxford University Press, 1987). The 1850s and the collapse of the political system are described in Michael F. Holt, *The Political Crisis of the 1850s* (New York: John Wiley, 1978).

21 *To the People of Ohio, Proceedings and Address of the Democratic State Convention Held at Columbus, May 10, 1848* (Columbus, 1848), 15.

BIBLIOGRAPHIC ESSAY

There is an enormous body of scholarly literature on U.S. politics in the 1840s. The following includes those works that have been most helpful in my research. Two studies of the election published in the early 1970s stand out for their coverage. Joseph Rayback, *Free Soil: The Election of 1848* (Lexington: University Press of Kentucky, 1970); and Homan Hamilton, *Zachary Taylor: Soldier in the White House* (Indianapolis, Ind.: Bobbs-Merrill, 1971). Hamilton's essay "The Election of 1848," in Arthur M. Schlesinger, Jr., and Fred L. Israel, eds., *History of American Presidential Elections*, vol. 2 (New York: Chelsea House, 1971), 865–918, is a shorter version that summarizes what happened. Richard Sewell, *Ballots for Freedom: Antislavery Politics in the United States, 1837–1860* (New York: Oxford University Press, 1976), and Frederick Blue, *The Free Soilers: Third-Party Politics, 1848–1854* (Urbana: University of Illinois Press, 1973), deal effectively with the rise of political antislavery.

On the nature of the political world in which the parties competed, Michael J. Heale, *The Presidential Quest* (London: Longman, 1982); William R. Brock, *Parties and Political Conscience: American Dilemmas, 1840–1850* (Millwood, N.Y.: K.T.O. Press, 1979); Joel H. Silbey, *The American Political Nation, 1838–1893* (Stanford, Calif.: Stanford University Press, 1991); Sean Wilentz, *The Rise of American Democracy: Jefferson to Lincoln* (New York: Norton, 2005); and Daniel Walker Howe, *What Hath God Wrought: The Transformation of America, 1815–1848* (New York: Oxford University Press, 2007) are ambitious and useful efforts to give shape and meaning to the antebellum United States. John Ashworth, *Slavery, Capitalism, and Politics in the Antebellum Republic*, vol. 1: *Commerce and Compromise, 1820–1850* (London: Royal Historical Society, 1995); Harry Watson, *Liberty and Power: The Politics of Jacksonian America* (New York: Hill and Wang, 1990); Roy Nichols, *The Invention of American Political Parties: A Study of Political Improvisation* (New York: Macmillan, 1967); Alex Keyssar, *The Right to Vote: The Contested History of Democracy in the United States* (New York: Basic Books, 2000); two books by Robert J. Dinkin, *Campaigning in America: A History of Election Practices* (Westport, Conn.: Greenwood, 1989) and *Election Day: A Documentary History* (Westport, Conn.: Greenwood, 2002); and Richard John, *Spreading the News: The American Postal System from Franklin to Morse* (Cambridge, Mass.: Harvard University Press, 1995) make important contributions to our understanding of the era as well. The underlying economic forces helping to shape the political realm are discussed in Douglas C. North, *The Economic Growth of the United States, 1790–1860* (Englewood Cliffs, N.J.: Prentice-Hall, 1961); George Rogers Taylor, *The Transportation Revolution, 1815–1860* (New York: Rinehart, 1951); and Paul Wallace Gates, *The Farmers Age: Agriculture, 1815–1860* (New York: Holt and Rinehart, 1960); among others.

The Whig Party has been well served by historians. George Rawlings Poage, *Henry Clay and the Whig Party* (Chapel Hill: University of North Carolina Press, 1936), still offers a great deal although it has been largely superseded, first by Daniel Walker Howe, *The Political Culture of the American Whigs* (Chicago, Ill.: University of Chicago Press, 1979), and exhaustively by Michael F. Holt's *The Rise and Fall of the American Whig Party: Jacksonian Politics and the Onset of the Civil War* (New York: Oxford University Press, 1999). There is nothing comparable for the Democrats, but Michael Holt has a brief, useful survey of the party in the antebellum years in his *Political Parties and American Political Development from the Age of Jackson to the Age of Lincoln* (Baton Rouge: Louisiana State University Press, 1992). There are fine biographies of the party's major political figures in the election in Willard C. Klunder, *Lewis Cass and the Politics 'of Moderation* (Kent, Ohio: Kent State University Press, 1996); Charles Sellers, *James K. Polk: Continentalist, 1843–1846* (Princeton, N.J.: Princeton University Press, 1957); John Niven, *Martin Van Buren: The Romantic Age of American Politics* (New York: Oxford University Press, 1983); Donald Cole, *Martin Van Buren and the American Political System* (Princeton, N.J.: Princeton University Press, 1984); and Joel H. Silbey, *Martin Van Buren and the Emergence of American Popular Politics* (Lanham, Md.: Rowman and Littlefield, 2005). Other important leaders are covered in Charles Going, *David Wilmot, Free Soiler: A Biography* (New York: Appleton, 1924); John Niven, *Gideon Welles: Lincoln's Secretary of the Navy* (New York: Oxford University Press, 1973); John M. Belohavek, *George Mifflin Dallas: Jacksonian Patrician* (University Park: Pennsylvania State University Press, 1977); Don E. Fehrenbacher, *Chicago Giant: A Biography of "Long John" Wentworth* (Madison: University of Wisconsin Press, 1957); Elbert B. Smith, *Magnificent Missourian: The Life of Thomas Hart Benton* (Philadelphia, Pa.: Lippincott, 1957); Roy F. Nichols, *Franklin Pierce: Young Hickory of the Granite Hills* (Philadelphia: University of Pennsylvania Press, 1931); Philip S. Klein, *President James Buchanan: A Biography* (University Park: Pennsylvania State University Press, 1962); Richard Sewell, *John Parker Hale and the Politics of Abolition* (Cambridge, Mass.: Harvard University Press, 1965); Robert Johannsen, *Stephen A. Douglas* (New York: Oxford University Press, 1973); James Shenton, *Robert John Walker: A Politician from Jackson to Lincoln* (New York: Columbia University Press, 1961); and John A. Garraty, *Silas Wright* (New York: Columbia University Press, 1949).

In addition to Sellers's biography of the president, understanding the Polk administration begins with Paul Bergeron, *The Presidency of James K. Polk* (Lawrence: University Press of Kansas, 1987); David Pletcher, *The Diplomacy of Annexation: Texas, Oregon, and the Mexican War* (Columbia: University of Missouri Press, 1973); Michael A. Morrison, *Slavery and the American West: The Eclipse of Manifest Destiny and the Coming of the Civil War* (Chapel Hill: University of North Carolina Press, 1997); Chaplain W. Morrison, *Democratic Politics and Sectionalism: The Wilmot Proviso Controversy* (Chapel Hill: University of North Carolina Press, 1967); Joel H. Silbey, *Storm over Texas: The Annexation Controversy and the Road to Civil War* (New York: Oxford University Press, 2005); William Dusinberre, *Slaveholder President: The Double Career of James Polk* (New York: Oxford

University Press, 2003); and, more generally, Leonard Richards, *The Slave Power: The Free North and Southern Domination, 1780–1860* (Baton Rouge: Louisiana State University Press, 2000).

The breakup of the New York Democrats is the subject of Herbert D. A. Donovan, *The Barnburners* (New York: New York University Press, 1925); and two unpublished doctoral dissertations: Walter Ferree, "The New York Democracy: Division and Reunion, 1847–1852," University of Pennsylvania, 1953; and Judah Ginsburg, "The Tangled Web: The New York Democratic Party and the Slavery Controversy, 1844–1860," University of Wisconsin, 1974. More recent analyses include Jonathan Earle, *Jacksonian Democracy and the Politics of Free Soil, 1824–1854* (Chapel Hill: University of North Carolina Press, 2004); and Yonatan Eyal, *The Young America Movement and the Transformation of the Democratic Party, 1828–1861* (Cambridge, U.K.: Cambridge University Press, 2007).

On the Whig leaders, in addition to Hamilton's biography of Taylor, see K. Jack Bauer, *Zachary Taylor: Soldier, Planter, Statesman of the Old Southwest* (Baton Rouge: Louisiana State University Press, 1985); Glyndon Van Deusen, *William Henry Seward* (New York: Oxford University Press, 1967); Robert Rayback, *Millard Fillmore: Biography of a President* (Buffalo, N.Y.: Buffalo Historical Society, 1959); Albert Kirwan, *John J. Crittenden: The Struggle for the Union* (Lexington: University Press of Kentucky, 1962); Robert Remini, *Henry Clay: Statesman for the Union* (New York: Norton, 1991); and Remini, *Daniel Webster: The Man and His Time* (New York: Norton, 1997). Two leading southern Whigs involved in nominating and electing Taylor are the subject of Thomas Schott, *Alexander H. Stephens of Georgia: A Biography* (Baton Rouge: Louisiana State University Press, 1988); and William Y. Thompson, *Robert Toombs of Georgia* (Baton Rouge: Louisiana State University Press, 1966). The two best biographies of Abraham Lincoln are David H. Donald, *Abraham Lincoln* (New York: Simon and Schuster, 1995); and, more recently, Richard Carwardine, *Lincoln* (Harlow, U.K.: Pearson-Longman, 2003). The leading antislavery Whigs are discussed in James Brewer Stewart, *Joshua Giddings and the Tactics of Radical Politics* (Cleveland, Ohio: Case Western Reserve University Press, 1970); David H. Donald, *Charles Sumner and the Coming of the Civil War* (New York: Knopf, 1960); Martin Duberman, *Charles Francis Adams, 1807–1886* (Boston: Little, Brown, 1960); and Frank O. Gatell, *John Gorham Palfrey and the New England Conscience* (Cambridge, Mass.: Harvard University Press, 1963).

The sectional tensions in the politics of the 1840s are well told from the southern perspective by William Freehling, *The Road to Disunion*, vol. 1: *Secessionists at Bay, 1776–1854* (New York: Oxford University Press, 1990); William J. Cooper, *The South and the Politics of Slavery, 1828–1856* (Baton Rouge: Louisiana State University Press, 1978); Eric Walther, *William Lowndes Yancey and the Coming of the Civil War* (Chapel Hill: University of North Carolina Press, 2006); John McCardell, *The Idea of a Southern Nation: Southern Nationalists and Southern Nationalism, 1830–1860* (New York: Norton, 1979); and in the several biographies of John C. Calhoun, most extensively in the somewhat dated but still helpful Charles M. Wiltse, *John C. Calhoun: Sectionalist, 1840–1850* (Indianapolis, Ind.: Bobbs-Merrill, 1951); and the most recent, Irving Bartlett, *John C. Calhoun: A*

Biography (New York: Norton, 1993). The southern Democratic loyalists of 1848 are represented well by William J. Cooper, *Jefferson Davis: American* (New York: Knopf, 2000); and John E. Simpson, *Howell Cobb: The Politics of Ambition* (Chicago, Ill.: Adams Press, 1973).

The antislavery impulse in the election of 1848 and its origins are the subject of Ronald G. Walters, *The Antislavery Appeal: American Abolition after 1830* (Baltimore, Md.: Johns Hopkins University Press, 1976); as well as Walters, *American Reformers, 1815–1860* (New York: Hill and Wang, 1978); Robert Abzug, *Cosmos Crumbling: American Reform and the Religious Imagination* (New York: Oxford University Press, 1994); James Brewer Stewart, *Holy Warriors: The Abolitionists and American Slavery*, 2d. ed. (New York: Hill and Wang, 1997); Bruce Laurie, *Beyond Garrison: Antislavery and Social Reform* (New York: Cambridge University Press, 2005); and John Niven, *Salmon P. Chase: A Biography* (New York: Oxford University Press, 1995).

Other facets of the 1848 challenge to the usual ways of politics are the subject of Judith Wellman, *The Road to Seneca Falls: Elizabeth Cady Stanton and the First Woman's Rights Convention* (Urbana: University of Illinois Press, 2004); Reeve Huston, *Land and Freedom: Rural Society, Popular Protest, and Party Politics in Antebellum New York* (New York: Oxford University Press, 2000); Richard Carwardine, *Evangelicals and Politics in Antebellum America* (New Haven, Conn.: Yale University Press, 1993); Elizabeth Varon, *"We Mean to Be Counted": White Women and Politics in Antebellum Virginia* (Chapel Hill: University of North Carolina Press, 1998); and Ellen C. Dubois, *Feminism and Suffrage: The Emergence of an Independent Women's Movement in the United States* (Ithaca, N.Y.: Cornell University Press, 1980).

There are many useful state-level studies of the politics surrounding the 1848 election, such as Stephen Maizlish, *The Triumph of Sectionalism: The Transformation of Ohio Politics, 1848–1856* (Kent, Ohio: Kent State University Press, 1983); Marc Kruman, *Parties and Politics in North Carolina, 1836–1865* (Baton Rouge: Louisiana State University Press, 1983); William G. Shade, *Democratizing the Old Dominion: Virginia and the Second Party System, 1824–1861* (Charlottesville: University of Virginia Press, 1996); John F. Kirn, "Voters, Parties, and Legislative Politics in New York State, 1846–1876," unpublished Ph.D. diss., University of Virginia, 2003; Lex Renda, *Running on the Record: Civil War Era Politics in New Hampshire* (Charlottesville: University of Virginia Press, 1997); Ronald P. Formisano, *The Transformation of Political Culture: Massachusetts Politics, 1790s–1840s* (New York: Oxford University Press, 1983); Kinley J. Brauer, *Cotton versus Conscience: Massachusetts Whig Politics and Southwestern Expansion* (Lexington: University Press of Kentucky, 1967); J. Mills Thornton, *Politics and Power in a Slave Society: Alabama, 1800–1860* (Baton Rouge: Louisiana State University Press, 1978); Manisha Sinha, *The Counter-Revolution of Slavery: Politics and Ideology in Antebellum South Carolina* (Chapel Hill: University of North Carolina Press, 2000); and William H. Adams, *The Whig Party of Louisiana* (Lafayette: University of Southwest Louisiana, 1973), were among the most pertinent for my purpose.

PRIMARY SOURCES

There are collections of the personal correspondence of many of the important political figures of the 1840s. Some of them are available in research libraries such as the Lewis Cass Papers in the William E. Clements Library at the University of Michigan; the Martin Van Buren Papers in the Library of Congress (also available on microfilm); the Stephen A. Douglas Papers in the University of Chicago Library; the William Henry Seward Papers in the University of Rochester Library; the John J. Crittenden Papers in the Library of Congress; the George M. Dallas Papers in the Historical Society of Pennsylvania; and the Greeley-Colfax Papers in the New York Public Library. In addition, there are letterpress editions of the papers of many of the prominent figures involved in the election, such as Clyde N. Wilson, ed., *The Papers of John C. Calhoun*, 28 vols. (Columbia: University of South Carolina Press, 1959–1993); James F. Hopkins et al., eds., *The Papers of Henry Clay*, 11 vols. (Lexington: University Press of Kentucky, 1959–1992); Milo M. Quaife, ed., *The Diaries of James K. Polk during His Presidency, 1845–1849*, 4 vols. (Chicago, Ill.: Jansen, McClurg, 1910); Ulrich B. Phillips, ed., *The Papers of Robert Toombs, Alexander H. Stephens, and Howell Cobb: Annual Report of the American Historical Association, 1911* (Washington, D.C.: American Historical Association, 1913); *Letters of Zachary Taylor from the Battlefields of the Mexican War* (Rochester, N.Y.: n.p. [Genessee Press], 1908); Frank Severance, ed., *Millard Fillmore Papers*, 11 vols. (Buffalo, N.Y.: Buffalo Historical Society, 1907); Robert Johannsen, ed., *The Letters of Stephen A. Douglas* (Urbana: University of Illinois Press, 1961); John Bigelow, ed., *The Writings and Speeches of Samuel J. Tilden*, 2 vols. (New York: Harper, 1885); and Roy P. Basler, ed., *The Collected Works of Abraham Lincoln*, 10 vols. (New Brunswick, N.J.: Rutgers University Press, 1953–1956). See also William Hanna, *Abraham among the Yankees: Abraham Lincoln's 1848 Visit to Massachusetts* (Taunton, Mass.: Old Colony Historical Society, 1983).

Party newspapers and campaign pamphlets provide a great deal of material about party outlooks, plans, and activities. Among the most useful newspapers are the Washington, D.C.–based flagship party publications, the *Daily Union* for the Democrats, the Whigs' *National Intelligencer*, and the antislavery *The National Era*. Other important newspapers that provide much insight are the *Albany Atlas*; Albany *Argus*; New York *Tribune*; New York *Evening Post*; Columbus *Ohio Statesman*; Columbus *Ohio State Journal*; Springfield *Illinois State Register*; Chicago *Journal*; and Philadelphia *Pennsylvanian*. The *Richmond Enquirer*; Richmond *Whig*; Milledgeville (Ga.) *Federal Union*; *Nashville Union*; Athens (Ga.) *Southern Banner*; Raleigh *Standard*; and Charleston *Mercury* are good illustrations of the southern political scene. Each of the parties also published special campaign newspapers throughout the fall, usually from Washington, D.C., and New York: the *Barnburner*; the *Campaign*; the *Battery*; the *Recruit*; the *Grape Shot*; and the *Young Guard*.

Other party publications that helped shape the campaigns begin with the *American Whig Review*; *Whig Almanac*; *United States Magazine and Democratic*

Review; American Free Soil Almanac; and George Hickman, comp., *The Democratic Textbook: A Compendium of the Principles of the Democratic Party.*

Extensive collections of Whig, Democratic, and Free Soil campaign pamphlets are located in the Library of Congress, the New York Public Library, and the Cornell University Library, among many other venues. The following are some representative titles (all published in 1848): *The Windings and Turnings of Martin Van Buren; Taylor Whiggery Exposed; Facts for Candid Men and True Democrats; Cass and Taylor on the Slavery Question; A Northern No! Addressed to the Delegates from the Free States to the Whig National Convention at Philadelphia, 1848;* and *The Cass Platform.*

Personal memoirs include Horace Greeley, *Recollections of a Busy Life* (New York: J. B. Ford, 1868); Henry B. Stanton, *Random Recollections* (New York: Macgowan and Slipper, 1887); George W. Julian, *Political Recollections* (Chicago, Ill.: Jansen, McClurg, 1884); Frederick Douglass, *The Life and Times of Frederick Douglass,* 2 vols. (Hartford, Conn.: Park, 1881); Thomas Hart Benton, *Thirty Years' View* (New York: Appleton, 1854–1855); Morgan Dix, comp., *The Memoirs of John Adams Dix,* 2 vols. (New York: Harper, 1883); Robert C. Winthrop, *Memoir of Robert C. Winthrop, Prepared for the Massachusetts Historical Society* (Boston: Little, Brown, 1897); and Henry Wilson, *History of the Rise and Fall of the Slave Power in America,* 3 vols. (Boston: Houghton Mifflin, 1872–1877).

Other publications of the time are Oliver C. Gardner, *The Great Issue, or the Three Presidential Candidates* (New York: n.p., 1848); *Proceedings of the Democratic National Convention Held at Baltimore . . . 1848* (Washington, D.C.: n.p., 1848); and Oliver Dyer, *Phonographic Reports of the Proceedings of the National Free Soil Convention* (Buffalo, N.Y.: n.p., 1848). The *Congressional Globe* contains many campaign speeches made while Congress was in session in the first half of 1848.

Election statistics are compiled in *Congressional Quarterly's Guide to U.S. Elections* (Washington, D.C.: Congressional Quarterly Press, 1975); and Michael J. Dubin, *United States Congressional Elections, 1788–1997* (Jefferson, N.C.: McFarland, 1998). Turnout percentages are recorded in the *Historical Statistics of the United States: Colonial Times to 1970* (Washington, D.C.: Government Printing Office, 1975).

The 1848 national platforms of the parties are collected in Kirk H. Porter and Donald B. Johnson, eds., *National Party Platforms, 1840–1964* (Urbana: University of Illinois Press, 1966).

INDEX

abolitionists, 12–13, 16, 39, 65, 74, 111

Adams, Francis, 76, 78, 99 (illus.)

Adams, John Quincy, 6

African Americans, 74, 76, 84, 96, 130

Alabama 1848 election results, 135, 136, 144

Alabama Platform, 41, 65, 66

Albany *Argus*, 90

Albany *Atlas*, 90

Albany *Evening Journal*, 87

Alexander, Thomas, 143, 144

Allison, John, 61, 103

American Antislavery Society, 12

American Party, 13

anti-immigrant nativist movements, 11, 13, 60, 114, 117, 125

Arkansas 1848 election results, 135, 136

banking institutions, 158

Barnburner Manifesto, 62

Barnburners
    anti-slavery sentiment of, 37, 44, 50
    on Cass, 64, 72
    1844 Democratic convention and, 22
    1848 Democratic convention and, 62–64
    Free Soil Party and, 78, 82
    separation from Democrats of, 38, 49–50, 62–63, 64, 67–68, 72–73, 151

Benton, Thomas Hart, 81, 95, 119

Birney, James, 14, 16, 142

Blair, Francis P., 8, 81

Blue, Frederick, 154

Brock, William, 152

Brown, Albert, 50

Buchanan, James, 47, 50, 64, 145

Buffalo Free Soil convention, 72, 74, 76, 123, 152

Butler, Benjamin F., 49, 77, 85

Butler, William O., 65, 92 (illus.), 161

Calhoun, John C., 15 (photo)
    on extension of slavery, 25, 50, 52
    on sectional politics, 13, 14, 41, 42, 83
    on territorial expansion, 25, 40–41

California statehood, 150

Campaign, 90

campaign organization, 88–101

campaign propaganda, 90–92, 93, 97, 99

Cass, Lewis, 92 (illus.), 148
    background of, 47
    Barnburners on, 64, 72
    character of, 100, 109–10, 117
    Democratic argument for, 117–18, 119, 120
    1848 nomination of, 47, 64, 67, 84, 85, 161
    Free Soilers on, 123, 124
    military background of, 110, 117–18
    on slavery issues, 52, 83
    southerners on, 111, 133, 141
    votes received by, 133, 134, 135, 136, 141, 144, 145
    Whig criticism of, 109–10, 111, 112, 113, 114–15

Chase, Salmon P., 39, 40, 73, 74, 77, 78, 95, 137, 148, 152

Chicago *Journal*, 114

Clay, Henry, 8
    in Congress, 17, 27, 150
    1844 election and, 5, 10, 16, 19, 145
    1848 campaign and, 54, 56, 57, 59, 61, 71, 79–80
    on slavery, 59–60
    on war with Mexico, 27, 31

Cobb, Howell, 121, 141

Columbus, Ohio, anti-slavery
    meeting, 72
Commander, James, 62
Congress, U.S.
    Democrats and, 19, 20, 30, 32, 37,
        137–38, 142, 158
    1846 election and, 36–37
    1848 election and, 136–37, 142
    Free Soilers and, 137, 138, 150,
        164–65
    sectionalism and, 34, 150–51
    slavery and, 52–53, 150–51, 158,
        164–65 (see also Wilmot Proviso)
    Taylor and, 61, 112, 149, 150, 169
    Tyler and, 17, 19
    Whigs and, 17, 20–21, 27, 37,
        56–57, 136–37, 142
Connecticut 1848 vote totals, 135, 136
Corwin, Thomas P., 54
Crittenden, John J., 54, 55 (photo), 132

Dallas, George, 47, 52, 95, 160
Davis, Jefferson, 84, 120
Delaware 1848 election results, 133,
    135, 136
Democratic National Committee, 88, 90
Democratic Party
    activists for, 8–9, 95
    beliefs of, 8, 10
    campaign activities and
        propaganda, 89, 90, 92, 95–96
    conflicts within, 21–24, 25–26, 29,
        37, 49, 62–64, 67–68, 72–73,
        80, 151
    Congress and, 19, 20, 30, 32, 37,
        137–38, 142, 158
    1840 election and, 3, 4, 10
    1844 election and, 10, 19–22, 63–64
    1846 election and, 37
    1848 campaign, 46–47, 115–21
    1848 election results, 133–38,
        142, 144
    1848 national convention, 62–67
    1848 party platform, 65, 157–61
    1852 election and, 151–52

Free Soil Party and, 80, 81–82, 142–44
    New York, 22–23, 37–38, 49–50,
        62–63, 64, 142, 144 (see also
        Barnburners)
    in North, 31, 32, 53, 120, 138
    partisanship and, 9–10, 16, 50, 64,
        81–82, 119, 121, 139
    sectional politics and, 39–40,
        43–44, 48–49, 83, 119–20
    slavery and, 16, 25, 31, 32, 37, 39,
        49–50, 52, 53, 65, 71, 72–73, 83,
        84, 105–6, 119–20, 121, 124, 158
    in South, 13, 16, 25, 41, 50, 52,
        65–67, 84, 120–21, 138, 140–41
    on territorial expansion, 23, 30–31, 45
    on veto power, 159
    on war with Mexico, 27, 29, 159
    Whig criticism of, 113–15
Dickinson, Daniel, 52
Dix, John A., 23, 82, 142
Dodge, Henry, 73
Douglas, Stephen, 48, 83, 95, 107
    (photo), 150
Douglass, Frederick, 74, 76, 84
Dow, Neal, 12

election of 1828, 5, 6
election of 1832, 5, 6
election of 1836, 4, 5
election of 1840
    Democrats in, 3, 4, 10
    election results in, 10
    voter turnout in, 4, 5, 141
    Whigs in, 3–4, 10, 14
election of 1844, 104
    Democrats in, 10, 19–20, 63–64
    election results in, 10, 16, 19, 64
    voter turnout in, 5, 141
    Whigs in, 10, 14, 19
election of 1846, 5, 32, 36–37
election of 1848
    day of, 129–33
    election results in, 133–37, 141,
        144, 145
    voter turnout in, 141–42

election of 1852, 151–52
Evans, George Henry, 12

Fillmore, Millard, 70, 97 (illus.), 111,
  147, 148, 150–51
Fillmore Ranger clubs, 93
Fish, Hamilton, 13
Florida 1848 election results, 135, 136
Free Soil Party
  African Americans and, 74, 76,
    84, 96
  Buffalo convention, 72, 74, 76,
    123, 152
  campaign activities and
    propaganda, 95, 96, 98, 99
  Committee of Conferees
    (Conference), 76, 77, 78, 79
  in Congress, 137, 138, 150
  diversity in, 96, 126, 142
  1848 convention, 76–77
  1848 election results, 133, 136, 137,
    142, 145
  1848 party platform, 77, 164–66
  1852 election and, 151–52
  impact on other parties, 79–83,
    104–5, 112, 125–26, 139–40,
    142–44, 145, 146, 148, 150, 151,
    153, 155–56
  nonpresidential races and, 87
  nonslavery issues of, 124–25, 126,
    143, 166
  organization of, 71–76, 89
  partisanship and, 125
  on slavery, 72–74, 77–78, 84, 122–
    23, 148, 153, 155–56, 164–66
  view of Whigs and Democrats,
    122–26
  women and, 74, 84, 96
Free Star, 84
fugitive slave law, 151

Garrison, William Lloyd, 12
Georgia
  Democratic State Convention, 84,
    89

1844 election and, 10, 104
1848 election results, 134, 135, 136
Giddings, Joshua, 39, 78
Gienapp, William, 16
Grape Shot, 90
Greeley, Horace, 8, 59, 80, 81

Hale, John P., 32, 35 (photo), 39–40,
  78, 137, 151
Hallett, Benjamin, 88
Harrison, William Henry, 3, 4, 17
Herkimer, NY, meeting, 49
Holt, Michael, 19, 115, 144
Hunkers, 22, 37, 38, 49, 62, 63, 64

Illinois
  1848 election results, 135, 136
  Whigs, 133
Illinois State Journal, 90
Indiana
  Democrats and, 144
  1848 election results, 135, 136
  Free Soilers and, 138, 143, 144
  Whigs and, 133
Iowa 1848 election results, 135, 136

Jackson, Andrew, 6, 8, 103, 104, 115
Julian, George, 96, 98, 138, 152, 154

Kentucky
  1848 election results, 135, 136
  Whigs, 132
King, Preston, 37, 138

Lawrence, Abbott, 69–70
Leavitt, Joshua, 79
Levin, Lewis, 11, 114, 137
Liberty League, 39, 74, 133
Liberty Party, 13
  in 1840–1844, 4, 14
  in 1846, 32
  in 1848, 39, 72, 73–74, 78, 142, 143
Lincoln, Abraham, 28 (photo), 140
  on Polk's policies, 27
  as Taylor supporter, 57, 81, 95, 149

Louisiana 1848 election results,
135, 136

Maine 1848 election results, 135, 136
"Maine Law," 12
Mann, Horace, 11
Marcy, William L., 22
Maryland 1848 election results, 133,
135, 136
Massachusetts
1848 election results, 133, 135, 136
Free Soilers in, 136, 138, 143
Whigs in, 39, 72, 73, 76, 95, 111–12
McLean, John, 54, 78
Mexico
treaty with, 30, 45
war with, 26, 27, 30, 56, 116, 159
Michigan
1848 election results, 135, 136
Free Soilers and, 138
Mississippi 1848 election results, 134,
135, 136
Missouri Compromise line, 41, 50, 52
Missouri 1848 election results, 135, 136
Morehead, James, 68
Morton, Marcus, 81

Nashville Union, 87
Nathan, Jonathan, 13
National Era, 90
National Intelligencer, 90
National Republicans, 6
Native American movement, 11, 12,
60, 114, 117, 125, 137
New Hampshire
1848 election results, 135, 136
Free Soilers and, 138
New Jersey
1844 election and, 10
1848 election results, 135, 136
Free Soilers and, 136
newspapers, partisan, 90–91
New York
1848 elections and, 104, 135, 136,
141–42

Free Soilers in, 136, 138, 142
Whigs in, 59, 142, 144
New York Democrats
division in, 22, 37–38, 49–50,
62–63, 64, 144
1848 congressional elections and,
142
at 1848 Democratic convention,
22–23, 62–63, 64
New York Evening Post, 90
New York Tribune, 90
Nicholson, A. O. P., 52
North Carolina
1848 election results, 135, 136
Whigs, 132

Ogle, Charles, 3
Ohio, 104
Democrats and, 133, 144
1848 election results, 135, 136
Free Soilers and, 136, 138, 143, 144
Oregon Territory, 24, 52

Palfrey, John Gorham, 39
Palo Alto Clubs, 93
partisanship, 146, 154
Democrats and, 9–10, 16, 50, 64,
81–82, 119, 121, 139
Free Soilers and, 125
Whigs and, 8–9, 16, 70, 80, 81,
95–96, 108, 110, 113, 115, 139,
140
Pennsylvania
1848 election results, 135, 136, 145
Free Soilers and, 136, 138, 143
Whigs and, 133
Philadelphia Pennsylvanian, 90
Pierce, Franklin, 151
Polk, James, 18 (photo), 65, 148
Democratic support for, 160
1844 election and, 5, 10, 16, 19,
20, 21–22, 23–24, 144, 145
1848 election and, 46
opposition to, 24, 27, 29, 48, 103,
104, 114

on slavery and South, 23, 24, 25,
26–27, 31
successes of, 25–26, 116
on territorial expansion, 20, 23–
24, 30–31
war with Mexico and, 26, 27, 30

Quitman, John, 65

Recruit, 90
Reform movements, 11–14, 16–17
Republican Party, 156
Rhode Island 1848 election results,
135, 136
Richmond *Whig,* 90
Ritchie, Thomas, 8
Rivers and Harbors Act, 114, 115, 116
Rough and Ready Clubs, 57, 93

Scott, Winfield, 56, 59, 69, 151
sectional politics, 32, 34, 113, 146, 150,
151, 153, 154
Calhoun on, 13, 14, 41, 42, 83
Democrats and, 39–40, 43–44,
48–49, 83, 119–20
in North, 39–40, 43–44, 48–49
in South, 13, 14, 16, 40, 41, 42, 83
Seward, William Henry, 59, 81, 95,
112, 140, 150, 154
Sewell, Richard, 153
*Sketch of the Life of General Zachary
Taylor,* 109
slavery, 42
abolition movement and, 12–13,
16, 39, 65, 74, 111
Calhoun and, 25, 50, 52
Cass and, 52, 83
Congress and, 52–53, 150–51,
158, 164–65 (*see also* Wilmot
Proviso)
Fillmore and, 111
Polk and, 23, 24, 25, 26–27, 31
Taylor and, 57, 60, 110, 111–12
See also under Democratic Party;
Free Soil Party; Whig Party

Smith, Gerrit, 39, 74, 133
Smith, Truman, 57, 58 (photo), 75
(illus.), 89
South Carolina, 6, 16
Democrats in, 62, 83, 133 (*see also*
Calhoun, John C.)
1848 election results, 135, 136
Whigs in, 68
Stanton, Elizabeth Cady, 12
Stephens, Alexander, 27
Stevenson, Andrew, 62
suffrage, 3, 130–31
Sumner, Charles, 39, 95, 148

tariffs, 17, 114, 160, 166
Taylor, Zachary, 97 (illus.)
Allison letters by, 61, 70, 103–4
character of, 100, 108–9, 150
Democratic criticism of, 117, 118
1848 nomination of, 56, 57, 60–
61, 69–70, 85, 162
election of, 133, 134, 135, 136, 138,
141, 142, 144, 145, 147–48
Free Soilers on, 123–24
inaugural address of, 148–49,
167–69
Lincoln's support for, 57, 81, 95,
149
military service and, 56, 60, 108,
109, 110, 117, 162, 163
political background of, 60, 108,
110–9
slavery and, 57, 60, 110, 111–12
support of Whig principles by,
61, 69, 70, 103, 110, 113,
149, 162
Whig argument for, 109–13
Whig opposition to, 69
temperance, 11–12, 125
Tennessee 1848 election results, 135,
136
Texas, 150
annexation of, 20, 21, 23, 25, 31
1848 election results, 135, 136
Trist, Nicholas, 45

two-party system
    dissent against, 11–14
    Free Soil Party threat to, 79–84
    rise of, 6–11
    sectional politics and, 43
Tyler, John, 17, 19, 20, 21, 23, 103

Van Buren, John, 49, 51 (photo), 89
Van Buren, Martin, 99 (illus.)
    Barnburners and, 22, 38, 49, 62,
        64, 72–73
    character of, 98, 100
    1828 campaign and, 6
    1840 campaign and, 3, 4
    1848 Democratic presidential
        selection and, 21, 22, 23, 47,
        49, 64, 67–68
    as Free Soil Party candidate, 72–73,
        78, 124, 125, 126, 133, 140, 142
    separation from Democrats of, 64,
        67–68, 119, 151
    on slavery, 78
    on Tyler's victory, 147
    votes received in 1848 by, 133, 134,
        135, 136, 145
    Whigs on, 103, 104, 112
Varon, Elizabeth, 96
Vermont
    1848 election results, 133, 135, 136
    Free Soilers and, 136
Virginia 1848 election results, 135, 136
voter eligibility, 3, 130–31
voter turnout, 4, 5, 141–42

Wade, Benjamin, 83
Walker, Robert J., 47
Walker Tariff, 114, 116
Washington Union, 90
Webster, Daniel, 54, 57, 59, 69, 81, 95
Weed, Thurlow, 8, 59, 87
Wentworth, John, 81, 119
Whig Executive Committee, 89, 90
Whig Party
    activists for, 8–9
    beliefs of, 7–8, 10, 17

campaign activities and
    propaganda, 89, 90, 93, 96, 97
conflicts within, 17, 26, 38, 79–80
in Congress, 17, 20–21, 27, 37,
    56–57, 136–37, 142
Democratic criticism of, 116–17,
    118–19, 121
1840 election and, 3–4, 10, 17
1844 election and, 10, 14, 19
1846 election and, 36–37
1848 campaign, 53–61, 108–15,
    136–37, 138
1848 convention, 53, 68–71
1848 election results and, 132–37,
    142, 145
1852 election and, 151
Free Soil Party and, 79–81, 83,
    142–44
in North, 31, 38–39, 57–59, 69,
    111–12, 138
partisanship and, 8–9, 16, 70, 80,
    81, 95–96, 108, 110, 113, 115,
    139, 140
on slavery, 16, 31, 32, 38–39, 57,
    59–60, 69, 71, 72–73, 105–6,
    111, 121, 124
in South, 13, 16, 31, 41, 57, 59–60,
    68, 69, 111, 138
statement of principles, 70, 162–
    63
territorial expansion and, 27,
    31–32, 34, 45
war with Mexico and, 27, 56, 116
Wilmot, David, 31, 33 (photo), 36, 39,
    49, 95, 137, 140
Wilmot Proviso, 36, 151
    Cass on, 83, 84
    Democrats on, 37, 38, 43, 48–50,
        53, 65, 68, 120
    Free Soilers and, 123
    northerners on, 34, 43, 53
    provisions of, 31–32
    southerners on, 40–41
    Whigs and, 34, 38–39, 83, 111, 112
Wilson, Henry, 39, 72

Wisconsin
1848 election results, 135, 136
Free Soilers and, 138
women's rights, 12, 74, 84, 96, 131
Woodbury, Levi, 47, 64
Wright, Silas, 22, 25, 36, 38

Yancey, William, 65, 66 (photo), 67, 83, 84
Young Indians, 56, 57